LATE STAR TREK

MASS MARKETS: STORYWORLDS ACROSS MEDIA

Gerry Canavan and Benjamin Robertson, Series Editors

Late Star Trek: The Final Frontier in the Franchise Era
Adam Kotsko

MASS MARKETS: STORYWORLDS ACROSS MEDIA

LATE STAR TREK

THE FINAL FRONTIER IN THE FRANCHISE ERA

ADAM KOTSKO

University of Minnesota Press
Minneapolis · London

Published by the University of Minnesota Press
111 Third Avenue South, Suite 290
Minneapolis, MN 55401-2520
http://www.upress.umn.edu

ISBN 978-1-5179-1909-2 (hc)
ISBN 978-1-5179-1910-8 (pb)

A Cataloging-in-Publication record for this book is available from the Library of Congress.

Printed in the United States of America on acid-free paper

Cover and interior design: Endpaper Studio
Typeset in Resolve Sans and Mercury Text

The University of Minnesota is an equal-opportunity educator and employer.

34 33 32 31 30 29 28 27 26 25   10 9 8 7 6 5 4 3 2 1

Captain, please. I'm trying to save you! I'm trying to save all of you!
—*Commander Michael Burnham, "The Vulcan Hello"*

I'm done worrying about the future. I want to help people now.
—*Ensign Bradward Boimler, "Those Old Scientists"*

CONTENTS

ACKNOWLEDGMENTS

My partner, Natalie Scoles, always deserves considerable thanks for her support and patience with my writing projects. But this time, she gets the credit for reawakening my interest in *Star Trek* as an adult by making the fateful suggestion that we rewatch *Next Generation* as well as for her indulgence and understanding as my *Star Trek* habit grew to encompass all the series and films, countless novels and comic books, and active participation in fan discussion forums. I also thank Gerry Canavan for showing me that my love of *Star Trek* could take an academic form, for introducing me to the Daystrom Institute Reddit fan forum (r/DaystromInstitute), and (with his series coeditor, Ben Robertson) for inviting me to contribute such an important volume to their series. Both Ben and Gerry provided valuable feedback, as did Sabrina Mittermeier and David K. Seitz. I am grateful as well to Malcolm Eckel (Thrawn) and James Grigg (8of5) for their permission to include a small portion of their massive diagram of *Star Trek* literature in this volume. I must also express my gratitude to my colleagues at r/DaystromInstitute, especially queenofmoons, kraetos, AlgernonAsimov, william_842, and uequalsw, for modeling the exact balance of intellectual rigor and good humor that every serious *Star Trek* fan should aspire to. North Central College provided grant funding for my writing process and for a professional indexer. Finally, I thank Doug Armato, Zenyse Miller, Mike Stoffel, Daniel Ochsner, and the rest of the staff at University of Minnesota Press, as well as my intrepid indexer Beatrice Burton.

ABBREVIATIONS

DSC: *Star Trek: Discovery*

DS9: *Star Trek: Deep Space Nine*

DTI: *The Department of Temporal Investigations* (novel series)

ENT: *Star Trek: Enterprise*

LDS: *Star Trek: Lower Decks*

PIC: *Star Trek: Picard*

PRO: *Star Trek: Prodigy*

SNW: *Star Trek: Strange New Worlds*

TNG: *Star Trek: The Next Generation*

TAS: *Star Trek: The Animated Series*

TOS: *Star Trek: The Original Series*

VOY: *Star Trek: Voyager*

INTRODUCTION

STAR TREK IN THE
TWENTY-FIRST CENTURY

E very *Star Trek* fan has a favorite series. For many older fans in
particular, *The Original Series* (1966–69)—which used its iconic
characters to hold up an allegorical mirror to one of the most tumultuous and influential areas of modern U.S. history while virtually
inventing fan culture as we know it[1]—remains unsurpassable. Others
prefer the franchise's most commercially and critically successful
outing, *The Next Generation* (1987–94), whose remarkable ensemble
cast and winning blend of workplace drama and detective proce-
dural turned the cerebral exploration of a postscarcity utopia into
must-see TV while essentially creating the market (and, as we will
see, the business model) for space opera. The other spin-offs of the
'90s, *Deep Space Nine* (1993–99) and *Voyager* (1995–2001), also have
their partisans, as each show's unique concept and setting allowed

it to explore more complex and darker themes than the sometimes one-sidedly optimistic *Next Generation*.

This book is not about any of those shows. Instead, I will begin my account of the franchise after all of those beloved series had run their course, a period that I dub late *Star Trek*. This designation evokes the concept of late capitalism, which has founded an influential stream of criticism that has attempted to measure the effect of the intensification of the workings of a capitalist economy on the cultural sphere.[2] The term may initially suggest the anticipation that capitalism will end soon. In its academic usage, however, late capitalism denotes something more like late-*stage* capitalism, the point at which, as in the late stages of cancer, the market and its values begin devouring the natural and social worlds that underpin it by infiltrating every area of life, even altering the workings of our natural world. (We can gauge the depth of this penetration by noting how often we use business jargon in our everyday lives—for instance, when we network instead of make friends, or attend to our regimen of productivity-refreshing self-care rather than simply resting or relaxing.) By analogy, then, late *Star Trek* marks the moment when *Star Trek* stops being a business out of necessity, simply because that's what it takes to keep new stories coming, and becomes more purely commodified. It is when story decisions are dictated by business strategy, when the quest for new audiences risks undercutting everything the established fans love, and when endless reams of material are churned out in the expectation that those same fans will shell out for anything with the name *Star Trek* on it. In short, it is the moment when a fictional universe and its distinctive fan culture transmogrify into a franchise in the fullest (and worst) sense.

In reality, of course, the distinction between the earlier and late-stage versions of capitalism and of *Star Trek* is not as clear-cut as my description might suggest. First of all, as long as there has been capitalism, its values have infiltrated and transformed the preexisting structures of everyday life, and by the same token, *Star Trek* has been a business from day one. Indeed, it has even been an entertainment franchise from an early stage, and arguably one of the most original and exemplary instances of the form. It is undoubtedly ironic that *Star Trek*—widely praised among academic commentators for its anticapitalist values—should be the pioneer of the ultracapitalist commodification of culture represented by the franchise form, but it is nonetheless undeniable. Science fiction scholar Dan Hassler-Forest defines franchise-style storytelling as a form of transmedia world-building that "takes place *across* media," "involves *audience participation*," and "is a process that *defers narrative closure*."[3] On all three points, *Star Trek* is exemplary. Early on, the franchise embraced not just live-action televised drama but also animation, film, novels, and comic books; it has since expanded to include video games as well. In terms of audience participation, I have already pointed out that *Star Trek* virtually invented contemporary fan culture, including practices like conventions, cosplay, fan fiction, and grassroots campaigns to save shows from cancellation. To this day, the *Star Trek* fan base remains among the most devoted and vocal in the world—something I have experienced firsthand as a participant-observer on the Reddit-based fan forum the Daystrom Institute (hereafter referred to as r/DaystromInstitute), which prides itself on rigorous intellectual discussion rooted in a command of the fine points of *Star Trek* canon (and which I will describe in more detail below). In fact, in the streaming era, shows have increasingly been created in explicit dialogue with the fans: *Strange New Worlds* (2022–present) was produced in part because of a fan campaign, and the creators of *Picard* (2020–23) are clearly angling for similar fan support for a new spin-off. Finally, the endless production of new *Star Trek* stories—even (and above all) when the official series are off the air—makes it, in Hassler-Forest's words, "one of those unusually expansive imaginary worlds that has become so vast that it is truly unlikely that even the most devoted fan can have experienced the resulting storyworld in its entirety."[4]

By the late 1970s or early '80s, then, the open-endedness of the franchise meant that anyone who was in the market for *Star Trek* would effectively never run out of things to buy. In turn, that meant that anyone who had the ability to produce more official *Star Trek* material had access to a considerable revenue stream—especially given that fans have been trained to accept only works produced by the legal intellectual property owners as authoritative canonical contributions to the storyworld.[5] The business model underlying the expansion of *Star Trek*'s postscarcity world is again in ironic tension with the uses to which that world is often put among academic commentators. For instance, in *Four Futures,* a work of "social science fiction"[6] that uses science fiction as a tool to think through possible consequences of mass automation and the environmental crisis, Peter Frase presents *Next Generation* as a postscarcity utopia where a combination of automation and instant replication of consumer goods has eliminated need and toil. He quotes the first-season episode "Neutral Zone," in which the *Enterprise* discovers some cryogenically frozen humans from the 1990s, including a businessman who is obsessed with learning how his stocks have performed over the course of three centuries. Captain Picard regards this character with open contempt and finally declares to him: "A lot has changed in the past three hundred years. People are no longer obsessed with the accumulation of things. We've eliminated hunger, want, the need for possessions. We have grown out of our infancy" ("The Neutral Zone," TNG 1.26).[7]

This monologue represents the high-water mark of Gene Roddenberry's utopian vision for *Star Trek,* and on a superficial level, it appears to be a stunning rebuke to the capitalist triumphalism of the 1980s and '90s. But things are not quite what they seem. To untangle exactly what is going on here, I must introduce a term sometimes used interchangeably with late capitalism: neoliberalism.[8] The term originated among thinkers like Milton Friedman and Friedrich Hayek, who advocated free market ideas (hence liberalism) but recognized a need to revamp them for the changed context of the post–New Deal world (hence neo-). After the postwar economic settlement began to break down, those neoliberal ideas were ultimately taken up by politicians like Margaret Thatcher and Ronald Reagan in the late 1970s and early 1980s. Only with the fall of the Soviet Union, however, did neoliberalism truly attain global supremacy. In the wake of that triumph, Francis Fukuyama issued his infamous declaration that all serious debate about the proper political and economic system had ended and we had therefore reached "the end of history."[9] In the long run, Fukuyama claimed, all major political conflicts would give way to a purely technical management of the economy according to neoliberal principles.[10]

In many ways, *Next Generation* fit seamlessly with the cultural optimism of that period, particularly on the geopolitical level. The most significant change in the *Star Trek* storyworld between *The Original Series* and *Next Generation* was the conversion of the Klingons—who often served as a stand-in for the Soviets in Cold War allegories—from enemies to allies. On the one hand, that move might appear prophetic in light of Gorbachev's opening to the West and the events that followed. On the other hand, it could appear equally ironic, because the "wrong" side wound up triumphing in *Star Trek*'s postcapitalist future.

We need to tread carefully here, though, because to this day, the franchise as a whole remains surprisingly incurious about the actual economic underpinnings of its utopian abundance, much less the path society took to get there. This gap alone should make us hesitate to identify *Star Trek* with Marxist values. Going a step further, we could observe that in other early episodes, Picard shows similar contempt for the idea that economic systems might be a site of political conflict. In "Lonely Among Us" (TNG 1.7), for example, he explains that on the backward planet of Antica, "these life-forms feel such passionate hatred on matters of custom, God concepts, even, strangely enough, economic systems." Here we can perhaps discern a more optimistic echo of Margaret Thatcher's infamous dictum that "there is no alternative" to the neoliberal order. When the economic system stops being a matter of dispute because the "correct" approach has been adopted, people are free to pursue their own destiny in a context of diversity and meritocracy. This strange indifference to economics leads Dan Hassler-Forest to conclude that the series, far from representing a thoroughgoing anticapitalism, "ends up celebrating and mythologizing capitalism's core values of individualism, entrepreneurialism, and hierarchical authority."[11] Instead of being an instantiation of Marxist values, as Frase claims, *Star Trek* gives us "a postcapitalist future in which class struggle is transcended and a technocratic utopia is realized."[12] This attitude surely explains its profound cultural resonance during the most optimistic and self-confident years of the neoliberal era, and from this perspective, the fact that the decline of the franchise began just as 9/11 shattered the "end of history" idyll seems like more than just a coincidence.

In short, *Star Trek* has always been more entangled with capitalism than a surface-level reading would suggest, in terms of both business practices and deeper ideological convictions. Coming at the concepts of late capitalism and late *Star Trek* from the other direction, however, we can also see that neither the market's interpenetration of our life nor the reduction of *Star Trek* to nothing but a business ever reaches the point of full saturation. In our own lives, we never fully identify with capitalist values—we still have sincere friends separate from our networking, and we never fully rebrand our rest and relaxation as self-care. Nor, I will argue, does the *Star*

Trek franchise ever really become purely commodified, if only because the writers, producers, and actors tend to love *Star Trek,* value what it stands for, and take pride in their work as creative artists. Though many fans are prepared to dismiss essentially all the products of this era of *Trek* as purely cynical cash grabs, my guiding assumption is that the creative laborers of *Star Trek* are doing their best.

This assumption of good faith on the part of the creators of late *Star Trek* contributes directly to one of my main hopes for this book: that the study of *Star Trek* as an exemplary franchise will provide scholars with intellectual tools that will be applicable to the study of what is arguably the hegemonic narrative mode in our contemporary world. This quest for useful concepts and paradigms will be served best by approaching all the franchise entries I study—television episodes, films, novels, comics, even fan theories[13]—as, first and foremost, stories, and further, stories that aim to contribute to an overarching story, in part by commenting on other existing stories. That is, I want to read all the varied texts that make up late *Star Trek* as narrative texts with their own artistic goals—among them the goal of vindicating their own existence as a contribution to *Star Trek.*

Thus, my approach will be a broadly literary one based on close readings of primary texts. Though I will supplement my analysis with the public statements of *Star Trek*'s creators where appropriate—particularly when it appears that commercial concerns or corporate interference have imposed aesthetically inorganic constraints on the writers and producers—I will primarily attempt to draw out the writers' and producers' intentions from what is implicit in the works themselves. And since their clearest intention is to produce new material that somehow fits into the *Star Trek* franchise, one of our biggest clues for discerning the creators' intention is how they take up and reshape their predecessors' work.

The quality of the results obviously varies, but I do not accept the common view that derivative works are low quality simply because they are derivative. One of my main models here is Dan Golding's *Star Wars after Lucas,* which analyzes Disney's attempts to revive the franchise without the continued input of its creator. Particularly striking is his analysis of *The Force Awakens,* which could easily be dismissed as a riff on the original film. Rejecting the tendency to "write off moments of citation . . . as simple plagiarism or lack of originality,"[14] Golding undertakes a stunning seventy-page analysis of the film from every conceivable angle, concluding with a reflection of how John Williams's use of the fugue form in the soundtrack echoes the citational style of the film itself. Given the much greater amount of material I plan to cover in this book, I cannot pretend to equal Golding's level of detail and rigor. I do, however, want to emulate him in spirit by insisting that the works under consideration here are consciously constructed aesthetic objects that reward analysis.

DYNAMICS OF *STAR TREK*'S DECLINE AND REBIRTH

Only if we take seriously the idea that *Star Trek*'s writers and producers are sincerely trying to do their best can we truly make sense of the franchise's failings, which are often blamed on some combination of creative burnout and fan stubbornness. That viewpoint is at the root of the most common narrative of *Star Trek*'s trajectory that emerged after the cancellation of *Enterprise.*[15] According to this oft-told tale, *Star Trek* (retronymed *The Original Series*), despite its modest ratings and ultimate cancellation, inspired a cult following that kept Gene Roddenberry's utopian dream alive. Following a successful revival as a film franchise, *Star Trek* returned to television with *The Next Generation.* After a rocky start, *Next Generation* ultimately proved to be the most successful iteration of the franchise on virtually every level. It defined science fiction television for a generation, for many fans even overshadowing its parent show as the definitive *Trek*. *Next Generation*'s success inspired a series of spin-offs (*Deep Space Nine, Voyager,* and the prequel series *Enterprise* [2001–5]) that witnessed steadily declining ratings and fan engagement. This dynamic bottomed out when *Enterprise*—whose hapless creators, Rick Berman and Brannon Braga, "were increasingly demonized" by fans, to the point where "even the mainstream press had picked up on the hostility by the time *Enterprise* ended"[16]—was canceled after only four seasons, far short of the seven-season run that the series of the 1990s had enjoyed. This was a sure sign that the once-triumphant franchise had collapsed into a state of creative exhaustion and cultural irrelevance.

There is a great deal of truth to this account, as far as it goes. At the same time, it faces significant limitations. First, it centers exclusively on the creative efforts of the production and writing staff and the reaction of fans, which combined to produce what longtime *Star Trek* executive producer Rick Berman called "franchise fatigue."[17] Such factors are obviously relevant, but this account ignores the broader market context that enabled *Next Generation* to enjoy such unique success and cultural resonance. In reality, if the prospects for a *Star Trek* spin-off depended solely on the interaction between the writers and the fan base, *Next Generation* would have been a major flop. Its first season in particular was poorly received by distrustful fans. Indeed, that season remains a byword for artistic failure, to the point where "growing the beard" (referring to the fact that the first officer, William Riker, adopted his signature facial hair only in the second season), designating the moment when "a series begins to become noticeably better in quality," has entered the pop culture lexicon as an antonym for "jumping the shark."[18]

In short, if *Next Generation* had been a typical network show, there is a good chance that it would have been canceled after the first season. The fact that it was able to endure and evolve into a beloved classic stems from two factors that Ina Rae Hark points out in an important study of the franchise's decline.[19] The first is quite simple: *Next Generation* had the field of televised science fiction to itself. Even if fans were disappointed in the series, they had nowhere else to go for their space opera fix. The second is that Paramount adopted a novel distribution model for the show: first-run syndication. In the 1980s and early '90s, cable TV was still in its infancy; broadcast stations reigned supreme. In addition to affiliates of the three major networks, there were many independent stations (most of which would ultimately become affiliates of the insurgent Fox network) that ran their own unique blend of syndicated reruns. Producing new content directly for the syndicated market allowed Paramount to sidestep the major networks. This move not only granted greater creative freedom but also allowed the series to outflank the competition. Every independent station could select the time slot that was most favorable for their particular market instead of receiving a single nationwide time slot from on high. In my local market, for example, new episodes of *Next Generation* ran at 7 PM Eastern time on Saturday night—a time slot that a network of the time would never have used for a big-budget drama, but one that guaranteed no one in my family had a better option to insist on when I wanted to watch *Next Generation*.

As with *Star Trek*'s pioneering of the franchise model, the fact that the success of *Next Generation* stems in part from an innovative business strategy is in some ways awkward, given *Star Trek*'s anticapitalist reputation. Redoubling this irony, however, we could say that the commercial success of *Next Generation* effectively freed *Star Trek* of capitalistic constraints during the heroic era of the 1990s and allowed it to achieve its own self-realization. With a guaranteed audience (and an initial order of two guaranteed seasons), *Next Generation* had ample time to find its feet, evolving into a satisfying ensemble drama as the writers and actors converged to find the right chemistry among the characters. It also allowed them to create a spin-off, *Deep Space Nine,* that took the franchise in surprising new directions. Yet the market giveth, and the market taketh away. *Next Generation*'s success in more or less single-handedly creating an audience for televised science fiction inevitably also created an opening for the competitors that would ultimately dethrone the franchise—in large part as a result of the poor decisions of its corporate owners rather than the failings of its writers or fans.

First, on the creative level, Hark argues that by the 1990s and early 2000s, the optimistic formula shared by both *The Original Series* and *Next Generation*—a futuristic drama set on a spaceship with no "twentieth-century human" as an audience proxy, in which our heroes "belong to the military branch of an interstellar federation presented as benevolent in its aims" and a "liberal humanist ideology underpins the action" such that "no species is seen as irredeemably evil"[20]—fell out of favor. Whether out of a simple desire to differentiate themselves or because the optimism of *Star Trek* had come to seem naive and unrealistic, a number of new space operas had debuted that focused on darker themes that made *Star Trek* "look like the outlier."[21] This failing was arguably self-inflicted: *Deep Space Nine* in many ways anticipated this darker thematic turn, as well as the more serialized storytelling method that later series tended to adopt, but it was treated as "the franchise's self-conscious 'middle child' in the 1990s."[22]

Many of those newer shows took advantage of the first-run syndication model. Some innovated further by debuting on cable networks that could tolerate lower ratings for cult hits that drew in faithful fan bases, allowing them to overcome the "paradox," pointed out by Hark, that "space-based science fiction. . . . has bigger budget requirements than the standard cop or lawyer show and yet appeals to a much smaller segment of the audience."[23] Meanwhile, the *Star Trek* franchise was looking backward to the very financial model it had overcome as Paramount attempted to create its own broadcast network, UPN, conceived as a rival to Fox. The newest spin-off, *Voyager,* was intended to serve as an anchor for the new network, which would allow *Star Trek* "to achieve the status of broadcast network hit that had eluded all previous entries in the franchise."[24]

In retrospect, the push to create UPN was obviously foolish. The studio had given up the advantages of first-run syndication and tied itself to a broadcast network with only a few affiliates. As Hark puts it, "*Voyager* did regularly top the UPN ratings, but that wasn't saying too much."[25] Yet after seven years of consistent ratings decline for *Voyager,* Paramount doubled down on the strategy by launching *Enterprise* on UPN as well. By the end of *Enterprise*'s run, as recounted by user Wowbagger on r/DaystromInstitute, the show was being regularly preempted and did not even have a stable time slot: "People then asked why *Enterprise*'s season 3 and 4 ratings were so low. Really? Could it have something to do with the fact that even its diehard fans don't know when it airs every week?"[26] Some degree of decline was likely inevitable, but—without minimizing their creative shortcomings—*Voyager* and *Enterprise* were both ultimately set up to fail by a misguided corporate strategy.

Nothing I have said so far represents a reason to abandon the decline narrative—in fact, just the opposite. The franchise did indeed go into a long fallow period after *Enterprise*'s cancellation. While the reboot films helmed by J. J. Abrams were critical and commercial successes, they were widely disliked by established fans and seemed to offer no prospect of a return to *Trek*'s natural home: television. The hard-core fan base that still sought out new material had to be content with scattered comic book miniseries, video games like *Star Trek Online,* or the dozens upon dozens of licensed novels that followed up on the characters and stories of the *Next Generation* era and filled out the fictional history of the *Star Trek* universe. *Star Trek* had seemingly bifurcated into one stream for casual blockbuster audiences and another for obsessive fans—neither of which seemed to promise any significant cultural impact in the darker and more paranoid cultural milieu that emerged after the supposed end of history.

More recently, however, there has been a veritable explosion of *Star Trek* material in the streaming era, inaugurated by the debut of *Discovery* (2017–24). Until the recent finale of *Star Trek: Picard* (2020–23), there were three live-action *Star Trek* series running concurrently—a feat not equaled even in the franchise's 1990s-era golden age. Alongside *Discovery* and *Strange New Worlds* (2022–present), viewers also have two animated options: the adult-oriented *Lower Decks* (2020–present) and *Prodigy* (2021–present), the latter the first-ever *Trek* series to be aimed squarely at a younger audience.[27] In a further experiment with different formats, the early seasons of *Discovery* were accompanied by a series of one-off episodes and teasers known as *Short Treks* (2018–20), and a direct-to-streaming movie is currently being in production. In fact, if we count *Short Treks,* there have been as many distinct *Star Trek* shows since 2017 as there had been in the fifty-one years of the franchise's history up to that point. Further, where the *Next Generation*–era shows up through *Enterprise* all shared similar production values and pacing—to the point where one could almost view them as a single unified show—the current series display a much wider range of styles. (See appendix 1 for detailed release dates.)

For many fans, this flurry of activity amounts only to further decline, or even betrayal. It is difficult to know for sure how widely watched these shows are in the absence of an industry-standard system for collecting and reporting ratings for streaming content. However, the fact that they are sequestered, for their primarily American audience, within the Paramount+ streaming service has surely limited their reach and cultural impact. Precise viewership figures aside, *Star Trek* is obviously not as central to our culture as it was in the early 1990s, or even the late 1960s, and from that perspective, we may well regard the present era as one of continued disappointment. Yet I hope it is clear by now that the huge success of *Next Generation* relied on first-mover advantages that are unlikely ever to be repeated. The commercial and cultural context for science fiction has changed, and at long last, the franchise's strategy has changed as well.

The use of *Star Trek* as an anchor for the Paramount+ streaming service could appear to be a reprise of the failed UPN strategy. Yet the proliferation of shorter series with different styles and approaches demonstrates an acceptance that science fiction is most often a cult product. The shows strive to appeal to as many small cult audiences as possible, even as Paramount is clearly relying on truly obsessive fans to maintain a constant subscription, so as not to miss the latest installment. It is difficult to know how sustainable this business model is. On the positive side, *Strange New Worlds* enjoys a multiseason commitment going forward, and new spin-offs (like *Starfleet Academy*) continue to be announced even as previous tentpole series like *Picard* and *Discovery* come to an end. At the same time, the tumultuous fate of *Prodigy*—which was canceled after only a single season (the only *Trek* series ever to suffer such a fate) and actively *removed* from Paramount+, before being revived for a second season on Netflix[28]—certainly does not seem like a good sign. Even worse, the shortsighted decision to cut off one of the biggest on-ramps for new fans by shifting from allowing older *Star Trek* series and films to be included among other streaming services' standard fare to requiring a subscription or upcharge may presage a new era of mismanagement on the part of the franchise's owners. The prospect of another company buying Paramount introduces another element of unpredictability, though the worst-case scenario of a purchase by Discovery—whose CEO, David Zaslav, is infamous for making bad decisions like removing the HBO name from the company's Max streaming service, or canceling completed films for the sake of generating a tax loss—has thankfully been averted.[29]

HOW TO READ RECENT *STAR TREK*

In any case, whether or not some shortsighted executive winds up pulling the plug, there is in principle no reason why the streaming model could not allow the exploration of *Star Trek*'s postcapitalist future to continue indefinitely into our dystopian capitalist present. My primary interest in this book is not business strategy, however, but creative strategy. I am less concerned with whether and how Paramount has managed to create a pipeline for churning out ever more *Star Trek*–branded material than in how the writers and producers have understood their task in that context. From what has been said so far, we might expect that their first step would be to pretend *Enterprise* never happened. After all, it was a flop, and it has not enjoyed any significant reappraisal by fans since its cancellation. Perhaps unexpectedly, however, subsequent *Star Trek* creators appear not to see it that way, because *Enterprise* has remained a consistent point of reference. In part, this attention comes more or less by default, as *Enterprise* is the only installment of the franchise set before *The Original Series* era that both the Abrams films and *Discovery* explore. Yet the insistence of the references goes far beyond the occasional Easter egg. The entire plot of *Star Trek Beyond* is structured around the fallout of events from the *Enterprise* era, and one of the primary plot arcs of *Discovery*'s first season follows directly on *Enterprise* installments. Even the final season of *Picard*—which clearly aims to return to the glory days of *Next Generation*—takes place around the 250th anniversary of Captain Archer's historic first voyage, which is to be marked by a massive commemoration that draws the entire fleet to Earth in celebration.

Neither fan service nor the demands of continuity can explain this pattern of references. Fans would rather forget *Enterprise* altogether,[30] and there are surely any number of stories to be told without any connection to the redheaded stepchild of the franchise. During the period of uncertainty and instability that the cancellation of *Enterprise* ushered in, the writers and producers freely chose to write themselves into a distinctively post-*Enterprise* tradition of *Star Trek*—one in which the doomed prequel is but a flawed first attempt to reinvent the franchise for a changed world. Although the more obvious approach would be to treat *Enterprise* and the Abrams films as a kind of interregnum between the golden age and the streaming age, the first step in really understanding what has become of *Star Trek* in the twenty-first century is to take seriously the deeper continuity that the writers and producers are signaling through these persistent references.

In this book, therefore, I will construct an alternative account of the franchise's recent history that starts from *Enterprise.* My goal in doing so is twofold. The overarching goal, as I have said, is to use late *Star Trek* as a case study for late capitalist franchise storytelling. But the second is simply to contribute to our understanding of a franchise that has always been noted for its relative intellectual sophistication and has therefore held a privileged place in the academic study of popular culture. The literature on *Star Trek* is in many ways rich and diverse, but it has been stuck in a rut, focusing on *The Original Series* and *Next Generation* to the relative exclusion of other series, as pointed out by David K. Seitz, whose 2023 book *A Different "Trek": Radical Geographies of "Deep Space Nine"* is, shockingly, "the first scholarly monograph devoted to a critical analysis of" a spin-off beloved by fans for its political and narrative complexity.[31] By recentering the narrative of *Star Trek,* I want to encourage scholars, even those who reject my framing in terms of late capitalism and franchise culture, to devote their serious attention to the later iterations of the franchise (including novels and comics) on their own terms, rather than dismissing them as dispensable knock-offs.

Let us, then, make a first pass at reading the story of late *Star Trek*. To get an initial sense of how the creators of *Star Trek* have understood their task in this strange new world, let us imagine the perspective of fans for whom *Enterprise* has served as their entry to *Star Trek*. Let us also assume that—against all odds—they were hooked and eagerly sought out all the new releases that followed. What would such fans think *Star Trek* is about? I think the answer would be that *Star Trek* is about terrorism. *Enterprise* debuted on September 26, 2001, mere weeks after the 9/11 terrorist attacks. The earliest episodes swam against the cultural tide by maintaining an optimistic focus on open-ended exploration, but the second season finale, "The Expanse" (ENT 2.26, aired May 21, 2003), opens with a devastating terrorist attack against Earth, which is revealed to be the opening gambit of an alien species bent on destroying the entire human race. The entire third season is given over to a heavily serialized narrative, inspired by the hit counterterrorism drama *24* (2001–10), that sees "the transformation of the usually peaceable Captain Archer into a man who tortures aliens to pursue the terrorists and protect Earth."[32] Once the alien threat is neutralized, humanity is threatened from within by prohuman radicals who, in the penultimate episode of the series, use a terror threat to attempt to disrupt the formation of the Coalition of Planets and rid Earth of alien interlopers.

The film *Star Trek Nemesis* (2002), the final outing for the *Next Generation* crew (up until *Picard*), opens with a terrorist attack on the Romulan senate that kills virtually all the members, clearing the way for a coup on the part of a younger clone of Captain Picard who plans to destroy Earth out of sheer resentment and spite. The first Abrams reboot film, entitled simply *Star Trek* (2009), features the destruction of Spock's home planet of Vulcan by a vengeful Romulan who is barely prevented from doing the same to Earth. The follow-up, *Star Trek Into Darkness* (2013), begins with a terror attack on a Starfleet facility on Earth, which turns out to be a false-flag operation to stoke a war with the Klingons. Rounding out the Abrams trilogy, *Star Trek Beyond* (2016) features a villain who served as a soldier in various conflicts during the *Enterprise* era, then crash-landed on an alien planet with miraculous properties that kept him and his crew alive—to nurse their grudge against the alien-loving Federation for their betrayal of humanity, which drives him to attempt a terrorist attack on an advanced, and densely populated, Starfleet facility.

The same pattern holds as we enter the streaming era. *Discovery*'s main character, Michael Burnham, is a human orphan adopted by Vulcan parents, who survives a terrorist attack by Vulcan Logic Extremists resentful of her contamination of Vulcan purity. Later, as an adult, she accidentally sets off a war with the Klingons, who—though not literal terrorists—are figured as religious fanatics and even indulge in suicide bombings toward the end of the conflict. For its part, season 1 of *Picard* takes place in the wake of a devastating terrorist attack on Starfleet's shipyards on Mars, which turns out to be a false flag carried out by a rogue faction of Romulans. While season 2 is mercifully free of terrorism, season 3 hinges on a secret plot by the cybernetic aliens known as the Borg to transform the younger generation of Starfleet personnel into mind-controlled zombies so that they can—you guessed it!—carry out a terrorist attack against Earth, as a prelude to the mass extermination of all Federation worlds. Even the lighthearted animated series *Lower Decks* features a false-flag terrorist plot, hatched by an idiotic alien species who hoped to frame the series' captain and guilt the Federation into giving them a better planet. Not to be outdone, *Prodigy* puts its tween protagonists in the middle of a terror plot by time-traveling aliens who hope to use a computer virus to destroy all of Starfleet—conceived as a preemptive attack to save their species, which, in the attackers' future, descended into a self-destructive civil war after making contact with the Federation.

In the early 2000s, a terrorism theme was an obvious response to the cultural zeitgeist. Over twenty years later, however, one begins to suspect that something else is going on. If our hypothetical fans would take a step back, they would realize that terror plots are only a subset of a broader sense of foreboding doom. I have noted that the second season of *Enterprise* ends with a terrorist attack and the fourth with the threat of one, but the other two seasons also end in apparent disaster. At the end of season 1, a time traveler removes Archer from his proper place in history, and the two arrive in a ruined future, where none of the "future" events of *Star Trek* took place. If anything, the finale for the third season is even more grim, as Archer finds himself thrown into an alternate history where the Germans triumphed in World War II, aided by what I can only describe as time-traveling space Nazis.

To return to the streaming era: *Discovery*'s first season presents us with a hugely destructive war with the Klingons that the Federation nearly loses. The second centers on a rogue AI that threatens to destroy all of sentient life unless Burnham and friends travel to the distant future, and once they arrive there in the third season, they discover that the Federation has been all but destroyed by a natural disaster known as the Burn. If the *Discovery* crew do not solve the mystery of how the Federation was shattered, its remnants will be absorbed by the oppressive Emerald Chain, a Mafia-like organization that has filled the power vacuum. Just when we think Burnham and friends deserve a rest, in the fourth season, a powerful spatial anomaly begins destroying planets; by the end, the story arc has the anomaly, like the Romulan terrorist from the first reboot film, on a collision course with both Earth and Vulcan. Not to be outdone, *Picard* season 2 has our heroes thrown back in time by the meddlesome Q, a godlike being who has been pestering the title character since the premiere of *Next Generation*. This time, the mischievous entity attempts to disrupt a decisive spaceflight, the failure of which will result in the erasure of the optimistic *Star Trek* future and replace the Federation with a violent and totalitarian empire run by bigoted human supremacists. The season 1 finale of *Strange New Worlds*—yet another prequel to *The Original Series,* centered on the crew from the original unaired pilot—sees Captain Pike threaten to avert his preordained grisly fate and thereby overwrite our familiar *Star Trek* timeline with a war-torn future. Even the novel continuity gets in on the fun, as the Federation is threatened with a destructive final showdown with the Borg that it only wins through what amounts to divine intervention.

None of this is entirely new territory for *Star Trek*. There have been many plots before where Earth has been threatened with destruction, where the Federation appeared to be on the verge of collapse, or where time-travel shenanigans nearly overwrote the *Star Trek* future with a more pessimistic alternative. The near-obsessive return to such themes, however, speaks to a shift in tone. Where *Star Trek* was breezily confident in the *Next Generation* era, in the post-*Enterprise* era, its future is under continual threat. It seems natural to infer that this theme is, either consciously or unconsciously, a reflection of the fact that the entire existence of the *Star Trek* franchise as an ongoing concern appears to be at stake with every new show.

We can see a similar metatextual gesture in the insistent recurrence of two closely related themes: loss and regret. Seemingly every major character has lost loved ones, is preoccupied with past mistakes or missed opportunities, or both. Here *Discovery*'s Michael Burnham stands out in a crowded field. When we start the series, she has already lost her biological parents (at least as far as she knows!) and alienated her Vulcan foster brother (Spock), and by the end of the two-episode debut, she has committed mutiny, sparked a war, witnessed the death of her beloved captain and mentor, and been sentenced to prison for life. In the Abrams films, Kirk loses a father figure in literally every film, while Spock struggles to cope with the death of his mother amid the destruction of his planet. Back in the Prime Timeline, Captain Archer is full of resentment of humanity's Vulcan allies, whom he believes to have held back his father's lifelong dream of developing a high-speed starship engine. Some 250 years later, decades after the *Next Generation* finale, "All Good Things," a now-elderly Picard starts off his titular series as an embittered recluse, haunted by the death of his friend, Data, who sacrificed himself to prevent the threatened terrorist attack in *Nemesis,* and obsessed with Starfleet's abandonment of a major humanitarian mission after the aforementioned terrorist attack on the shipyards. The theme even carries through to the animated fare: *Prodigy*'s youthful heroes are all, in some sense, orphans who start the series in a slave camp, and the main character of *Lower Decks* is a habitual rebel who has been constantly transferred and demoted despite her obvious talent.

Again, none of these themes are new, but the intensity of this pattern surely points toward an awareness of the loss of *Star Trek*'s easy cultural authority and appeal. As in the ambivalent relationship with an absent parent, the writers undoubtedly sometimes resent the *Star Trek* legacy for setting up an impossible standard, even as they wish to reconnect with it. Sometimes the sheer number of stories centered on the corruption or infiltration of Starfleet—a theme that seems to cluster around the figure of Jean-Luc Picard, who for most fans embodies the *Star Trek* ethos to a degree rivaled only by Spock—leads one to suspect a certain amount of hostility toward the people in charge of the franchise. In his streaming series, Picard's sense of bitter betrayal turns out to be warranted, as Starfleet was in fact infiltrated by a Romulan mole who set all the terrible events in motion. Shortly thereafter, we learn that a faction from the Dominion, the big bad from *Deep Space Nine,* has teamed up with the Borg to infiltrate Starfleet, raising the specter of two simultaneous conspiracies to undermine Starfleet from within. (One wonders if the various moles all met for cocktails.) In the different storyline of the novels, Picard is arguably complicit in a scheme by the nefarious Starfleet dark ops unit, Section 31, to assassinate and replace a Federation president, and our heroes later uncover the disturbing fact that Section 31 is led by a rogue AI that has been manipulating events behind the scenes for essentially all of *Star Trek*'s fictional history. The occasional plot about Starfleet moles is surely par for the course, but the recurrence of the theme may point to a suspicion on the part of *Star Trek*'s creators that they have been set up to fail.

FAN SERVICE, FREEDOM, AND FEDERATION

We seem to have come a long way from the optimistic vision of *The Original Series* and especially *Next Generation*. In those series, humanity had healed its divisions, overcome material scarcity via humanistic values and technological progress, and dedicated itself to peace and discovery. As the franchise evolved, those values came under increasing pressure, above all in *Deep Space Nine,* which took place in a milieu far from the center of Federation space, where war, bigotry, and greed still held sway. Nevertheless, idealism remained the center of gravity throughout the *Next Generation* era. Now, in contrast, *Star Trek* mostly presents us with a world where humanity's very survival is constantly under threat, where the authorities are hypocritical when they are not outright infiltrated by malevolent forces, where the residents of a supposed utopia are often isolated, filled with regret, and even bitter.

Yet their bitterness—speaking here of both the characters and their creators—is not a sign of pure cynicism but rather of disappointed idealism. Just as the characters ultimately want to vindicate Starfleet values, so too do their creators want to be doing *Star Trek*—that, at least, will be one of my guiding assumptions as I work my way through this strange and varied mass of material. Indeed, as I have already said, I will be even taking it a step further and approaching these materials with the assumption that they are created by talented people who are doing their best. As the reader will see, I have serious questions about the direction many of these well-intentioned people have collectively taken the franchise and about the judgment displayed in any number of individual plot points and creative decisions. Yet I have made every effort to set aside the lordly disdain of the judgmental fan for whom any new *Trek* is guilty until proven innocent and instead to judge each installment on its own terms, always trying to come to an empathetic understanding of why each installment took the approach it did before considering whether it may have done better had it done otherwise. In other words, none of the creative laborers involved in contemporary *Trek* is a Romulan mole, and none is trying to alter *Star Trek*'s DNA to turn it into a force for evil—not even Berman and Braga or (though I admit that here I hesitate) J. J. Abrams.

The creators of contemporary *Trek* obviously vary in their vision and approach, as well as in the quality of their results. What is more important from my perspective, however, is what they share. All of them are under tremendous pressure, and all of them are working under significant constraints. Judging from my initial inventory of overarching themes, they all feel those pressures and constraints acutely. They have been put in charge of something that is very important to a considerable number of people, and its future may depend on the choices they make. They must somehow keep that legacy alive, vibrant, and relevant while making sure that everything they do squares not only with people's ideas of what *Star Trek* is (or should be) all about, but with the plot points established in a mass of canon production that is rapidly approaching seven hundred hours of material.[33] I would be stressed out too.

In addition to the specific constraints of *Star Trek,* they also face a range of broader challenges that confront all contributors to a shared storyworld, whether it be a corporate franchise, a mythological tradition, or a scriptural canon. Broadly speaking, there are three primary strategies available to creators who have to thread the needle between originality and continuity in such a context. The first is fan service, which emphasizes continuity above all else and results in giving the faithful more of the same. The risk here, obviously, is redundancy. If the supposedly new series simply retreads old material, why does it need to exist? This approach thus dialectically calls forth its opposite, which is the attempt to maximize artistic freedom through a declaration of novelty or discontinuity. Perhaps the most radical example of this move is the premiere of *Deep Space Nine,* which broke decisively from the template set by *The Original Series* and *Next Generation*—and brought Captain Picard on as a guest star exclusively so that Benjamin Sisko, the new commander, could inform him how much he hates and resents him. This strategy carries its own contradictions, raising the question of why the creators are doing *Star Trek* at all if they are so determined to break with precedent. These two opposing approaches thus find an uneasy synthesis in the assertion that the new installment is a necessary moment in the overarching story—not of particular characters (which would be mere fan service), but of the *Star Trek* universe as such. In practice, this usually means that the installment gives us crucial information about the fate of the Federation as a whole, but any unexpected fresh world-building could serve the same purpose.

As the *Deep Space Nine* example illustrates, the existence of these three strategies is not limited to the current era of *Star Trek*. Nor are they usually found in isolation, because each would necessarily fail on its own. Pure fan service would be indistinguishable from simply rewatching the old episodes. Pure artistic freedom would amount to watching a different show entirely. And pure world-building would reduce an entertainment property to a weird kind of fictional reference work—a prospect that, to be fair, some *Star Trek* fans might welcome. Rather, in any given production, one strategy will tend to predominate, but it will necessarily call forth one or both of the others. Among the current shows, for instance, *Lower Decks* is predominately about fan service, yet it brings a level of novelty with its new characters and comedic tone as well as providing some fresh worldbuilding in clarifying the Federation's approach to second contact with alien species. *Strange New Worlds* is, if anything, even more purely fan service, but it still provides the minimal novelty of updating *Original Series*–era visuals to match contemporary production values while building out the implications of the Federation's ban on genetic engineering. More ambitious efforts will tend to strike a balance between two of the three strategies, as when season 1 of *Picard,* for example, continues the title character's narrative (fan service) with a radically different tone, setting, and supporting cast (freedom). Most interesting, though, are the attempts to pull off a tour de force by implementing all three simultaneously and with equal vigor.

On the level of *Star Trek* scholarship, one could posit a similar triad: fan commentary, dispassionate critical analysis, and contributions to the academic literature.[34] I have already noted that I hope to engage in the second and third pursuits, but in case this is somehow not already clear, I also write as a fan. One of my earliest memories as a child is of watching *The Original Series* with my dad. As a teenager, I cherished the comforting weekly ritual of watching *Next Generation* and was eager to get on at the ground floor when *Deep Space Nine* premiered. Though I drifted away from *Star Trek* in college and grad school, I returned to it as an adult at the suggestion of my partner, with whom I watched all of the *Next Generation*–era shows up through *Enterprise,* and all the new productions since. (I also watched all of *The Original Series,* which she does not enjoy, on my own time.)

The seeds for this book were only really planted when I discovered r/DaystromInstitute. Named after an in-universe research center, it cut against Reddit's smashmouth reputation by hosting carefully moderated discussions with strict rules of engagement: stay on topic, explain your answer, assume good faith, and no jokes or memes. Even after being a regular for nearly a decade—and being promoted to the rank of commander in recognition of the quality of my posts—I still sometimes run afoul of the regulations and have my posts pulled for insufficient rigor. Amid a group of obsessive fans debating the true implications of *Star Trek* canon, my academic training in theology rendered the various modes of fan analysis hauntingly familiar, and a combination of a contrarian's streak and a scholar's nose for gaps in the literature pushed me toward a series of detailed analyses of the neglected *Enterprise*. When *Discovery* finally arrived, I found myself among its most ardent defenders amid a broadly hostile fan reception—a dynamic that reversed when I was one of only a few critics of the well-received first season of *Picard*. In the meantime, a combination of morbid fascination and sheer desire to see the story continue prompted me to pick up an *Enterprise* novel, which proved to be my gateway drug. For nearly a decade now, I have always had a *Star Trek* novel going on my Kindle. With the onset of the Covid-19 pandemic, I finally found the time to dive into the Abrams-era tie-in comics as well.

CHARTING A PATH DOWN THE LONG ROAD FROM THERE TO HERE

This is to say that I write as a fan—not just of *Star Trek* in general, but of this strange, unloved era of *Star Trek* in particular. With that disclosure out of the way, all that remains is to provide a preview of what will follow in the main body of the text. I will proceed broadly chronologically, devoting each chapter to a particular tranche of contemporary *Trek* material and tracking the unique balance of strategies deployed at each stage. While my focus will be on the canonical on-screen material, I will also train my eye on the tie-in novels and comics, which tend to be neglected by scholarly commentators but which took on a fresh significance for fan culture and the development of the franchise during this period.

In contrast to most commentators on *Star Trek,* I will not be focusing primarily on the franchise's political or ethical implications, nor on its status as a mirror of American society. While such scholarship is often insightful and valuable, I cannot help but detect a certain insecurity in its emphasis, as though we can only justify our interest in less prestigious cultural artifacts by drawing out of it some broader cultural insight—or, best of all, normative political guidance. Though my analysis is grounded in my sense of the current political-economic conjuncture and how it shapes popular culture, much of the discussion will focus on what may seem to be trivial "inside baseball" about franchise continuity. This approach, which could sometimes appear to be mere fan commentary, is dictated not only by my focus on the development of the franchise as such but by the nature of the material, which in this period becomes highly self-referential. Indeed, much of my argument in this book will focus on the ways that foregrounding the franchise or fictional universe as such gets in the way of producing the kind of engaging characters, moral allegories, and thought experiments that actually hook fans to begin with. This book is the story of the ways that the writers and producers made *Star Trek* that is *about* its status as *Star Trek,* rather than simply *doing* what people like about *Star Trek.* The latter obviously includes political allegories, but I will assume that the value of analyzing the development of a storyworld in which so many people have invested so much of themselves does not depend on the existence of some kind of political payoff.

The first chapter will focus on the star-crossed prequel series *Enterprise.* I will argue that its creators, the much-maligned Berman and Braga, effectively transformed *Star Trek* into a different kind of franchise that would have a quite different relationship with its fans, demanding a much more disciplined approach to world-building. At every step, however, they failed to grasp the implications of what they had done and consistently prioritized their creative freedom over all other concerns, until they were finally replaced by Manny Coto, who placed a similarly one-sided emphasis on fan service during his brief run at the helm.

The second turns to the tie-in novels, which in the 2000s began to construct a vast, intimidating continuity that extended the stories of all the *Next Generation*–era series in complex, intertwining ways. While tie-in literature has largely been neglected by scholars, I argue that the so-called novelverse is the most creatively successful iteration of *Star Trek* in this era, focusing on three authors in particular—Christopher L. Bennett, Kirsten Beyer, and David Mack—who respectively exemplify my strategies of fan service, creative freedom, and fresh world-building.

In the third chapter, I investigate perhaps the most metaphysically audacious attempt to reimagine the *Star Trek* universe, namely the series of reboot films helmed by J. J. Abrams, which created an entirely fresh history (known as the Kelvin Timeline) to avoid the entanglements of past world-building and maximize creative freedom. Yet despite the heroic efforts of the comic books—which took on an unprecedented importance for the franchise during this period—the absence of a television incarnation of this version of *Star Trek* (largely the result of corporate infighting, not creative choices) doomed the Kelvin Timeline to superficiality and even futility.

The fourth chapter treats the series that returned *Star Trek* to the small screen after more than a decade, *Discovery*. Its first season exemplifies the unique storytelling possibilities opened up by franchise universes. By using detailed references to established lore to accomplish unexpected world-building that opens up narrative freedom, *Discovery* achieves a veritable tour de force, telling a prestige drama–quality story that only *Star Trek* could tell. The writers and producers quickly distanced themselves from the first season's innovations, however, and ultimately launched our heroes into the distant future of the franchise, thereby achieving creative freedom but undercutting fan investment by making the series largely irrelevant to other installments.

In the fifth chapter, I turn to *Picard,* which generated more excitement than any *Star Trek* production since the end of *Next Generation.* In place of the reunion show most were expecting, however, the first season reimagined the iconic captain and his world in much darker terms. This unexpected world-building provided creative freedom and potentially set the series up to meet or exceed the creative achievements of *Discovery* season 1, but poor planning made it a missed opportunity. After a meandering second season, the series finally reunited the *Next Generation* crew in a convoluted story aimed at superficial fan service. In the end, I argue, what should have been the streaming era's greatest triumph turned out to be its worst creative failure.

Rounding out the main body of my text, the sixth chapter discusses three series with more modest ambitions: *Lower Decks, Prodigy,* and *Strange New Worlds.* Where *Discovery* and *Picard* all sought to reinvent the *Star Trek* universe and defy fan expectations, all three of these series pick an unobtrusive corner of franchise continuity to pursue more episodic and character-driven stories. *Lower Decks* and *Strange New Worlds* in particular demonstrate that *Star Trek* still has a lot to give—if it can stop making bold statements about its fictional world and simply live in it.

I conclude with a reflection on what *Star Trek*'s travails tell us about the pitfalls of franchise storytelling as well as the unique potentials it opens up. Against the prevailing common sense that reusing characters and storyworlds is in itself a sign of cultural decay,

I will flesh out my claim that franchise storytelling revives an approach that has been perennial in essentially all known human cultures. In contrast with the contemporary prejudice that derivative stories are by definition inferior, many of the most beloved stories of all time are based on preexisting characters and settings. What holds back franchises is not their reliance on the familiar but rather the unique status of our modern myths as corporate intellectual property rather than common cultural heritage.

1

ENTERPRISE

THE END OF ONE LONG ROAD
AND THE BEGINNING OF ANOTHER

T
he promise, and peril, of *Enterprise* is immediately evident from
the opening moments of its feature-length premiere, "Broken
Bow" (ENT 1.1). The cold open places us in the middle of a tran-
quil domestic scene where a young boy is painting a model spaceship
by hand. The scene feels like it could take place in our contemporary
world or even in the past, but the dialogue tells us that we are in a
different world. The boy quotes a speech by Zefram Cochrane, the
famed inventor of faster-than-light warp drive, and his father turns
out to be a warp engineer whose ambitions are being thwarted by
the Vulcans. For the inveterate *Star Trek* fan, it is clear that we are
in the world that emerged in the wake of the events of the film *First
Contact* (1996). In this most (perhaps even only) beloved *Next Generation* film, Picard and colleagues travel back in time to prevent the
nefarious Borg Queen from disrupting the most important day in

human history: April 5, 2063, the day when Cochrane's inaugural warp flight caught the attention of passing Vulcans, who made First Contact with humanity and set us on the path to *Star Trek*'s optimistic future. Far from being pleased at the immediate fan service, however, a viewer familiar with *First Contact* would be surprised to learn that the relationship between humans and Vulcans has soured into resentment and distrust.

In the space of a single scene, then, *Enterprise* provides fan service while taking the story in an unexpected direction, which immediately opens up a space for creative freedom and promises fresh world-building. The gesture here is similar to that of the 2019 HBO series *Watchmen,* which is set decades after the events of Alan Moore's classic comic book series of the same name (1986–87).[1] Moore's original work explored the question of what would happen if a superhero—the near-omnipotent Doctor Manhattan—emerged in our real world. The answer turns out to be that Doctor Manhattan's allegiance on the American side escalates the Cold War to the point where a brilliant billionaire hatches a plan to fake an alien attack on Earth in order to prevent nuclear war, bring about global unity, and convince Doctor Manhattan to leave the planet. The TV series takes these absurd events with deadly seriousness, imagining what life would be like for people in that world while also folding in an unexpected exploration of racial justice. As in *Enterprise,* the guardedly optimistic ending of the parent text is undermined as it turns out that the new human unity discovered in the wake of alien contact does not erase all conflict. The result, in both cases, is a strange new world that is recognizable as our own, yet uncannily different—and a story that rewards, without strictly requiring, knowledge of the source text.

This trend continues in the next scene, which is perhaps the most memorable of any *Star Trek* premiere. A caption tells us that it is now thirty years later in Broken Bow, Oklahoma, as the camera pans over a small spacecraft that has crashed in a cornfield. An alien emerges, a Klingon, pursued by two aliens of an unknown species that might initially appear to be simply little green men. The Klingon lures his pursuers, who evince the ability to shape-shift, into a grain silo, which he escapes and then demolishes with his disrupter. Meanwhile, a farmer enters the scene, brandishing a shotgun that turns out to be some kind of energy weapon. The Klingon addresses him in his alien language, but the farmer—in typical American style—tells him, in highly idiomatic English, that he does not understand, then opens fire.

The Klingon's crash-landing on Earth is irresistible, a sudden and shocking disruption of a stereotypical American idyll by *Star Trek*'s most iconic aliens. On my first viewing, many years after the episode first aired and with full knowledge of the show's negative reputation, I was immediately won over and wondered what fans were so upset about. Then the theme song started. I was stunned to see that the title card distanced us from *Star Trek,* designating the show simply as *Enterprise* (a nomenclature that continued until *Star Trek* was added as the main title in the third season). Most jarring, though, is the music itself. In place of the traditional orchestral score are the opening strains of a cover version of Rod Stewart's power ballad "Where My Heart Will Take Me," the original of which had served as the theme song for the sentimental Robin Williams film *Patch Adams* (1998). At the same time, the visuals are in my opinion perhaps the best designed of any *Star Trek* title sequence, showing moments from the history of human naval and space exploration and culminating in footage of Zefram Cochrane's historic flight from *First Contact* (a strange decision, given the apparent desire to distance the show from *Star Trek*) and a shot of the title ship, the *Enterprise* NX-01.

Here the show's dual mandate—to appeal to *Star Trek* fans with a deep dive into the universe's fictional history while simultaneously winning over casual viewers—is on full display, as the fan-service and creative-freedom strategies collide incoherently. On the one hand, the song itself is tacky and alienating, especially for the younger audiences that the show's success or failure would hinge on. On the other hand, the attempt to inscribe *Star Trek*'s fictional history into real-life space exploration leads to a lazy American triumphalism—*Sputnik* and Yuri Gagarin are conspicuously absent—that contradicts the cosmopolitan spirit of a franchise that dared to put a proud Russian on the bridge crew at the height of the Cold War. As Lincoln Geraghty points out in his analysis of the infamous title sequence, the latter aspect was not lost on fans, who complained vociferously in the letter pages of fan publications about the erasure of Soviet contributions to the space race.[2]

For many viewers, the theme song represented an insuperable obstacle to taking the show seriously—apparently including Geraghty, whose only references to *Enterprise,* aside from the section analyzing the title sequence, either simply note its existence as a *Trek* series or refer to its cancellation. This pattern of minimal, dismissive reference to the series also occurs in the work of other scholars, though the trend may finally be breaking, as evidenced by the recent *Routledge Handbook of Star Trek,* in which Zaki Hasan performs a more recuperative reading.[3] Another notable exception is Ina Rae Hark, who continues to be a major point of reference for my thinking in this chapter. Unlike most other commentators, for instance, she highlights the tumultuous production history of the show,[4] which essentially reinvented itself three times during its brief run. Even Hark's insightful analysis, however, starts from a negative premise: "*Enterprise,* the supposed new beginning, was never more than tired repetition of ideas executed better in other *Treks,* as if I were watching reruns."[5]

My attitude was similar on first viewing. However, on returning to it, especially in the context of debates with fellow obsessive fans on r/DaystromInstitute, I found myself coming around to a position like Christopher Bennett's, the author of the *Rise of the Federation* tie-in novels set in the *Enterprise* era: "When I watched [*Enterprise*] in its original run, my perceptions were filtered through 'Oh, that's not what I expected' or 'That's not how I would've done it,' and that colored my reactions, as I think it did for a lot of us. But on revisiting the series, I was able to accept that this was how it was and evaluate it on its own terms. And I think it held up pretty well overall."[6] Obviously that positive reassessment does not apply to everything, but in terms of its intervention into the *Star Trek* universe—which is Bennett's primary concern as a tie-in novelist who aims to turn *Enterprise* into a usable history for his own stories—the show's original world-building is often more creative and sophisticated than it is given credit for.

In the pages that follow, I will argue that far from simply filling in the gaps of *Star Trek*'s fictional timeline, *Enterprise* reconceives the *Star Trek* universe by taking seriously, for the first time, that the universe's history matters as something other than fodder for one-off time-travel plots. In doing this, it self-consciously writes its dilemma as a prequel into the literal text of the show, introducing the kind of meta, or self-reflective, level into *Star Trek* that will characterize all subsequent installments of the franchise. It is ultimately this meta element, I claim, that marks *Enterprise* as the beginning of the new era that I call late *Star Trek,* not simply as "the last standard-bearer for *Star Trek*'s middle period," as Hasan puts it.[7]

Before delving into analysis, however, I believe a brief rundown of the show's production history would be helpful. *Enterprise* is unique among *Star Trek* entries in having a single writer-producer team for the majority of episodes, namely Rick Berman and Brannon Braga, known to fans as "Berman and Braga"—and regarded as a byword and a curse. The fact that *Enterprise*'s cancellation has so tarred their names is unfortunate, because both had previously made major contributions to the franchise. Rick Berman essentially served as Gene Roddenberry's successor at the helm of *Star Trek,* so that the franchise's '90s golden age is often referred to as the Berman era. For his part, Braga served as showrunner for *Voyager* as well as the writer of several beloved *Next Generation* episodes (e.g., TNG 5.18 "Cause and Effect," 6.21 "Frame of Mind," and 7.11 "Parallels") and cowriter, with Ronald D. Moore, of the critically acclaimed series finale "All Good Things" (TNG 7.25–26) and the films *Generations* (1994) and *First Contact* (1996). Though Berman had never taken on significant writing duties, Braga had shown himself to be one of the most creative *Star Trek* writers—above all by inventing the "recurring time loop" concept in "Cause and Effect," which, as pointed out by Sarah Böhlau, actually debuted shortly before *Groundhog Day* turned the story format into a widely known trope.[8]

This overreliance on two individuals to churn out the vast majority of episodes for the lengthy twenty-six-episode seasons of the time was a missed opportunity. As Hark notes, the *Star Trek* writers' room had witnessed a mass exodus at the end of *Voyager,* which could have opened the door to "new staff writers" to give "the series new perspectives."[9] The failure to do so arguably meant that *Enterprise* "soon showed the results of this myopia combined with creative exhaustion."[10] At the same time, it did have the advantage of guaranteeing a unified vision for a show whose prequel format necessitated a more disciplined approach to its world-building than previous installments. As I will argue, the first two seasons show both of these traits: first, a meandering feel that is often indistinguishable from previous shows, and second, thoughtful building out of the show's historical era and its regional politics.

Declining ratings led to a radical revision of the show in its third season, still under the leadership of Berman and Braga. The prospect of cancellation seems to have sharpened the duo's focus and led to a final burst of genuine creativity. The overarching terrorism arc, which was billed as a kind of "*24* in space," made room for the development of a unique alien enemy, the multispecies Xindi, and the systematic exploration of a dangerous region of space known as the Delphic Expanse. Above all, the season represents, to this day, *Star Trek*'s longest-running serialized story arc. Despite these creative successes, persistently low ratings led to Berman and Braga's removal from day-to-day writing and production duties for season 4. They were replaced by up-and-coming TV producer Manny Coto—a name as praised among fans as Berman and Braga's are reviled—who inaugurated a third era with a focus on fan service, oriented primarily around solidifying the relationship between *Enterprise* and *The Original Series*. Only once the show's cancellation was confirmed did Berman and Braga return, penning a self-indulgent and embittered series finale, framed as a historical holodeck program interwoven into a middling *Next Generation* episode, that functioned less as a proper series finale for *Enterprise* than as an epitaph of televised *Trek* as a whole. This chapter will trace the long road to that grim outcome. I will begin by treating seasons 1 and 2 as a unit and exploring how they manage *Star Trek*'s unwieldy fictional timeline and build out the world of the show. I will then discuss seasons 3 and 4 in turn, with an eye to the show's ultimately failed attempts to reinvent itself by doubling down on the strategies of artistic freedom and fan service, respectively.

HOW NOT TO BLOW UP A TIMELINE

To get a sense of the novelty of *Enterprise*'s intervention, it may be helpful to reflect on *Star Trek*'s general approach to its own fictional backstory. Even the most devoted fan must concede that, especially when it comes to events that are close to the real-world historical present, the franchise's continuity management has been a mess. Distant historical events are invented for the sake of individual stories and treated as well-known by the characters, with no apparent effort to coordinate the dates. This strategy allows writers to nimbly respond to current events—arguably most successfully in the beloved *Deep Space Nine* two-parter "Past Tense" (DS9 3.11–12), whose prophetic message about the marginalization of the homeless David K. Seitz ably analyzes in his book[11]—but the final result is a confusing and contradictory timeline.

One example is the date of First Contact. When the *Enterprise* crew discovers the Borg have gone back to April 5, 2063, they all immediately know what that means—but the audience has never heard that date before. The only reference to that general time period is in the *Next Generation* premiere, "Encounter at Farpoint" (TNG 1.1–2), in which the mischievous Q transports our heroes to 2079, an era of dystopian totalitarianism on Earth. How can we square such a scenario with the world-shaking events of First Contact over a decade earlier? Fan theories can achieve great wonders, but it is not immediately evident that these plot points make sense together.[12] We could say something similar about "Past Tense" (DS9 3.11–12), in which Sisko and friends find themselves transported back in time to 2024. There they accidentally cause the death of an important activist and must reenact his heroic actions on behalf of the homeless in order to restore the timeline. Yet World War III and its attendant nuclear holocaust, which would presumably reset all political coordinates, are supposed to have taken place subsequently. What long-term historical difference could a shift in national U.S. policy toward the homeless have made in that context?

The episodic format of '90s *Trek,* combined with the relative inaccessibility of past episodes in the pre-streaming era, meant that such discrepancies made no real difference. As long as the broad outlines remained consistent, no one but the most obsessive fan would notice the problem. (In fact, such fans would likely take a perverse joy in trying to figure out how to resolve the apparent continuity error.) This attitude was sustainable as long as *Star Trek*'s past was someplace our heroes just visited. With *Enterprise,* in contrast, it is where they live. For the *Next Generation* crew, the events of First Contact are over three hundred years in the past, and Zefram Cochrane is a figure in history books. For the crew of the NX-01, which launches in 2151, First Contact and its consequences are world-shaping historical events that took place during their grandparents' lifetimes. Archer and his father both met Cochrane in person, work at the warp 5 facility that he founded, and see themselves as building directly on his legacy. For Captain Picard, Cochrane's warp flight and First Contact with the Vulcans are an important step in the long history of the Federation, but for Captain Archer, they are the biggest, most important thing—in a way, even the only thing—that has ever happened.

Appropriately, then, the show's first two seasons are effectively bookended by *First Contact.* As we have already seen, a young Jonathan Archer mentions Zefram Cochrane and his achievements in the first scene of "Broken Bow." Later, when Archer has prevailed on the Vulcans to allow him to transport a comatose Klingon to his home world as the inaugural mission for the *Enterprise* NX-01, they mark the occasion with a video recording of Zefram Cochrane (James Cromwell) dedicating the warp 5 facility—and incidentally coining the key phrases in the famous voice-over from the title credits of *The Original Series* and *Next Generation.* We might call this the official Cochrane, whom Picard would have viewed as the original version before their involvement in the time-travel plot. The great man returns in one of the final episodes of season 2, "Regeneration" (ENT 2.23), in which unfortunate human scientists unwittingly revive some Borg soldiers who fell to Earth during the events of *First Contact* and who have been cryogenically preserved in the Antarctic ice. In their attempt to make sense of what is going on, Starfleet uncovers a speech by Cochrane, who—reverting from his status as historical icon to the shambling drunk we meet in the film—reveals that his warp drive was destroyed by cybernetic aliens (viz the Borg), and a human crew from the future helped him carry out his historic launch. This speech demonstrates that the time-travel shenanigans of *First Contact* are already baked in as the real, though secret, history of that momentous day.

Given the show's prequel concept, asserting that *Star Trek*'s fictional timeline represents a cohesive history with ongoing consequences rather than a series of isolated object lessons was a logically necessary step. But Berman and Braga then take the less logically necessary step of asserting that the kind of time-travel interference attempted by the Borg is actually commonplace. In fact, various rival factions will have weaponized time travel in order to divert the timeline onto courses more to their advantage, leading to a conflict known as the Temporal Cold War. Already in "Broken Bow," we learn that the unfortunate Klingon, Klaang, is a temporal agent and that his pursuers are members of the Suliban Cabal, a rogue faction of aliens who serve an unnamed figure (known to fans as Future Guy) in exchange for advanced technology and genetic modifications (hence the ability to shape-shift). Later, in "Cold Front" (ENT 1.11), it is revealed that the unassuming Lieutenant Daniels (Matt Winston) is a temporal agent from the thirty-first century who is tasked with making sure that Archer fulfills his world-historical role as founder of the Federation.

The Temporal Cold War injects a clever meta element into *Enterprise,* setting an example that virtually all subsequent installments will follow. From an out-of-universe perspective, the events on screen really are constrained by future characters and events as a result of the need to maintain continuity with the other shows (which aired in our past but exist in the characters' future), and this in-universe campaign of temporal meddling writes that dilemma into the literal text of the show. In principle, it also creates some productive ambiguity in terms of its relationship to the "future" shows.

Is all of this time-travel interference baked in like the events of *First Contact,* or does it result in a separate timeline? Some disgruntled fans took advantage of the Temporal Cold War to effectively write *Enterprise* out of their personal vision of the *Star Trek* timeline (a perennial theme on r/DaystromInstitute before the streaming era). A less extreme path would have been to use the conflict to excuse or overwrite continuity discrepancies, but as Hark points out, "it never ended up being used this way," presumably in part because "a universe in which history could be changed over and over again would be terrifyingly unstable."[13]

Given the on-screen evidence, it seems clear Berman and Braga intended just the opposite of the ambiguity most viewers perceive. The conflict's designation as a cold war seems to imply that the various proxy battles all cash out into a more or less stable status quo, while Daniels's role as a voice from the future allows them to assert that, despite never being mentioned in other shows, Archer and the crew of the NX-01 are essential to the *Star Trek* timeline. As I mentioned in the introduction, this world-historical importance is asserted most dramatically in the first season finale, "Storm Front, Pt. 1" (ENT 1.26), in which Daniels removes Archer from the twenty-second century and inadvertently erases the entire *Star Trek* timeline (Figure 1). Other than providing a platform for these dramatic declarations, in the early seasons, the Temporal Cold War mainly takes the form of the Suliban Cabal interfering with Archer's mission at Future Guy's behest, for no stated reason. Hence the Temporal Cold War neither delivers the world-building function the writers seem to have had in mind nor provides compelling plots—particularly for a casual viewer, who would presumably be confused by the prospect of a science fiction future that is being manipulated by an even more distant science fiction future.

The handling of *Star Trek*'s fictional history is representative of Berman and Braga's tendency to unwittingly write themselves into

FIGURE 1. *Captain Archer and temporal agent Daniels look out over the ruins of the future after Archer is removed from the timeline. ("Storm Front, Pt. 1," ENT 1.26).*

a corner. On the one hand, they have chosen a prequel setting that both requires and rewards fan knowledge of obscure franchise lore by making one-off references to the *Star Trek* past count for present storytelling. On the other hand, they have been remarkably inattentive to the very details they invoke, leading to near-universal nitpicking by fans. In a contemporary news story on the show's decline, Dave Itzkoff reveals that Jolene Blalock, a dedicated *Star Trek* fan long before she was cast as T'Pol, "was dismayed by early *Enterprise* scripts that seemed to ignore basic tenets of the franchise's chronology, and that offered revealing costumes instead of character development. 'The audience isn't stupid.'"[14] The skepticism is not limited to fans. When reviewing "Broken Bow" to prepare for this chapter, I found that the X-ray feature on Amazon Prime, which provides pop-overs with trivia, includes detailed accounts of the apparent continuity errors—for example, Klaang should look like the ridgeless Klingons of *The Original Series,* and his crash landing is the wrong time for humans to make first contact with the Klingons.

In my view, nothing happens on-screen that cannot be squared with existing canon, but Berman and Braga could have built trust by making it easier for fans to make the connections. Instead, their strategy of seeking creative freedom and eschewing fan service while forcefully asserting that they are contributing to Federation history seems calculated to alienate *Star Trek*'s most loyal audience. Rather than seek conciliation, however, the unfortunate duo dedicated a whole episode to mocking fan concerns. In "Singularity" (ENT 2.9), the NX-01 is trapped by a stellar phenomenon that slowly pulls the ship in while causing obsessive-compulsive behavior among the crew that manifests as a desire to fix minor continuity glitches. Trip ignores engine problems in favor of providing Archer with a chair more reminiscent of Kirk's, for instance, while Reed develops a system to put all systems on high alert simultaneously, which he calls the Reed alert (implicitly the origin of the familiar red alert). Ultimately, of course, they break the spell and escape the trap. It is a valuable lesson, though the allegory could easily be turned around on Berman and Braga, who appear more concerned with picking fights with fans than moving the story forward.

BUILDING A STRANGE OLD WORLD

I have argued that the strategies of fan service and creative freedom both jostle for position in the opening scenes of "Broken Bow" and in *Enterprise*'s infamous title credits. What allows them to hold together is the show's claim to be presenting a crucial historical moment for the Federation, and their effort to imagine the political and cultural dynamics of that transition is often successful. I must admit up front, however, that at times their vision of that history is lazy, even retrograde. The narrowly American perspective displayed in the title sequence marks a more conservative turn for the franchise in general, which Sharon Sharpe has dubbed "retro-futurism."[15] Far from appealing to new audiences, this move alienated existing fans, including journalist Donna Minkowitz, whose critique of *Enterprise* in the *Nation* can be summed up in its title: "Beam Us Back, Scotty!"[16] In terms of representation, for instance, the opening scenes of "Broken Bow" are overwhelmingly white and male. The only Black actor with a speaking role is Tommy "Tiny" Lister Jr., who plays the errant Klingon, Klaang—a fact that casts a shadow over the farmyard scene from our post–Stand Your Ground perspective. Scholar David Greven even goes so far as to proclaim an overlap between *Enterprise*'s implicit ideology and the neoconservatism of the Bush administration that effectively marks "the death of *Star Trek*."[17]

The retrograde trend continues after we have endured the title credit sequence. We are reintroduced to the little boy from the opening scene, this time as the full-grown Jonathan Archer (Scott Bakula), painting his very real spacecraft, the *Enterprise* NX-01, along with chief engineer Charles "Trip" Tucker III (Connor Trineer), who is portrayed as a Southern good old boy. When we reach the hospital where Klaang is alive but comatose, we meet the top officials from the Vulcans and Starfleet. In a shocking reversal of the trend of ever-greater diversity and inclusion in *Deep Space Nine* and *Voyager,* all are played by white men. They are accompanied by T'Pol (Jolene Blalock), the first female character to speak on screen. Later she will become Archer's science officer and loyal comrade, but when she utters her first line, urging restraint, he responds, "You have no idea how much I'm restraining myself from knocking you on your ass." Within a few scenes, we round out the rest of the main crew: the Denobulan chief medical officer, Phlox (John Billingsley); armory officer Malcolm Reed (Dominic Keating); pilot Travis Mayweather (Anthony Montgomery); and communications officer Hoshi Sato (Linda Park). Aside from the latter two (a Black man and Korean woman, respectively, both of whom hold the lowest rank of ensign), all major recurring characters are portrayed by white actors.

The producers justified this major step backward from previous series with reference to the prequel concept. Adopting a strictly linear concept of progress, they simply triangulated from *The Original Series* to our present day and selected a level of diversity that was ostensibly halfway between. Even on its own terms, though, this explanation fails—the dystopian Bush administration displayed greater diversity than the leadership of the supposedly utopian United Earth 150 years later. And it is not just that there are not enough nonwhite, nonmale characters. Those who fall outside that demographic tend to be marginalized in plot terms. T'Pol is relentlessly sexualized throughout the series, beginning with an infamous scene in which she and Trip strip down to their underwear to rub decontamination gel on each other, and continuing through a series of episodes in which Archer and Trip appear to develop a rivalry over who will eventually get to sleep with her. (In the end, Trip wins out.)

Despite this sexualization, however, T'Pol is a central, fully developed character, forming a triad with Archer and Trip that is similar to Spock's iconic interplay with Kirk and McCoy. The other minoritized characters are less fortunate. Mayweather has a unique background as a Boomer, a member of a human subculture that has been living aboard interstellar cargo ships for generations, but he never gets an A-plot unrelated to that cultural background, and by the end of the series, he hardly even gets any lines. Hoshi is an absurdly gifted linguist, whose skill set is indispensable in an era before *Star Trek*'s universal translator had been perfected (a process to which she will contribute significantly), but her apprehension about space travel wins her the contempt and disrespect of her colleagues. Archer in particular treats her as a secretary, at one point ordering her to secretly ascertain Reed's favorite food so that they can surprise him for his birthday. (It turns out to be pineapple.) There are times when Archer's beloved beagle, Porthos, seems like a more integral part of the crew than Hoshi or Mayweather.

All of these critiques of *Enterprise* have long been commonplace, but they are no less true for that. Clearly Rick Berman and Brannon Braga were, at the very least, uninterested in *Star Trek*'s progressive tradition of diversity and inclusion, and they appear to have used their simplistic account of historical progress as an alibi for ignoring it. On issues that they do care about, however, they show a remarkable thoughtfulness, taking seriously the idea that it took time to get from the historic encounter of First Contact to the optimistic future of *Next Generation*. In terms of aesthetics, they err on the side of continuity with present-day space exploration rather than anticipating *The Original Series,* for instance by putting the crew in loose-fitting blue jumpsuits reminiscent of NASA garb (aside from T'Pol, who must of course wear a skintight Vulcan uniform) rather than the iconic primary-color uniforms of Kirk's era. On the level of technology, they remove certain capabilities (energy shielding for the ship chief among them), render some others new and unreliable (such as the transporter, which the characters fear and only consent to use in the gravest emergency), and sharply downgrade others (like the tractor beam, which is replaced by a literal grappling hook attached to a really long rope). It is arguably too close to the familiar setup of the other shows, but they take these constraints seriously and generate some genuinely tense plots out of them (e.g., "Silent Enemy" ENT 1.12 and "The Catwalk" ENT 2.12). In terms of human culture, they recognize that not everyone would be eager to go into space, as illustrated by Hoshi's reticence, and they introduce the aforementioned Boomer subculture as humanity's mercantilist pioneers. Their development of Phlox's previously unseen species, the Denobulans, is another highlight, particularly his alien style of medicine, which deploys the special properties of a menagerie of alien animals that he keeps in sick bay.

Their greatest invention, however, is the plot point that has come in for most criticism from both fans and critics (including Hark): the troubled relationship between humans and Vulcans. We learn in "Broken Bow" that the Archer family's complaints about Vulcans are warranted, as our alien benefactors have been closely supervising and at times impeding human efforts to get past the painfully slow warp speeds endured by the Boomers. Their attitude toward humans is suspicious and patronizing, though that surely makes sense when we realize that Vulcans have a two-century life-span and hence remember when they first came across the war-torn humans struggling through nuclear winter. If we keep in mind that the charming Mr. Spock is an outlier, their disdain for emotional humans is in keeping with the characterization of Vulcans throughout the *Next Generation* era.

Unfortunately, world-building often comes at the expense of character development, as many of the main cast exist primarily to stand in for some particular aspect of the twenty-second-century milieu. As I have already mentioned, Hoshi represents humanity's curiosity but also apprehension about space, Mayweather stands in for the Boomers, and Phlox serves as a "good," open-minded alien who welcomes humanity into the cosmos. For his part, Reed embodies the perennial tension between Starfleet's scientific and military mandates, coming down in favor of the latter. Only Phlox, whose novel Denobulan background allowed for the periodic injection of new backstory elements, really transcends this one-note characterization.

The main trio of Archer, T'Pol, and Trip fare better. Archer and T'Pol's gradual progress toward a relationship of mutual trust and sincere (platonic) friendship is perhaps the strongest character arc in the series, while Trip emerged as a fan favorite due to his tendency, in Hasan's words, "to find himself in situations that expose his anthropocentrism with a view to harnessing it as a narrative vehicle for character growth."[18] This aspect of Trip's character is gradually submerged, however, in the later seasons, where he loses his happy-go-lucky attitude after the death of his sister in the Xindi attack on Earth, and where his primary role is to pick up where Archer left off in assisting with T'Pol's embrace of humanity (this time romantically).

As the NX-01 explores local space in the first two seasons, we learn that the Vulcans are a regional power, engaged in an ostensibly benevolent colonialism that aims to keep other, more volatile species under control. Among the species chafing at Vulcan domination are the blue-skinned, antenna'ed Andorians, who were a mainstay of *Original Series*–era background art but are fully developed here for the first time. Over the course of the series, Archer's friendship with an Andorian, Captain Shran (Jeffrey Coombs), one of the most compelling recurring guest stars in the franchise's history, proves crucial to the early development of the Federation. Rounding out the species portrayed in the beloved *Original Series* episode "Journey to Babel" (TOS 2.10), which introduced the idea of fractious intra-Federation negotiations, the argumentative and commercially oriented Tellarites also emerge as an increasingly important presence.

This reimagination of the Vulcans as a kind of proto-Federation unto themselves implicitly calls into question the familiar values of the established Federation of the "later" series. The Vulcans' caution in enabling human technological progress and introducing them into the galactic community in many ways echoes (or anticipates) the famous Prime Directive, which forbids undue interference in the natural development of "primitive" planets. For American viewers, who tend naturally to identify with the Federation's perspective, it appears benevolent and progressive. When humanity is on the receiving end, it feels different.

Do Berman and Braga intend us to ask these questions? Given that they treat the Federation as a transhistorical destiny and even attempt, somewhat clumsily, to demonstrate the necessity of the Prime Directive (e.g., "Dear Doctor," ENT 1.13), the answer must be no. In fact, *Enterprise* appears to be strikingly uninterested in real-world political commentary throughout its run. There are certainly some political allegories. For instance, in "Fusion" (ENT 1.17), we meet a reviled Vulcan minority who engage in the disgusting practice (familiar to viewers of other series) of mind-melding and who give T'Pol a disease, clearly meant as an allegory for AIDS, by forcibly melding with her. In "Detained" (ENT 1.21), where Archer and Mayweather are held in an internment camp for Suliban, we are reminded that not all members of that mysterious species are involved with the Suliban Cabal—a salutary message in the heat of the War on Terror, which at this point could be taken into account in the writing. More often, though, they deal in the kind of broad-strokes ethical dilemmas that are the stock-in-trade of *Star Trek,* and any innovations—such as the fraught encounter with a three-gendered species in "Cogenitor" (ENT 2.22) or Trip's experience of male pregnancy ("Unexpected," ENT 1.5)—are more likely reiterations of previous plots than responses to headlines. In terms of the broad strokes of the setup of the series, it is unlikely that they are intending to send any particular contemporary political message. To borrow what Dan Golding says of *The Force Awakens, Enterprise* "is simply too bound up in the franchise itself and in commercial considerations to comment in such a direct way" on politics.[19]

To the extent that Berman and Braga care about politics, it is the fictional politics of the *Star Trek* universe—and the internal politics of the franchise, in which they attempt to assert *Enterprise*'s essential place. They therefore shy away from the one burning issue they are best positioned to address: how exactly humanity went from a postapocalyptic hellscape to a postscarcity utopia. Instead, to the extent that they fill in the backstory of their own era, it is focused on historical footnotes, as in "Carbon Creek" (ENT 2.2)—one of the most charming installments of *Enterprise,* and my sentimental favorite *Star Trek* episode—which portrays a group of Vulcans stranded in small-town America in the 1950s, or else on the background of the warp program itself (e.g., "First Flight," ENT 2.24). What they can never account for, however, is why United Earth, possessing only one high-speed ship, would assign it to simply wander around aimlessly, to see what it can see. Even without temporal agent Daniels's guidance, everyone somehow just *knows* they are supposed to do *Star Trek*.

"NONE OF THIS WAS SUPPOSED TO HAPPEN"

I have mentioned previously that the mid-twenty-second century has only rarely been name-dropped in *Star Trek*'s fictional backstory. Numerically, that is true—essentially only two events with ongoing consequences have been mentioned, but they are big ones. In "Balance of Terror" (TOS 1.14), set in the mid-twenty-third century, Spock mentions that a war between Earth and the Romulans broke out "a century ago"—putting it in 2166 if we take him absolutely literally—which was waged "with primitive atomic weapons and in primitive space vessels" between combatants who were incapable of "ship-to-ship visual communication." The immediate purpose of this line in the episode is to set up the big reveal that the evil Romulans look exactly like the Vulcans, sparking racist antagonism against Spock. For fans, though, it set a hard ceiling for the technology of the twenty-second century, which *Enterprise* flagrantly violated. The other significant date is 2161, which a throwaway line in *Next Generation* had established as the date the Federation was founded ("The Outcast" TNG 5.17).

The relationship between these two dates—established decades apart, by completely different writing staffs—does not seem to have prompted much reflection before *Enterprise*'s debut. Surely only the most obsessive fans would note the apparent contradiction that arises if we picture Earth fighting a war on its own *after* the foundation of the Federation, but that is easily solved by assuming that Spock was using a ballpark figure. *Enterprise* forced the issue, however. By starting off in 2151, the producers doubtless intended to end the series with the foundation of the Federation ten years later. This means that they were obligated to address the Romulan war in some way: it logically had to take place before the Federation was founded.

Portraying both of those major events—humanity's first real experience of interstellar conflict and the beginnings of the organization that guarantees *Star Trek*'s utopian future—would forever cement *Enterprise*'s importance to the franchise, in ways that no amount of empty assertion by a shadowy temporal agent ever could. More than simply putting the events on screen, they would have an opportunity to make them newly meaningful by clarifying the relationship between what had essentially been two bits of trivia for hard-core fans. Had the war convinced a restive humanity to reach out to its neighbors? Had progress toward a major alliance prompted the Romulans to attack? Either way, they had a unique chance to develop and deepen *Star Trek*'s account of its own past—exactly what the prequel concept promised fans *Enterprise* would do.

Given the ongoing decline in ratings over the course of the first two seasons, they had a potentially limited window to achieve those goals and ensure their legacy. Yet instead of leaning into fan service in order to shore up their claim to be building the history of the Federation, Berman and Braga responded to the emerging ratings crisis by leaning into artistic freedom. Far from building the show's connections to *Star Trek* canon, they invented a previously unmentioned terrorist threat, from a previously unmentioned species (or group of species) known as the Xindi, who lived in a previously unmentioned and self-enclosed region of space known as the Delphic Expanse. Both the adversary and the setting represented major innovations. The Xindi are the first species to be portrayed with radically different subspecies: Primates, Arboreals (something like sloths), Reptilians, Insectoids, Aquatics (cetaceans), and the sadly extinct Avians (presumably birds), who all developed on the same now-lost world. In a rare unqualified compliment, Hark declares the Xindi "a welcome change from *Trek*'s tendency to treat alien worlds as having a single race and culture, down to lock-step clothing and hairstyles."[20] In terms of setting, the Delphic Expanse is riven by dangerous spatial anomalies created by large alien structures known as spheres, which turn out to have been built by the Xindi's shadowy benefactors (the creatively named Sphere Builders) in order to transform the properties of our galaxy so that they can take over. Only a substance known as trellium-D—which initially appears to drive Vulcans mad, complicating the NX-01's effort to adapt to local conditions—can protect against the anomalies, meaning that much of the Expanse's economy is centered on mining it. The existence of the spheres also distorts the region's culture, even inspiring religious devotion on the part of some misguided souls, who seek out the spatial anomalies as a spiritual high ("Chosen Realm" ENT 3.12). Aside from *Deep Space Nine*'s exploration of its local environs, necessitated by its stationary milieu, *Star Trek* has never dwelled on a distinct region of space in this way.

Further, Berman and Braga proposed a radical break with the history of *Star Trek* storytelling, committing themselves to a single overarching plot that would occupy the entire season (reduced to twenty-four episodes from the previously standard twenty-six, but still long by contemporary standards). Only *Deep Space Nine* had attempted such sustained serialization, and that only in its final eleven episodes, which sought to tie up the complex plot threads that had developed, more or less organically, over the show's long run. Beginning-to-end serialization was new.

The end result still feels far more episodic than a typical serialized streaming drama, sometimes jarringly so. We can see this clearly in a sequence of three episodes. The first, "Twilight" (ENT 3.8), opens with Captain Archer stumbling, confused, onto the bridge only to witness the destruction of Earth by the Xindi. It turns out that he has been affected by a kind of time tumor, which periodically resets his memory in a way familiar from the film *Memento* (2000). Without Archer's leadership, the mission to thwart the Xindi failed, and the remainder of the episode follows the last remnants of humanity as the Xindi ruthlessly hunt them down—until Phlox discovers a way to remove the time tumor and return Archer to the moment he was first afflicted with it. The third, "Similitude" (ENT 3.10)—incidentally the first writing credit for future showrunner Manny Coto—opens with the apparent death of Trip, but it is actually a rapidly aging clone that Phlox grew in order to collect organs to save the real Trip. As the clone ages, he turns out to share Trip's memories and quickly endears himself to the crew—who ruthlessly murder him, over his impassioned protests, to get their irreplaceable chief engineer back. (In their defense, the clone would have soon died on his own, rendering the whole effort wasted.) Both episodes send a clear message: from our characters' perspective, the Xindi could well succeed in their genocidal goals, meaning that desperate measures are warranted. Yet this urgency is hard to square with the intervening episode, "North Star" (ENT 3.9), in which they discover a human settlement from the 1800s on an alien planet and dress up in fun cowboy outfits to investigate.

The most significant problem Berman and Braga faced in writing this plot was precisely the prequel concept. Even if we empathize with our characters' ignorance of the future, we can confidently infer from the hundreds of hours of previous *Star Trek* material set in the twenty-third and twenty-fourth centuries that humanity was not, in fact, wiped out by the Xindi in 2153. Hence, in contrast to their approach in the early seasons, they initially use the Temporal Cold War to generate explicit ambiguity. The seed is planted in "The

Expanse" (ENT 2.26), in which Future Guy reverses his usual meddling ways and reveals to Archer that the Xindi terrorist attack represents a dangerous new front in the temporal conflict. An unknown faction has manipulated the Xindi, convincing them that they will be wiped out by humanity unless they strike first. Thankfully, the Xindi have made the questionable tactical choice of revealing their intentions by testing their weapon on Earth, giving Archer a chance to head them off. Later, Daniels further muddies the waters, declaring that from his future perspective, "none of this was supposed to happen" ("Carpenter Street" ENT 3.11). The figure who previously served as our anchor, guaranteeing Archer's place in history, has now opened up the possibility that the Xindi attack has diverted the timeline onto an unpredictable path. Eventually, Daniels appears to be satisfied that the timeline is healing and the Xindi will even be welcomed into the Federation ("Azati Prime" ENT 3.18), but for most of the season, a cloud of ambiguity hangs over the outcome.

The Xindi arc represents another shift in strategy from the early seasons: an extended, literal "ripped from the headlines" plotline. Yet aside from the initial premise, there appears to be a concerted effort to avoid making a direct political comment. For instance, at one point, Hark justifiably asks, "Having established the Suliban Cabal as the chief adversary for two years, what would have been more logical than to have it developing the weapon within the Expanse at the behest of Mr. Future Guy, who turned out to represent the Sphere Builders?"[21] The answer is probably that they perceived that the Suliban had failed to grab audiences. But I would also suggest that part of the motivation to avoid the involvement of the Suliban (and even to recruit Future Guy as an unexpected ally) stems from the fact that, in a bizarre coincidence, Berman had spent time in Afghanistan and, developing *Enterprise* many months before the 9/11 attacks, based the name "Suliban" on "Taliban," simply because of its "mysterious" sound.[22] Doubling down on that connection would have been fraught, to say the least. I would say the same for another more organic choice of villain, namely the Romulans. Would Berman and Braga really want to tie such a central part of *Star Trek* lore to the War on Terror?

Thinking in terms of the aftermath of 9/11, the fact that Earth is the victim of a preemptive attack based on false information might prompt a sympathetic identification with Iraqis. Nevertheless, the majority of the "*24* in space"–style plot seems to adopt a contemporary American perspective on terrorism and the extreme measures it supposedly justifies. The internal diversity of the Xindi and the fact that some of the subspecies are convinced by Archer's diplomatic appeals provides a potential optimistic spin on the us-versus-them rhetoric of the time. However, that message is undermined by the fact that members of the Xindi subspecies who take humanity's side are all mammalian (Primate, Arboreal, and Aquatic), while the more radically alien Reptilian and Insectoid groups remain committed to the attack to the bitter end. The biological affinity on display seems more likely to play into racial stereotypes than undermine them.

Whatever political impact the message of the Xindi arc was intended to have was bound to be muted, given the show's continued decline in ratings. As mentioned in the introduction, this likely had as much to do with *Enterprise*'s limited reach as part of the UPN broadcast network and its constantly shifting time slot as with any artistic successes or failures. Yet judging from conversations on r/DaystromInstitute, a hard core of engaged fans—both hate watchers and sincere supporters—continued to watch faithfully and debate each episode's merits in the emerging online fan culture. In response to a thread of mine asking what it was like to watch the Xindi arc as it aired,[23] several fans expressed fatigue or frustration—an understandable response given that *Trek* fans had never before been asked to focus on one plotline and one adversary for so long. Nevertheless, an unforgettable anecdote from a contemporaneous viewer shows that many fans were still engaged. As Wowbagger (already quoted above in connection with the show's ever-shifting time slot) recounts, one Wednesday, *Enterprise* had been preempted yet again, and one user saw an opportunity:

> That night, just after the Enterprise time slot finished, some wag on the TrekBBS posted a new thread, "Grade 'The Interregnum.'" Standard post-episode reaction & review thread. He had a poll set up for letter grades, and offered his own comments. Something along the lines of, "I appreciated this week's attempt to give Travis and Hoshi something to do, but I felt that, given the premise, they could have gone a lot darker. What did the rest of you think?" There were an awful lot of wags on the BBS at the time, and a good chunk of them immediately "got" the joke. There was no episode called "The Interregnum," this was just something [the original poster] had made up.

What followed was a distillation of the joy of fan culture:

> The reviewers dove in, dissecting the plot and character arcs of an episode that did not exist. Much ink was spilled over how difficult it is to give Hoshi storylines, and how this was a transparent but effective attempt to do that. Many people complimented the episode's Romulan bounty hunter—especially the decision by the writers to put him in "awesome" full-body armor so that (respecting canon) the crew never saw his face. Others said they cried when the bounty hunter finally caught up with his prey, the last Xindi-Avian, aboard Enterprise, and admired Hoshi for her bravery in that climactic scene. Then the haters showed up, and started tearing apart TPTB for another "derivative plot" that "betrays the premise of the series" and uses all its characters as "plot devices." Even the armor came under withering fire: "the bird-of-prey

design makes no sense for personal armor, and would be completely impractical in real life." Fights broke out about whether the Hoshi/Avian relationship was touching or just uncomfortable and weird. Berman and Braga were cursed, and hailed. The whole thing ended up shaking out almost exactly the same way any other episode review thread would.[24]

I share this story not only because it is so charming, but to show how badly Berman and Braga had misjudged their own fans. The participants in this thread were not pedantic nitpickers—or not only that. They were creatively invested in the show, building on existing *Star Trek* lore and the new concepts introduced in the Xindi arc in strikingly inventive ways. In any ranking of Xindi episodes, "The Interregnum" surely deserves a place near the top.

FAN SERVICE: THE FINAL FRONTIER

The third season finale, "Zero Hour" (ENT 3.24), marks the end of the Xindi arc as well as the end of Berman and Braga's control over the writing and day-to-day workings of the series—a humiliating repudiation for two men who had helped to shepherd the franchise for so long. At the same time, it must have been something of a relief. As we have seen, the infamous duo wrote their impatience with the fans into the text of the show ("Singularity," ENT 2.9), and when given one final chance to revive its fortunes, they ran as far away from its prequel concept as they could. As Hark acutely observes, a general sense of being trapped pervades the series:

> Three out of every ten episodes have plots that involve someone being kidnapped, held hostage, or imprisoned, and this doesn't count a number of others that deal with characters being marooned and cut off from rescue by their shipmates. The anxiety may come with the territory of an American narrative post-9/11,

but I cannot help but think that it also reflects the mindset of those running the show. Producing and writing still another *Trek* show had become a constricting and stressful process.[25]

Whatever feelings of relief they may have been experiencing, however, it is hard to argue that they left the stage with grace. Though they wrap up the Xindi plot, clarifying that the timeline is back on track from Daniels's future perspective, they immediately throw a confusing curve ball. The destruction of the Xindi weapon, just minutes away from a final attack on Earth, appeared, to T'Pol and the rest of the crew, to come at the cost of Archer's life—but in the season's final minutes, we see him awaken in a primitive medical tent, where we see an alien in a Nazi uniform.

In the thread mentioned above, several contemporaneous viewers recalled feeling excitement at the cliffhanger, which drove fevered fan speculation. In the DVD commentary to the episode, Connor Trineer (Trip) speculates that Berman and Braga ended in such an ambiguous way that the corporate higher-ups would not dare to spark fan outrage by canceling the show.[26] For my part, I find it difficult not to conclude that they wrote such a bizarre ending to create problems for their replacement, Manny Coto, a young writer-producer who had joined the writing staff in season 3 and had no previous *Star Trek* experience. It would have been a simple matter to tie up all the loose ends and leave Coto with a more or less blank slate. Instead, he had to start off the season by figuring out how to resolve the bizarre scenario his predecessors (and former bosses) had foisted on him.

Whatever the motivation for this strange plot twist, Coto rose to the challenge with creativity and vigor, penning a feature-length fourth season premiere ("Storm Front," ENT 4.1–2) that not only restored the pre-Nazi alien status quo but tied off the problematic Temporal Cold War arc once and for all. In Coto's resolution of Berman and Braga's scenario, Archer has found himself in a timeline created by the Na'kuhl, a temporal faction that had traveled back in time to aid the Nazi side. Daniels, in the process of transporting the NX-01 into the damaged timeline, explains that their radical intervention came at a cost: they could make only a one-way trip and had to use Earth's primitive technology to build a time machine to get back to their home period and see the results of their handiwork. Aided by an unlikely alliance of Black Americans and mafiosi, as well as the Suliban (in their final appearance), Archer and friends manage to prevent them from closing the circle, which means that they . . . will have never gone back in the first place? The temporal mechanics are admittedly complex, but in his final message from the future, Daniels once again confirms that the timeline has been restored to its intended condition and promises that Archer will never again have to deal with temporal meddling, because the Temporal Cold War is (or will have been?) "over." Aside from some brief references to the Xindi crisis, one of the central concepts of the show is unceremoniously dropped and never spoken of again. The identity and motives of Future Guy accordingly remain unknown, even to this day.

Thus far, little seems to have been achieved other than resetting the status quo to where it was before Archer's rude awakening in the Nazi timeline. Two episodes out of the season's reduced run of twenty-two thus take place in a bubble timeline, with no wider consequences, and are in that sense wasted. Thematically, though, the connection between time travel and Nazism introduces the leitmotif of season 4: genetic engineering, which the Na'kuhl promise to the Nazis and which comes up again and again in the remaining episodes. Like the time-travel theme that dominated the first three seasons, genetic tinkering raises questions of ancestry and legacy. But whereas Berman and Braga used time travel to seek freedom from the constraints of the franchise's past telling of their story's future,

Coto's focus on genetic manipulation clearly aims to demonstrate that *Enterprise* has authentic *Star Trek* DNA—above all by establishing as many connections as possible to the lore of *The Original Series*.

In some cases, this fan service is compatible with moving the story forward. For instance, perhaps the most successful arc of the season aims to explain and fix the Vulcans' unexpected behavior in the series by showing how Archer and T'Pol set off a reformation that helps Vulcans return to the true teachings of their spiritual founder, Surak ("The Forge," "The Awakening," and "Kir'Shara," ENT 4.7–9). This plot leads to the unwinding of the Vulcan High Command, laying the groundwork for the Federation to fill the power vacuum, and it also reveals that previous Vulcan leadership had been influenced by the nefarious Romulans, setting up the war. Another arc does similar double duty, as the Romulans develop an advanced drone ship that can appear to be any type of vessel, allowing it to sow chaos by staging false-flag attacks—a clear prelude to war ("Babel One," "United," and "The Aenar," ENT 4.12–14). The effort to track and destroy the drone ship also winds up strengthening ties among humans, Andorians, and Tellarites, again pushing toward the foundation of the Federation. As we will see, the novels seamlessly pick up these threads when they tell the story of the Romulan war; presumably *Enterprise* would have done much the same if it had not been canceled.

In other cases, the fan service is unforgivably self-indulgent. For instance, "Bound" (ENT 4.17), Coto's only solo writing credit in season 4 other than the two-part premiere, revisits one of Gene Roddenberry's most misogynistic creations, Orion slave girls, and aims to redeem the concept by clarifying that the apparent sex slaves actually dominate Orion society through their irresistible pheromones. One wishes Coto had followed the example of all post–*Original Series* writers and quietly left the Orion slave girls aside. We are also treated to a two-episode voyage into the Mirror Universe

("In a Mirror, Darkly," ENT 4.18–19), in which everyone's moral character is reversed. As in most treatments of this odd parallel world, the concept is played up for campy fun—one imagines that the writers started from the image of the normally timid Hoshi seizing power over the totalitarian Terran Empire and worked back from there. Yet the story has no relevance for the show's main plot, other than to emphasize the importance of Zefram Cochrane to the Prime Timeline by having his Mirror Universe equivalent murder the Vulcans and steal their ship on First Contact Day. The primary payoff of the episode is to put an *Original Series*–era ship—the *Defiant,* which disappeared into an alternate universe in "The Tholian Web" (TOS 3.9) and is here revealed to have been sucked into the Mirror Universe's distant past—on screen so that we can see that Archer and his colleagues appear in the ship's logs, confirming that the events of the series were known to "future" characters in the franchise.

Even more bizarre is the story arc that aims to explain why the Klingons of *The Original Series* did not have the forehead ridges seen in later productions, including *Enterprise* ("Affliction" and "Divergence," ENT 4.15–16). A *Deep Space Nine* outing ("Trials and Tribble-ations," DS9 5.6) in which the crew was digitally inserted into fan-favorite *Original Series* episode "The Trouble with Tribbles" (TOS 2.15) had played up this contradiction for laughs. But the season 4 writing staff joined the fan consensus in taking the joke literally as confirmation that it was not just a matter of different makeup budgets—the Klingons really looked that way during Kirk's five-year mission. The two-part arc in which the Klingons lose their ridges as a result of a contagious genetic alteration builds on a previous three-part arc focused on the fate of genetically augmented humans from the Eugenics wars, meaning that five total episodes—nearly one-fourth the running time of what was potentially the final season of televised *Star Trek*—were devoted to the Klingon ridge problem.

In the previous section, I chided Berman and Braga for being too dismissive of fans, but the creative trajectory of season 4—which most fans remember as the season when the show finally hit its stride—surely shows the dangers of pure fan service. What possible meaning or interest could "Bound" or "In a Mirror, Darkly" or the Klingon ridge plot have for anyone other than hard-core *Star Trek* fans? There are some real creative successes, such as the decision to structure most the season into arcs of two or three episodes, which turned out to be a good balance between episodic and serialized formats. And the penultimate arc ("Demons" and "Terra Prime," ENT 4.20–21), about a reactionary human group that attempts to sabotage the formation of the Coalition of Planets, represents a return to the distinctiveness of the characters and world of *Enterprise* after a full season that had been primarily about a show that had aired decades before. Hasan claims that Coto "quickly demonstrated his affinity for both these characters and the *Star Trek* universe,"[27] but in my view, the latter far overshadows the former. The fourth season reduces the *Enterprise* characters to little more than chess pieces in plots that aim to reconcile every perceived contradiction with established lore.

Once the show's cancellation was announced, Berman and Braga were brought back to craft a series finale ("These Are the Voyages . . . ," ENT 4.22), which Hasan rightly calls "an unfortunate, ignominious end."[28] Repeating the Mirror Universe arc's gesture of confirming that "later" characters knew about the events of *Enterprise,* they staged the NX-01's final mission—delivering Archer to the event where he will oversee the signing of the Federation charter—as a holodeck episode, set during the commercial breaks of the *Next Generation* episode "Pegasus" (TNG 7.12). There Will Riker (Jonathan Frakes) must face a difficult choice between loyalty to Picard and to his former commanding officer, and he and Deanna Troi (Marina Sirtis) use the events of that fateful historical mission as fodder to think through his dilemma. Along the way, the episode namechecks both the events of "Broken Bow" and the consequences of the Xindi arc, erasing any ambiguity about *Enterprise*'s place in the franchise by showing that the Temporal Cold War is indeed baked into the later timeline.

As an attempt to guarantee a connection between *Enterprise* and *Next Generation,* however, this framing is not fully convincing. They did not choose a particularly memorable or recognizable plot, the actors' more advanced age is unmistakable, and their characteristically loose handling of details returned as they did not even bother to make sure that Troi's hairstyle was the same as in the original episode. The lesson that Riker is supposed to learn is also difficult to discern, as Trip's tragic death in defense of Archer could be construed as pointing toward loyalty to either Picard or the former commanding officer. It even falls short as an attempt to give some closure to *Enterprise*'s arc by showing the Federation's foundation in 2161. Not only has no crew member been promoted or changed roles over the course of a decade, but Riker "unceremoniously ends the program just as Archer is beginning to speak" at the signing ceremony.[29] Finally, it is not a satisfying—or even minimally respectful—ending from the perspective of the show's main cast, who are reduced to bit players in a *Next Generation* holodeck episode. Braga reports that the filming of the episode "was the only time Scott Bakula was ever mean to me,"[30] and rightly so.

We may never fully know Berman and Braga's intentions, but I suspect that we are dealing with a level of self-indulgence even greater than the solution to the Klingon ridge problem. Though Berman conceded in 2017 that "Manny [Coto] had finally found the voice of the show, and season 4 should've been season 1,"[31] at the time, his abandonment of many of the show's key concepts and plotlines as well as his failure to develop the characters meaningfully must have rankled. This accounts, I believe, for the fact that all our heroes remain stagnant after a decade. More broadly, they seem to have taken the finale as an opportunity to process their emotions about the show's cancellation, using the fan-favorite character of Trip as a stand-in for the series as a whole. In a final dialogue before his never-heard speech, Archer complains to T'Pol: "When I took command ten years ago, I saw myself as an explorer. I thought all the risks would be worth it because, just beyond the next planet, just beyond the next star, there would be something magnificent, something noble. And now Trip is dead, and I have to give a speech about how worthwhile it's all been" ("These Are the Voyages . . . ," ENT 4.22). This use of Trip as a proxy for the show perhaps also explains T'Pol's odd declaration that she would like to meet Trip's parents. Though it does not fit plotwise—why would she not have met Trip's parents long before, given their romantic relationship?—it does make sense as an expression of hope that fans of *Enterprise* would revisit the "parent" shows. Yet presumably this recommendation was redundant for anyone still watching at that late date. Even in the series' closing moments, Berman and Braga show themselves to be out of touch with their audience.

In the end, *Enterprise* is a fragment, riven by contradictions and continually making promises its creators could not—and perhaps did not even want to—fulfill. It attempted to render *Star Trek*'s fictional history weighty and meaningful for the first time, and it built out a previously unseen era in often quite creative ways. Yet in many respects it continued the franchise's fast and loose approach to the details of continuity and spent much of its time, especially in the early seasons, on plots that were indistinguishable from *Next Generation*–era episodes. Its attempt to establish its crucial place in the *Star Trek* canon through the future perspective of Daniels only introduced confusion (and ultimately gave many fans an excuse to write the show out of the franchise entirely), while its lackadaisical pace prevented it from filling in the genuinely momentous events it was best positioned to address. Finally, Berman and Braga's often hostile attitude toward fans demonstrates, as Hark puts it, "how [*Star Trek*] creative personnel lost sight of how to function as a cult phenomenon in the new world of internet fandom"[32]—a task that their successor, Manny Coto, arguably botched to an equal degree by overcorrecting in the opposite direction.

Nevertheless, this failed prequel set the terms for the late *Star Trek* era. After *Enterprise,* all *Star Trek* creators were aware of the inherent tension between seeking artistic freedom and indulging in fan service, and all would make use of in-text meta gestures to reflect explicitly on their place in the franchise. As we will see next in chapters 2 and 3, the two main streams of official *Star Trek* material that followed, the novelverse and the Abrams reboot films, were true successors to *Enterprise* in two ways. First, they both benefited from fans' openness to new creators after the last men standing from the *Next Generation* era—indeed, the last producers to be in "apostolic succession" with Gene Roddenberry—had discredited themselves. Second, both also agreed that *Enterprise* had the right idea but did not go far enough. They differed profoundly on what that right idea was: the novelverse doubled down on continuity and fan service, while the new film series went all in on artistic freedom by establishing a new timeline. But both wrote their intention to follow in *Enterprise*'s halting footsteps into the text by making the redheaded stepchild of the franchise an explicit and even indispensable point of reference. Unexpectedly, characters and lore from the prequel series prove to be foundational for the novelverse's boldest and most creative world-building and for the Abrams films' most radical assertion of artistic freedom. Unwittingly and unwillingly, Berman and Braga had done more than close up shop on a waning era of *Star Trek*—they had laid the groundwork for a new one.

2

THE NOVELVERSE

THE LONGEST *STAR TREK* STORY EVER TOLD

N either *Enterprise*'s premiere nor its finale fared well in the tie-in novels. The first outing was taken up in the strange genre of the novelization, which expands on an episode or film in prose form. In an unusual but amusing move, Diane Carey, a prolific *Trek* author who had penned both novelizations and original tie-in novels, used her novelization of "Broken Bow" as a vehicle for essentially mocking her source material.[1] The implicit criticism usually takes the form of long stretches of indirect discourse purporting to relate characters' innermost thoughts as they attempt to reconcile themselves to a situation that Carey regards as contrived or nonsensical. The critique is subtle at first, as when Klaang—a fierce Klingon warrior—struggles to reconcile himself to the fact that he is running from the Suliban rather than engaging in combat.[2] By the halfway point, though, it becomes unmistakable. When she recounts Reed and Mayweather's visit to a seedy corner of the station where the *Enterprise* crew is seeking information about Klaang and the Suliban, Carey has Reed give voice to justified complaints: "Ah, yes, a brothel. What a shock. If he had been sketching out the most stereotypical mecca in all literature, this would be at its center. Didn't anyone do anything subtle anymore?"[3] Later, Reed's internal monologue expresses dread at the prospect of reporting what they have seen: "he didn't want to tell this story. Perhaps he could make something up that would be more interesting to hear about and less trite in the telling."[4]

Another awkward flirtation, this time with Sarin, a dissident former member of the Suliban Cabal who is disguised as a human woman, elicits a critique from Archer: "Oh, brother. This dame had seen too many steamy movies. She had the sticky dialogue down pat, not to mention the unoriginal seductive stare and liquid lips. What did they take him for?"[5] Archer cannot serve as readily as a pure projection screen, however, because the script gives him a more distinctive characterization than Reed—one Carey clearly does not care for. His internal monologue is petulant and hostile from beginning to end, especially in his interactions with T'Pol, for whom Carey has obvious (and understandable) sympathy. Part of her task in the novelization is to make the reasons for T'Pol's inclusion on the crew more explicit, and she settles on the idea—repeatedly contradicted in later episodes—that the Vulcans see humanity's unique potential and want "a formally logged record of humans and Vulcans working together under duress, with two completely different methods of command—and doing all right together."[6] At a crucial point in their mission, Archer declares that the partnership has already proven successful: "Her technical expertise and ability to stay cool, side by side with my irrational leaps of anger and whatever else I've got . . . it worked."[7]

In Carey's telling, though, even the erratic, impulsive Captain

Archer can discern that the Temporal Cold War makes no sense. In the same lengthy passage of invented dialogue where Archer and Tucker reason that the Vulcans are testing themselves as much as they are the human crew, the duo venture unexpectedly into the realm of theoretical physics: "The farther in the future they are, the more crazy and dangerous it is that they would be doing these things. While it has marginal effects on people here, it could completely change their own time. So what do they want?"[8] Reflecting on the tendency for the butterfly effect to wreck even the best-laid plans of temporal meddling, Archer and Tucker gradually conclude that the participants may well be insane.[9] This pattern of editorializing did not escape Berman and Braga, who discuss the issue at some length on a DVD commentary and report complaining to the book's editorial team. As the TrekBBS poster who transcribed the exchange notes: "By the way, Carey had written over 30 Trek books before *Broken Bow* in 2001, and none since. Coincidence?"[10] Even if they were able to get Carey blacklisted, however, the book was still published, snark and all.

The indignities did not wane in the original tie-in novels that continued the *Enterprise* story in the wake of its cancellation. In their novel *Last Full Measure,* which centers on conflict between Starfleet and Earth's military during the Xindi arc, authors Andy Mangels and Michael A. Martin include a framing narrative in which a young James T. Kirk meets the legendary Trip Tucker, unexpectedly alive and well.[11] Their follow-up effort, *The Good That Men Do,*[12] set in 2155 (the year in which *Enterprise* season 5 would have taken place), reveals the shocking truth: the story of Trip's death on the NX-01's final mission was falsified! Using a framing device in which *Deep Space Nine* characters Jake Sisko and Nog meet up to discuss some recently declassified files, the novel traces Trip's intuition that war with the Romulans is coming and his fateful decision to join Section 31 in order to do everything he can to tip the balance. To facilitate this career change, Archer and Reed arrange to fake Trip's death, in a sequence of events eerily reminiscent of the holodeck program Riker had pondered in "These Are the Voyages . . ." (ENT 4.22). (It is never explained why or how these events would then be transposed to a different mission six years later in the historical record.) With everyone but Archer and Reed believing he had died, Trip then begins his quest to penetrate behind enemy lines and, disguised as a Romulan scientist, disrupt a crucial military research project.

This improbable narrative begins a series of adventures in which Trip does un-Trip-like things while isolated from his friends, making his resurrection an ambiguous achievement in terms of plot and character development. From the perspective of the franchise's real-world history, however, it is a milestone: the first time that a tie-in novel was allowed to explicitly contradict and undo an on-screen event. As Sean Guynes and Gerry Canavan discuss in their chapter on the novels in the *Routledge Handbook of Star Trek,* the franchise's owners have long stipulated that only on-screen events are fully canon, meaning binding for future stories, whereas "an event that happens only in the novels is treated by *Star Trek* fans and creators alike as if it had never happened at all."[13] For a work of the so-called beta canon of the novels to overwrite an official event from the on-screen alpha canon therefore marks a major departure—and, like Carey's novelization, represents a particularly striking demonstration of "the capacity of franchise fiction, like fan fiction, to critique through reimagination."[14]

Guynes and Canavan use the term franchise fiction to underline their belief that franchise tie-in literature represents a distinctive genre unto itself, which they view as being "as readily open to the sort of in-depth, at-length critical writing regularly leveled at individual *Star Trek* episodes or films."[15] Yet—whether because it falls between the two stools of fully official *Star Trek* and the unofficial fiction produced by fans, or because of its reputation as purely derivative and therefore dispensable—*Star Trek* franchise fiction has rarely been discussed in the scholarly literature. (One notable exception is andré carrington's vindication of Steven Barnes's novelization of fan-favorite *Deep Space Nine* episode "Far Beyond the Stars," which David K. Seitz builds on in his book on the series.[16]) The tide may be turning, however, as an edited collection on the topic of tie-in fiction, incorporating both academic articles and reflections from *Trek* authors, recently appeared.[17] Nevertheless, at the time of its publication, Guynes and Canavan's chapter was to my knowledge the only extended scholarly discussion of the genre as such. This history of neglect is unfortunate, because the hundreds of extant novels "vastly outweigh all other media—including television—in the number of stories told about and set in the franchise's fictional universe" and accordingly "have operated as an imaginative space for fans to collectively work out the implications of concepts from televisual *Star Trek,* as well as to identify and attempt to resolve apparent contradictions in the character portraits, fictional history, and philosophical themes of the series."[18]

Any account of *Star Trek* that leaves out the novels is therefore bound to be incomplete, because "no franchise has produced more franchise fiction, nor produced it more consistently, than *Star Trek*"[19]—and never was this more true than in the awkward interregnum between *Enterprise* and *Discovery.* For that period of over a decade—and arguably for some indeterminate number of years before *Enterprise* was finally canceled—the novels became the primary driver of *Star Trek,* developing a sprawling continuity that draws in all eras and characters from the franchise and significantly changes the status quo of the *Next Generation*–era shows. The staggering complexity of this body of *Star Trek* literature is perhaps best captured by the frankly intimidating fan-produced diagram known as "The Almighty Star Trek Lit-verse Reading Order Flow Chart" (Figure 2).[20]

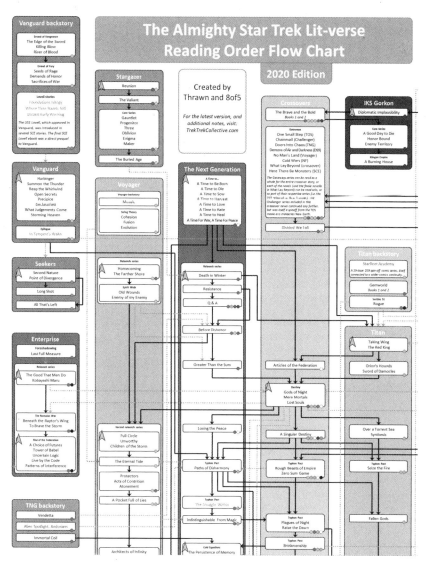

FIGURE 2. *A small portion of the flowchart of the novelverse created by Malcolm Eckel (Thrawn) and James Grigg (8of5), representing the stories connected to* Original Series, Enterprise, Voyager, *and* Next Generation, *along with a column for large-scale crossovers.*

I cannot hope to capture the full breadth and depth of all those stories, in part because my human finitude has prevented me from reading them all. In place of a full accounting—which surely almost no one is in a position to offer—I will attempt to provide a basic orientation to this rich and varied body of work. After a brief introduction to the history of the novels in general and their importance for fans, I will recount the slow emergence of the novel continuity beginning in the late 1990s and give an overview of its full flourishing in the wake of the commercial failure of *Enterprise* and the *Next Generation* film *Star Trek Nemesis.* I will then turn to a study of three of the most important authors of the novelverse, Christopher L. Bennett, Kirsten Beyer, and David Mack, who respectively exemplify the fan service, artistic freedom, and Federation (or fresh world-building) strategies and provide further confirmation that each of the three dialectically calls forth the other two. Finally, I will conclude with a consideration of the novelverse's strange denouement in the *Coda* trilogy, where the authors continue late *Star Trek*'s trend of integrating meta reflections into their work by writing their struggle with the unexpected arrival of *Star Trek: Picard*—and the consequent overwriting of the beta canon novel timeline by fresh alpha canon material—into the story itself.

THAT DANGEROUS SUPPLEMENT . . .

I have never met a serious *Star Trek* fan who has not read at least a few novels. This may be changing for younger generations of fans, as I will discuss in later chapters, but for both *Original Series*– and *Next Generation*–era fans, novels are an integral part of the *Star Trek* experience, in some cases even overshadowing the aired episodes. For many fans my age, for example, Peter David's tie-in novels are more vivid and memorable touch points than the show itself. I can picture myself eagerly tearing through *Vendetta,* feeling that I was finally getting the inside truth about the Borg.[21] I am presumably also far from the first young teenage *Star Trek* fan to feel vaguely embarrassed yet undeniably intrigued by *Imzadi*,[22] which provides a sometimes *very* intimate look into the early courtship of Will Riker and Deanna Troi. The outsize impact of these novels is easy to understand. Given their greater length, they are able to go into more depth than any episode ever could, and they also represent a far greater time investment on the reader's part. Perhaps more importantly, though, they provide the unique experience of choosing what to explore—a rare privilege in the pre-streaming (and even pre-DVD) days, when access to *Star Trek* was typically limited to one or two weekly time slots or the random vagaries of late-night syndicated reruns.

In the earliest days of the franchise, maintaining reliable access to the existing stories was the number one priority. James Blish's novelizations of *The Original Series* episodes started a long tradition of translating on-screen content to prose. This tradition ended shortly after Diane Carey's sarcastic adaptation of "Broken Bow," as the streaming shows understandably chose to forego novelizations. At a time when the whole *Star Trek* archive is available on demand, such works are clearly redundant, but in previous eras, they were the most reliable way to relive favorite episodes. (In fact, Alan Dean Foster's adaptations of *The Animated Series,* which was almost impossible to find for decades after its brief Saturday morning run, were for years effectively the only way for fans to experience those stories.) Obviously the novelization is an extremely constricting genre, but even here, authors have found room for creativity, filling in background and adding supplementary internal monologues that can strongly influence fans' experience of the canon text. Perhaps the most exemplary case here is Gene Roddenberry's own novelization of *Star Trek: The Motion Picture*,[23] which enjoys a quasi-canon status and has even proven essential to understanding some baffling moments in the film (such as one character's seemingly unmotivated declaration that she has taken a vow of celibacy).

Of greater interest are the licensed original stories, which began to be published in the late 1960s but which, as Guynes and Canavan point out, only became truly popular once fan culture reached a critical mass in the late 1970s, starting "a surge in *Star Trek* novel publishing that never abated."[24] Most tie-in novels aspired to be little more than lost episodes, giving fans new one-off adventures that reliably reset to status quo ante. By the mid-1980s, however, some authors began attempting to go beyond simply providing more *Star Trek* adventures and instead sought to deepen our understanding of the universe. The most remarkable contributor from this era is Diane Duane, whose 1988 novel *Spock's World* offers an astonishingly ambitious account of Vulcan culture and history, starting even from the early evolutionary history of life on Spock's home planet.[25]

Rival species especially benefited from the new ambition among *Trek* authors. Before the publication of *Spock's World,* Duane had made a name for herself with a series in which she provided a similarly comprehensive account of the Romulans. The inaugural effort, *My Enemy, My Ally* (1984),[26] paints a strikingly sympathetic portrait of the enemy species, and the sequel, *The Romulan Way* (1987),[27] is told from an almost entirely Romulan perspective, alternating between a history of the Romulans' quest to leave their native Vulcan and found a new society and a present-day story about a deep-cover Federation spy who has all but gone native. Duane's account of the Romulans was so popular that, in an unprecedented move, she was allowed to continue her series on its own terms, even after on-screen events contradicted her account of Romulan culture and history. The Klingons receive a similarly nuanced treatment in John M. Ford's *The Final Reflection* (1984),[28] which adopts an entirely Klingon perspective aside from a framing device in which the *Enterprise* crew is obsessively passing around the novel that we are about to read. Ford's portrait of a Klingon society marked by the contradiction between its stated value of honor and its sordid power politics, together with his account of the ways that the Federation and the Klingons often need to save each other from themselves, proved so popular among fans that it wound up shaping the on-screen portrayal of *Star Trek*'s ultimate rival species, who up to that point had only been vaguely sketched out in the on-screen canon. That influence continues to be active, as *Star Trek: Discovery*'s cocreator, Bryan Fuller, assigned *The Final Reflection* as "required reading for those dealing with Klingons and *Discovery*."[29] Here the novels become a supplement in the full Derridean sense, substituting for and even subverting what they presumably exist to serve.

It is no mistake that the most ambitious beta canon entries of this era tended to address *The Original Series* rather than *Next Generation*. Given the novels' secondary status, they are constantly in danger of being overwritten by new on-screen events. Only once a show is safely off the air can authors be fully confident that their efforts will not be rendered redundant. Guynes and Canavan point out that Pocket Books "began to develop a loose internal continuity independently of reference to the series in the 1980s and 1990s,"[30] but any effort at a more thoroughgoing consistency and development across the novels was largely doomed as long as *Next Generation*–era series were still airing. One notable exception, however, was the *New Frontiers* series, cocreated by Pocket Books editor John Ordover and author Peter David (who also served as the sole writer of the series). Centering on an entirely new crew tasked with keeping peace in a never-before-seen region of space, the series could not rely on readers' preexisting familiarity and thus was at once constrained and empowered to create its own internal continuity to flesh out its characters and setting.

The first decisive move toward a shared continuity for the tie-in series was the development of a *Deep Space Nine* relaunch series by editor Mark Palmieri, who gave his writers the chance to continue the story beyond the finale. Given that *Deep Space Nine* had done so much to introduce serialization and systematic world-building into the franchise, it is fitting that it served as a template for subsequent development of the novelverse. While building on existing characters and scenarios, the relaunch novels, beginning with S. D. Perry's *Avatar* duology (2001),[31] also changed the status quo by creating new characters and tying existing characters from other series into the *Deep Space Nine* story, both of which would become hallmarks of subsequent novelverse series. A short-lived *Voyager* relaunch series followed, starting with Christie Gold's *Homecoming* (2003),[32] though it proved difficult to keep the story going once the show's natural arc had concluded with the crew's return home from the Delta Quadrant.

The moment when the novelverse truly emerged, however, was in the wake of *Next Generation* films *Insurrection* (1998) and *Nemesis* (2002). Both films introduced plot points that were difficult to reconcile with previous canon events. For instance, the exact timing of *Insurrection* in relation to *Deep Space Nine*'s Dominion war is ambiguous, and *Nemesis* features appearances by Worf and Wesley Crusher that are difficult to understand, given the former's role as Klingon ambassador and the latter's conversion into a transcendent being known as a Traveler. The attempt to create a scenario that could account for these and other apparent discrepancies ultimately gave birth to a massive nine-book miniseries—all released rapidly over the course of a single year—that tied together the events from the existing series and films while laying the foundation for a radically altered galactic status quo. In what became known as the *A Time To . . .* series (2004),[33] with each book named after a phrase from Ecclesiastes 3:1–8, the various authors craft an increasingly dark narrative of corruption and betrayal on the part of Starfleet Command, which culminates in the assassination of a Federation president by the off-book black ops organization Section 31—a plot in which Picard is unwittingly complicit. Along the way they introduce characters who will ultimately serve under Captain Riker on the USS *Titan* and provide a tantalizing glimpse into the workings of the Federation government. Indeed, the assassination clears the way for a special election, which is won by no-nonsense Nanietta "Nan" Bacco, perhaps the most charming and popular character ever created directly for the novels. She and her closest aides would go on to star in Keith R. A. DeCandido's fan-favorite novel *Articles of the Federation* (2005),[34] which serves as a kind of *West Wing* in space, giving fans an unprecedented window into the nitty-gritty details of intergalactic politics while centering characters who had never appeared on screen.

Clearly the series far exceeds its initial mandate to account for Worf's strange career trajectory from ambassador back to security officer and Wesley's unexpected ability to reappear in human form, just as it far exceeds what anyone could reasonably expect the authors to spin out of the straw of these unloved *Next Generation* films. It is hard for me to imagine a better example of the necessary relationship between my three franchise strategies: the initial attempt at pure fan service gives way to a development of *Star Trek*'s worldbuilding that makes room for considerable artistic freedom. Following in the footsteps of the *Deep Space Nine* relaunch and the *A Time To . . .* series, the rotating cast of *Trek* tie-in writers would ultimately use this new novel-only status quo as the basis for showing us the following:

- The Romulan war and early years of the Federation.
- A new cast of characters on board *The Original Series*–era space station *Vanguard*.
- What Kirk and friends were up to in the years between *The Motion Picture* (1979) and *Wrath of Khan* (1982).
- A whole bunch of Mirror Universe stories involving not-so-evil-after-all counterparts to the *Next Generation* crew.

- A devastating war with the Borg that would lead to the death of Admiral Kathryn Janeway, the revelation of the Borg's origin, and their near-miraculous defeat.
- The marriage of Captain Picard and Dr. Beverly Crusher and the birth of their son, along with the marriage of Riker and Troi and their (ultimately successful) struggle to conceive a child.
- The Department of Temporal Investigations' various attempts to work with its counterparts in future centuries to maintain a stable timeline.
- The destruction and rebuilding of the *Deep Space Nine* station in the wake of Benjamin Sisko's unexpected return from "dwelling with the Prophets."
- The revelation that Section 31 has been run by an artificial intelligence known as Control that has been manipulating events from the earliest days of Starfleet history, leading to the final defeat and liquidation of that morally ambiguous organization.
- The return of the USS *Voyager* at the head of a fleet tasked with exploring the Delta Quadrant, where Janeway is resurrected by Q and ultimately leads a mission beyond the boundaries of our galaxy.
- The formation of a kind counter-Federation of "bad guy" species known as the Typhon Pact.
- Picard's desperate effort to erase all these events from existence to save the Prime Timeline from destruction.

Along the way, the established characters and a large cast of new ones experience all manner of reshuffling in terms of posting, career role, and at times even romantic involvement. It is, in short, a lot to process.

THREE APPROACHES TO THE NOVELVERSE

I have read multiple novels in nearly all of these plot trajectories and am happy to provide recommendations. For the sake of our present enterprise, however, I will leave aside any effort to tackle the novelverse as a whole in favor of a brief overview of the work of three authors who have made significant contributions, and whom I take to be exemplary of my three strategies: Christopher L. Bennett (fan service), Kirsten Beyer (freedom), and David Mack (Federation or world-building). As always, though, the strategies cannot exist alone, and one thing that makes these three authors so accomplished is the way that they use their preferred strategy as a starting point for weaving them all together in their own unique ways.

Christopher Bennett is a *Star Trek* fan's *Star Trek* fan. He is a veritable scholar of franchise lore, with an intimidating grasp of the smallest details. This scholarly impression is reinforced by his publication of detailed annotations for every one of his *Star Trek* publications, clarifying his references to both alpha and beta canon as well as real scientific articles that support his speculations. His *Trek* fiction also has an impressive range, as he is one of only a few authors to complete what he calls a "grand slam": writing "tie-ins for every onscreen [pre-streaming] Trek series, as well as several book-only ones."[35] He is best known as creator and sole author of the fan-favorite book-only series *Department of Temporal Investigations,* which, in Guynes and Canavan's words, "attempts the impossible task of rationalizing every *Star Trek* time travel story ever filmed into a single, coherent system."[36]

The series takes as its starting point the framing device of "Trials and Tribble-ations" (DS9 5.6), in which representatives from the Department of Temporal Investigations (DTI) grill Sisko about his actions when time-traveling to Kirk's era. As in *Enterprise*'s Klingon ridge saga, something that was clearly a joke—the agents are named Dulmur and Lucsly, in tribute to *The X Files'* Mulder and Scully, despite both being men—is taken deadly seriously. Dulmur (the fun one) and Lucsly (the by-the-book one) become our primary point-of-view characters, and their adventures give us a window into the structure of the DTI, the way it trains new agents, and its relationship to future temporal agencies (both the thirty-first-century outfit that sent Daniels to watch after Archer and an earlier one introduced in *Voyager*). The bulk of the conceptual work happens in the first novel of the series, *Watching the Clock*,[37] which reveals that by Daniels's time, the *Star Trek* universe has settled into a single timeline where the Borg have been eliminated (more on that later) and peace reigns. Using actual research in quantum physics, Bennett uses conversations among his characters to bridge the gap between *Star Trek*'s frequent claim that characters are changing or even overwriting a single timeline and more common contemporary portrayals of time travel in which altering a past event produces a fork, or a new parallel universe. In his account, both are happening: time travel does introduce forks, but in the long run, the various timelines are competing according to how probable they are. Guided by temporal agents within the single dominant timeline of the thirty-first century, the DTI's task is to manage the number and type of time-travel events so that the desired outcome remains the most probable. Sometimes this means tolerating brazen violations of the Temporal Prime Directive—most notably when DTI has to look the other way and tolerate Admiral Janeway's illicit use of time travel to deliver a crushing blow to the Borg ("Endgame," VOY 7.25), simply because there are so few possible timelines where the Borg are defeated.[38] Most often they need to prevent tampering, though there are cases where they find themselves, much to their horror, participating in a temporal incursion for the greater good.

On one level, the series is pure fan service, and in fact the weight of reconciling continuity for its own sake often distracts from plot and character development. Some of Bennett's clarifications—such as the true identity of Future Guy, who turns out to be a random minor player in the Temporal Cold War—are disappointing, but some moments of fan service are pure joy, as when he presents all the time-travel episodes of *The Original Series* and *Animated Series* as part of an overarching plot and includes "deleted scenes" where the characters acknowledge the dangers of what they are doing.[39] Yet the project of the series required significant scientific research and reasoning on Bennett's part, and his theory of time travel—though motivated by the effort to impose coherence on a preexisting body of stories written by many hands over the course of decades—strikes me as a creative one that could serve as the basis for a new science fiction franchise that took it as its starting point. In other words, a thoroughgoing, rigorous effort at fan service wound up producing something that was at once deeply creative and a major contribution to the franchise's world-building.

Bennett does not always hold together all three elements as successfully. At times he uses *Trek* as an excuse to puzzle out a science fiction concept of his own invention, as when he uses an adventure of Riker's *Titan* to explore what it would be like for a fully aquatic species to develop technology.[40] More often he takes fan service too far, as in *The Captain's Oath,* where he attempts to account for everything that is said on screen about Kirk's early service record by telling a story that jumps across three different time periods in a way that winds up making the plot unsatisfying and difficult to follow.[41] Even less engaging is his *Enterprise* novel *Tower of Babel*,[42] which is bogged down by his effort to synthesize the franchise's many references to Rigel (a readily visible real-life star). At times, though, the self-indulgence loops back to a kind of brilliance, as in *The Collectors,* where the DTI discovers a species that "collects" extinct species from across the galaxy and our hero's ill-considered intervention into their menagerie leads to the creation of a Borg *Tyrannosaurus rex.*[43]

Aside from *The Department of Temporal Investigations,* Bennett's only other opportunity to do large-scale world-building was in the *Rise of the Federation* series, which continued the story of *Enterprise* after the finale. This series constituted a second relaunch of *Enterprise,* after Martin and Mangels's effort to extend the series was abruptly cut short when a projected trilogy on the Romulan war was reduced to two books, resulting in a garbled, confusing resolution to that conflict. Bennett was able to pick up the pieces and tell the story of the Federation's early years in a way that is (with the exception noted above) elegant and convincing. He maintains his characteristic eagle eye for details of the lore and tries to make all of *Enterprise* a usable history by following up on one-off species and concepts in a way that makes the original episodes feel more meaningful, most notably "Dead Stop" (ENT 2.4), which sets up a two-novel arc that includes significant independent world-building.[44] The mysterious automated station from that episode, which offers repairs ostensibly free of charge while kidnapping crew members to use their brains as computers, turns out to be a widespread phenomenon. The Coalition of Planets tries to eliminate it but encounters a major moral dilemma when it turns out that some species submit to it voluntarily in order to gain access to technology—and in some cases, to achieve sentience. At the same time, he develops a new storytelling style, dividing the original *Enterprise* characters across multiple ships so that he can have a window into a wider range of scenarios. The result is a much more convincing account of the emergence of things like the Prime Directive than Berman, Braga, or Coto were ever likely to offer, showing that rigorous fan service is fully compatible with creative world-building.

In many ways, Kirsten Beyer is the polar opposite of Christopher Bennett. She has written for only one *Star Trek* property, namely *Voyager,* and has been much more intent on moving the story forward than filling in continuity gaps. Yet she shares with Bennett the task of reviving a failed relaunch series for a segment of the franchise that the novel continuity had left in shambles.

After the failure of Christie Gold's initial relaunch, the *Voyager* characters largely fell into disuse. Even worse, the main character, Kathryn Janeway, was no longer available because she had been killed. In *Before Dishonor*,[45] Peter David introduced a new and even more sinister turn for the Borg. Driven mad by the crushing blow delivered by Janeway's aforementioned time-travel shenanigans, they had turned from abducting and assimilating people (that is, surgically altering them to include cybernetic components and incorporating them into a hive mind) to simply destroying as much of the Federation as possible. Their campaign began on an apparently abandoned Borg ship, which Janeway, in her hubris, chose to investigate firsthand—only to be assimilated and, worse, turned into a Borg Queen, leaving Picard no choice but to destroy the ship, and her along with it. The storyline is deeply disrespectful of Janeway's character, reducing her death to a powerful object lesson for Picard, who of all people needs no reminder that the Borg are dangerous. Breakout character Seven of Nine had not fared much better. Throughout the Borg arc that began with *Before Dishonor*, her role was essentially to attend meetings where she said fatalistic things about the Borg's likely victory. Even worse, when the Borg were finally eliminated, she was "cured" of her Borgness—a profound violation of the character's story arc, which was grounded in her struggle to find a positive use for her oppressive upbringing in the Borg Collective.

In Beyer, the novel continuity found someone who combined a genuine talent for storytelling with a real respect and affection for the *Voyager* characters. Unfortunately, it had only found her once the novels had written all the *Voyager* plotlines into bizarre corners. Rather than follow Bennett's procedure of trying to recover a usable history from the previous novels, Beyer's first entry in the second relaunch series, *Full Circle,* is dominated by the attempt to write her way *out* of all of those corners.[46] Indeed, her goal is to get out of the milieu of the tie-in novels altogether by returning the *Voyager* characters to the remote Delta Quadrant—but this time voluntarily. As he struggles to cope with his former captain's death, Chakotay, Janeway's erstwhile first officer and long-smoldering love interest, discovers that she had been working on a secret project called Full Circle, which would send a small fleet of vessels to the Delta Quadrant using a newly perfected high-speed propulsion technology known as quantum slipstream. Now another admiral has taken up the charge.

Even more than Bennett's focus on multiple ships, Beyer's use of a fleet marks an innovation in *Star Trek* storytelling. In addition to setting up all manner of potential conflicts and complications, it allows her to explore new concepts like a medical vessel staffed entirely by sentient holograms like *Voyager*'s Emergency Medical Hologram (known only as the Doctor). The need to replace Janeway also sets up an interesting story arc for the character Beyer invents to replace her, Afsarah Eden. While at first she seems like a simple stand-in, Eden is revealed to have her own motive for exploring the Delta Quadrant: she is an orphan seeking to be reunited with her species in that remote area of space. Her relationship with her ex-husband, fellow admiral Willem Batiste, is not only the first extended portrayal of divorce in *Star Trek* history but also sets up a further continuing plot arc when he is revealed to be a sleeper agent for the hostile Species 8472. The invention of these new characters and arcs may be a partial silver lining of the death of Janeway, because an immediate return to the original cast may have tempted Beyer to return too quickly to the old status quo of the series. By the time she arranges Janeway's resurrection (through the help of god-like Q),[47] a new status quo has emerged, and her return introduces further complications rather than representing a reversion to the norm. Similarly, the way that Beyer deals with Seven's apparently cured condition takes a scenario imposed on her by the novel continuity and effectively undoes it (the cure is no cure at all and in fact is driving her insane), using it to deeply explore Seven's relationship to her Borg identity in a world where she is the only remaining representative of that species.[48]

One could say that Beyer's signature gesture as a tie-in novelist is precisely to acknowledge the existing continuity in order to get away from it. The events of the novelverse are continually referenced yet strangely inessential. Put differently, the series is in perfect continuity but tells exactly, and only, the story it wants to tell. This makes it the only *Next Generation*–era segment of novel continuity that can be read and enjoyed on its own. She does not contribute to the novelverse's world-building so much as navigate it. Her priority is character, and she makes every returning character from *Voyager* and most recurring characters from the broader fleet vivid and believable. It is perhaps this unique combination of skills, along with the fan and critical acclaim her *Voyager* novels enjoyed, that led to her joining the streaming-era writing and production team, where she was "hired as a staff writer on *[Discovery]* before becoming co-creator of *[Picard]*"—a trajectory that Guynes and Canavan rightly characterize as "unique."[49]

At the time she joined the television crew, Beyer's *Voyager* series was unfinished, and she herself had a hand in the development of the show that would effectively overwrite it. Yet Beyer returned one last time to the novelverse to give the *Voyager* crew an appropriate send-off, as Janeway and the fleet embark on an unprecedented mission to a neighboring galaxy.[50] This redoubling of the choice to return to the Delta Quadrant on purpose not only cements Janeway's status as the greatest explorer in Starfleet history but also shields the *Voyager* crew from any entanglement in the events that would wind down the novelverse—and any further abuse at the hands of other authors. Though her role on *Prodigy* means that this novel cannot stand as the last word on the ultimate trajectory of Janeway's career, the ending feels so undeniably true to the character that I am sure that, if given the opportunity, Beyer would find a way to get there from whatever starting point the franchise provided.

Of the authors I am considering, the third, David Mack, has been by far the most prolific. According to their respective Memory Alpha wiki pages, Mack has written thirty-five *Star Trek* novels (with one more published subsequently), Bennett twenty-two, and Beyer eleven.[51] No current *Trek* author has written more, and even the sheer volume of his output arguably understates his impact on the novel continuity. He had his hand in every major event in the novelverse's sprawling narrative, most often taking charge of the moves that most decisively broke with the televised status quo.

The most dramatic example is the *Destiny* series, in which he draws together all *Next Generation*–era shows (including *Enterprise*) to craft a narrative that at once reveals the origins of the Borg and documents their defeat.[52] Even more than Beyer, this story uses the existing continuity as a jumping-off point for creative development, but it implicitly justifies itself by positioning the elimination of the Borg as deeply necessary for the very survival of *Star Trek*. He achieves this within the narrative itself by building on the series of Borg-focused novels that began with Peter David's *Before Dishonor,* presenting the Borg as absolutely undefeatable, except by a miracle. From the perspective of the franchise as a whole, this portrayal forces an issue that has long been noted by fans: the Borg are simply too powerful. Even one of their distinctive cube-like ships—which is, unaccountably, the maximum number they ever send to a battle—is enough to pummel whole fleets of Starfleet vessels. Once they conquer a species or region, it is totally and irrevocably conquered because the population has been incorporated into the hive mind. The only way to imagine a happy future for the Federation and the galaxy as a whole is for them to be defeated, but that outcome seems absolutely impossible.

Mack's novel trilogy not only achieves that impossible goal but also answers long-standing fan questions about the origin of the Borg—indeed, he seamlessly does both at once. On the one hand, he confirms the widespread fan intuition that these cybernetic villains must have some necessary relationship to humanity. To achieve this, he plucks Captain Erika Hernandez and the crew of the *Columbia* NX-02, bit players in *Enterprise* season 4, from obscurity, making a forgotten character from the hated prequel foundational to his ambitious plot. Hernandez's crew suffers a major systems failure during the Romulan war and can travel only at near-light speeds, meaning that they can only reach the nearest planet at the cost of losing decades of time, the result of relativistic temporal paradoxes. They eventually make contact with a godlike species known as the Caeliar, who are able to use an advanced technology known as ca-toms to manipulate matter directly with their minds. While Hernandez ultimately joins the Caeliar society, exchanging her normal human body for one made of catoms, a segment of her crew tries to hijack the Caeliar's technology to go back in time and help fight the Romulans. They wind up overshooting the mark by several centuries and then interfacing with the Caeliar catoms in a way that turns the ringleader into the first Borg Queen, whose paranoia and fear drive her to create the Borg Collective. The Caeliar thus provide the ultimate origin of the Borg as well as the means to defeat them, as Hernandez is able to interface with the Collective and use her Caeliar powers to simply eliminate them all from our heroes' dimension.

This summary makes the story sound absurd (as all *Star Trek* stories ultimately do). Yet the three novels are undeniably absorbing and provide meaningful development for many favorite characters—not to mention giving a believable account of Hernandez's deepening relationship with the Caeliar, and especially her primary handler. The main thrust of the story is classic *Star Trek:* a Starfleet captain (one of the first, in fact) is able to accept and even join with something more radically alien than almost any species we have ever seen on screen while maintaining her humanity, and this combination is what ultimately saves the *Star Trek* universe. It is also the kind of meta moment characteristic of late *Star Trek,* since Mack's account of the human origin of the Borg echoes the implicit claim that the Borg's overwhelming power was a trap of the franchise's own making. Despite eliminating arguably the coolest concept ever developed by *Star Trek,* the *Destiny* trilogy was well received among fans. In a recent retrospective review on TrekCore, for instance, Alex Perry declared that *Destiny* is "the best *Star Trek* story ever published in prose. A stunning achievement of audacious scale, I doubt anything will quite shake *Destiny* from the top spot of my all-time favorite *Star Trek* books."[53]

Destiny is not Mack's only major contribution to the novel continuity. He got his start by contributing two volumes to the foundational *A Time To* . . . series, which set up the story of the Federation president's corruption and ultimate assassination by Section 31[54]—an arc that laid the foundation for the novelverse's unique exploration of Federation politics as well as its exploration of Section 31's role in Federation history. The latter plot came to a head in *Control,*[55] which claims that Section 31 is ultimately run by a centuries-old AI that has been surveilling Starfleet and manipulating major events since Archer's time. As with the Borg arc, this at once confirms fan intuition and eliminates a major threat to the *Star Trek* project. While Section 31 has appeared in only a few episodes, it has been a major object of fan speculation, especially when *Enterprise* revealed that it had existed from the earliest days of Starfleet. During the long interregnum between *Enterprise* and *Discovery,* in fact, one of the most popular topics for fan theories on r/DaystromInstitute (other than writing *Enterprise* out of the Prime Timeline) consisted of attributing various shady events to Section 31 or claiming that well-known characters were actually Section 31 agents. Mack takes those fan theories and radicalizes them, positing that all of *Star Trek* history has been corrupted by Section 31—but only as a prelude to eliminating it for good, when Data and friends defeat the AI and publicize its nefarious schemes.

Mack's ambitions are not always so world shaping. For instance, the *Vanguard* series, set in *The Original Series* era, emphasizes creative freedom above all,[56] inventing a whole new cast of characters, an unforeseen set of complex political dynamics, and a godlike species wielding powerful ancient technology. Though it does feature cameos from Kirk's *Enterprise* crew and name-drops major events from the series, the overall goal is to avoid affecting the existing continuity, since the series ends with the station's destruction and the sealing of all records related to the tumultuous events we have just seen. In contrast, the *Cold Equations* miniseries attempts little but the fan service of resurrecting Data at long last.[57] Once again, he confirms widespread fan theories that downloading his memories into B4, a more primitive prototype introduced in *Nemesis,* would prove decisive. Yet even here he introduces his own twist—Data's "father," Doctor Soong, faked his own death and uploaded himself into a superior android body, which he donates to Data once he learns that B4's programming is degrading under the strain of storing Data's, well, data. When Data takes over the new body, he is affected by Doctor Soong's memories and personality, causing him to become a noticeably different character who is not content simply to return to the status quo.

Overall, we could say that David Mack's signature world-building gesture, at least in his most ambitious works, is to push *Star Trek*'s contradictions to their limits, then swoop in with a resolution that allows the story to move forward. While there are many other authors who made creative contributions to the novel continuity and broke with the status quo in major ways, it is this sense of conceptual necessity that makes me identify Mack as the real architect of this corner of the franchise. He is not simply reshuffling the characters in soap opera fashion. He is thinking deeply about the implications of the franchise's existing world-building and what needs to change to save *Star Trek* from itself. Yet even if the ultimate payoff of his narratives is negative—finally getting rid of the Borg or Section 31— the path he takes to get there combines the fan service of satisfying character development with the creativity of totally new concepts (such as the Caeliar or the Control AI). Mack was never able to attain the levels of sheer franchise erudition that Bennett specialized in, nor (with the possible exception of *Vanguard*) did he ever find his way to the same kind of blank canvas that Beyer created for herself. Instead, he drew on both of their strategies in the service of building the world of the relaunch novels into something that demands to be taken seriously—not as a churning out of endless new material for obsessed fans, but as a thoughtful and distinctive iteration of *Star Trek*.

"ARE WE SURE WE SHOULD BE DOING THIS?"

However we determine its boundaries, and however we calculate the amount of plot in a novel versus a TV episode or a film, the novelverse is easily the longest continuous *Star Trek* story ever told. This feat was only possible because, as David Mack puts it in the acknowledgments to the final installment of the novel continuity, "no one—not the authors, editors, or licensing executives—expected there to be more films or series continuing the narratives of *Star Trek: The Next Generation, Star Trek: Deep Space Nine,* and *Star Trek Voyager.*"[58] That expectation held even with the arrival of *Star Trek: Discovery* in 2017. Because the show was set before *The Original Series* era—where, aside from the hermetically self-enclosed *Vanguard* series, the novels had all been episodic one-offs for decades—it was not in a position to overwrite or contradict anything from the main novel continuity.

That all changed with the announcement of *Star Trek: Picard* in

August 2018. In Mack's words, "Within a few episodes, it became clear that the literary continuity we had conceived and crafted for nearly twenty years could not be reconciled with the future described in *Picard*'s backstory. One revelation after another pushed our vision of the late twenty-fourth century farther and farther out of concurrence with the newly established canon."[59] When the announcement was first made, the novelverse authors must have felt that all their efforts were accurately described by the title of the first *Next Generation*–era novel to be released in the wake of the announcement: *Collateral Damage*.[60] The main story of that novel winds down one of Mack's longest-running plot threads, as Captain Picard is put on trial for complicity with Section 31's assassination of the Federation president—a charge of which he is of course ultimately cleared. Reading it at the time, I thought that it provided at least some closure for a continuity that would soon have to end. But Mack and his collaborators had other ideas. Rather than accept a situation where "our labors of two decades would be cast aside, abandoned *in medias res* . . . we would need to find a way to bring them to a conclusion."[61] Joined by longtime *Trek* novelists James Swallow and Dayton Ward, Mack spearheaded one final novelverse event: a trilogy, to be published at the breakneck pace of one novel a month, which would bring the continuity to a definitive end.

The plot is suitably complex. The first novel, by Dayton Ward, introduces the basic scenario.[62] Wesley Crusher, using his mysterious powers as a Traveler, discerns that something terrible is happening. The Devidians—an alien race that feeds on suffering, last seen in the *Next Generation* two-parter where they find Data's head in a cave and hang out with Mark Twain ("Time's Arrow," TNG 5.26–6.1)—have discovered that they can gain unimaginable power by creating and then collapsing alternate timelines, to harvest the suffering of the billions upon billions of lives snuffed out. Their home base appears to be the novelverse timeline, and Picard and friends try and fail to stop their ghoulish time-travel manipulations. In a signal of seriousness that many readers found cheap,[63] we see the death of late-season *Deep Space Nine* regular Ezri Dax (who had been promoted to captain of a highly advanced ship in previous novels) and beloved novel-only character T'Ryssa Chen (a half-Vulcan with attitude).

The second installment, by James Swallow, kicks the series into high gear.[64] The focus shifts to *Deep Space Nine* characters, as our heroes discover that the Bajoran wormhole, which houses the nontemporal beings the Bajorans worship as the Prophets, is a major tool for the Devidians. They make the unimaginable decision to collapse the wormhole, and it is ultimately Kira—a faithful worshipper of the Prophets, who has long since given up her military commission in favor of joining the Bajoran clergy—who must pull the trigger and kill her own gods. But Picard begins to feel that even this radical move is not enough. He approaches Starfleet Command with an unthinkable plan: they must travel back in time to erase the forked timeline they have been living in, lest the Devidians gain access to the Prime Timeline. Not only does this write the novel continuity's existence as an alternate timeline into the text of the story itself, but it also specifies that the fork began with the time-travel manipulations of the film *First Contact,* reflecting the fact that the novelverse first fully emerged in the gap between the final two films. Naturally, Starfleet Command is skeptical, and here they have the support of Riker, who unexpectedly becomes the main antagonist when Picard predictably goes rogue to do what he thinks is best.

In the conclusion, fittingly penned by David Mack, events come to a head—but not before Mack pays one last visit to his version of the *Next Generation*–era Mirror Universe. The in-text excuse for this excursion is that they have a piece of technology needed for their grim quest, but it feels like an uncharacteristic self-indulgence, as though Mack is trying to follow up on every distinctive novelverse scenario one last time. Ultimately, through a complex sequence involving "simultaneous" actions at two different points in the time-line and one nontemporal realm, Picard and company succeed in erasing themselves from existence. In this, they get some help from Riker, whose short-lived enmity turns out to be the result of his being haunted by the shadows of the different timelines that the Devidians are erasing. Aside from Riker, the other characters all show remarkable confidence in their plan to erase themselves—and untold billions of others—from existence. The one major exception is Data's recently resurrected daughter, Lal, who provides the quotation from this section's heading.[65] Data assuages his daughter's doubts with characteristic logical rigor: "Lal, I helped create this plan based on the best evidence available. I would not have suggested so drastic a measure if I thought a less-extreme solution were possible. The facts in hand tell me this is the way."[66] This response convinces Lal, who then begins pondering the metaphysical consequences of their actions: "After we prune our branch of time from the tree of the multiverse . . . what will take our place?"

Data concedes that the answer may well be nothing at all, but Mack knows better. In the final surreal pages of the novel, he adopts Picard's perspective as he is wiped out of existence and travels through a number of possibilities. We then enter the apartment of Benny Russell, the mid-twentieth-century Black science fiction author who appeared in the beloved *Deep Space Nine* episode "Far Beyond the Stars" (DS9 6.13). There he had been portrayed as the author of *Deep Space Nine,* but here we learn he has also written the novelverse books—including *Coda* itself, which we are watching him finish. Content that this tale of self-sacrifice "is a fitting end to a tale of heroes,"[67] he then realizes there are more stories to be told with this cast of characters and sets to work on a fresh start, namely the opening line of the first *Picard* tie-in novel, Una McCormack's *The Last Best Hope,* which had been released the previous year.[68]

Of all the many meta gestures we will see in the era of late *Star*

Trek, Coda's is the strangest and most complex. Not only does it write the novel continuity out of existence within that continuity itself—explicitly distinguishing itself from the main alpha canon Prime Timeline, in print—but it also introduces a further framing device that allows a kind of handoff to the next phase of *Next Generation*-era novels. Here I must admit that I share Lal's skepticism. Was this really the only way? By the long-standing rules of the franchise, the events of the novelverse already never happened. Was there really a need to explicitly write it out of existence? Why this wanton destruction and tragedy instead of a final installment where we learn that everyone lived happily ever after?

We may never know. I suspect that part of the reason for this radical course of action was the perception by the studio executives that the sheer volume of novelverse material, together with its authority among fans, could produce confusion, or even expectations that *Picard* would maintain consistency with the novels. At the same time, the fact that this climax is so inorganic to the existing plots, calling on a forgotten villain from a silly late-season *Next Generation* episode and providing no meaningful closure to any of the novels' remaining plot threads, may represent a tacit admission that the novel continuity had reached the point of diminishing returns and there was simply not much left to do within the terms that it had set. Yet reading between the lines of Mack's account of the motives behind the *Coda* series, I wonder if the most decisive factor was a sense of pride. After all, for decades, the novels had so dominated *Trek* that they could even overwrite the final televised episode. Passively allowing themselves to be overwritten in turn may have felt anticlimactic—better, perhaps, to go out in a blaze of glory, with the exorbitant gesture of overwriting themselves.

3

THE KELVIN TIMELINE

A BLANK SLATE

After the commercial failure of the last *Next Generation* film, *Star Trek Nemesis* (2002), and the cancellation of *Enterprise* in 2005, many fans worried that, in Lincoln Geraghty's words, they may have witnessed "the end for the world's most famous, and once most popular, science fiction franchise."[1] Surprisingly, though, the *Star Trek* film franchise was revived in relatively short order, under the leadership of nostalgia auteur J. J. Abrams. As we will see, this segment of the franchise—encompassing three films: *Star Trek* (2009),[2] *Star Trek Into Darkness* (2012), and *Star Trek Beyond* (2016)—would prove to be highly controversial among fans, and its attempt to maximize freedom from canon constraints by creating an alternate timeline would ultimately render it a digression or even a dead end.

Yet what is variously known as the J.J.-verse, the Abramsverse, or (most officially) the Kelvin Timeline did produce one *Star Trek* installment that is both widely praised by fans and foundational for later storytelling: the promotional comic book series *Countdown* (2009).[3] Published over the four months leading to the film's theatrical release, it tells the story of Spock's discovery that a star called Hobus would soon go supernova, endangering the Romulan home world, and of his efforts—aided by Romulan mining ship captain Nero as well as the *Next Generation* crew—to stave off that disaster. As viewers of the film know, his efforts were not only unsuccessful but also resulted in both Spock's and Nero's ships being thrown back in time, creating a fork in *Star Trek*'s timeline. What fascinated fans about the comic, however, was less the background to the film itself than its tantalizing glimpse into the futures of Prime Timeline characters. Most notably, the last page of the first issue reveals that Data is captain of the *Enterprise,* and we later learn that he was resurrected from memories imprinted onto B4 in *Nemesis.* Other characters have similar career changes—for instance, Picard has been named ambassador to Vulcan, Worf has joined the Klingon military, and LaForge has become a designer of experimental ships—but what is compelling about the comic series is less the detail of the plot than the sheer fact that we are learning more information about beloved characters whose stories seemed to be over.

Of course, as we just saw in chapter 2, fans looking for more information about Picard and friends already had a superabundance of material in the novelverse. What made *Countdown* different was the widespread belief that it had been anointed as canon. The source of this misconception—which contradicts the official rule according to which only television episodes and films can ever be canonical—is an interview by Anthony Pascale with *Star Trek* (2009) screenwriter Roberto Orci, who collaborated on the comic book series. When asked whether *Countdown* is canon, Orci initially hedges: "I always say that I arrived in Star Trek where the rules of what is canon had already been established." But when the interviewer pushes him, he jokingly reveals his own preference: "OK, based on that then with you Anthony Pascale as a witness, I hereby declare anything that we oversee to be canon."[4]

For a comic to achieve even the appearance of canonicity was unprecedented. As Gerry Canavan points out, the tie-in comics "occupy a position close to the very bottom of the authority barrel" within *Star Trek*'s hierarchy of officialness.[5] While many plot points and themes have graduated from the beta canon of the novels to the true on-screen alpha canon, "almost nothing from the comics has had a lasting influence on *Star Trek*."[6] The same would ultimately prove true of *Countdown*'s plot, nearly all of which is contradicted by the backstory to *Picard*. Nevertheless, Canavan is right to claim that "the comic's story of the Federation's failed attempt to evacuate Romulus before its destruction has quite unexpectedly become the foundation stone of all *[Picard]*-era *Star Trek*."[7] What the comic's popularity and quasi-canonical status achieved was to turn the backstory of Spock's voyage back in time—clearly intended solely to explain his presence and provide Nero's motivation—into an unshakeable fact of Prime Timeline history. Even though the *Picard* writers chose to tell a different, and in many ways darker, story about the supernova that destroyed the Romulan home world, it was arguably the unique authority of *Countdown* among fans that forced them to treat it as a foundational plot point rather than a throwaway reference.

The success of *Countdown*—together with the decision to focus on tie-in comics for the new films, to the exclusion of original novels—ushered in an unexpected golden age for *Star Trek* comics. The new prestige of the genre would lead to the production, by collectibles company Eaglemoss, of a series of high-quality hardcover compilations that aimed to collect all extant comics since the franchise's beginning. That project was ultimately never completed, but longtime *Star Trek* comics rights holder IDW began a collected edition of all the stories published under its own aegis. Unsurprisingly, both series chose the same comic to highlight in their respective first volumes: *Countdown*.

From the standpoint of franchise history, the elevation of a four-issue comic book series to such an august perch is an interesting curiosity. From a creative perspective, though, the fact that a promotional comic could so overshadow three blockbuster films (with nine-figure budgets) in fan esteem surely shows that something went wrong along the way. In this chapter, I will trace the root of the problem to the one-sided reliance of Abrams-era *Trek* on the strategy of freedom. Yet I will not simply echo the fan refrain perhaps best encapsulated by the title of an article by Megan Leigh, "Star Trek: How J. J. Abrams Ruined Everything."[8] Instead, in keeping with my policy of assuming that late *Star Trek*'s writers and producers are talented people doing their best, I will try to discern why the Kelvin Timeline's creators thought this transdimensional byway was the appropriate next step for the franchise and how their efforts laid the foundations for what came next, for good and for ill.

FROM HALF-MEASURES TO FULL MEASURES

For a film that was supposed to get back to basics, transforming the franchise from a cult phenomenon to a summer blockbuster factory, *Star Trek* (2009) is remarkably convoluted. As noted above, the narrative as a whole is framed by a time-travel incursion from the post-*Nemesis* future of *Star Trek*. Most *Trek* time-travel narratives work on the assumption that our heroes are intervening in the past of the same timeline, resulting in disastrous changes that completely overwrite their familiar future and requiring them to restore the basic shape of past events so that history can resume its proper course. Here, however, the logic is different. Spock and Nero come from the future of the timeline of the previous shows and films. But when Nero destroys the USS *Kelvin*—killing Kirk's father and irrevocably changing the course of his life in the process—he does not overwrite

Trek's fictional future. Instead, he introduces a fork that leaves the original timeline (retronymed the Prime Timeline by fans, after the designation of Leonard Nimoy's character as Prime Spock in the credits) untouched while also opening up a space of creative freedom within the new timeline (ultimately called the Kelvin Timeline, because the destruction of the USS *Kelvin* was the cause of the fork). Just in case the audience has not followed the temporal mechanics involved here, the Kelvin Timeline's version of Spock (Zachary Quinto) declares: "Nero's very presence has altered the flow of history beginning with the attack on the USS *Kelvin* culminating in the events of today, thereby creating an entire new chain of incidents that cannot be anticipated by either party. . . . Whatever our lives might have been, if the time continuum was not disrupted, our destinies have changed." Both the time-travel plot itself and the young Spock's in-text declaration count as two of the most explicit self-reflective meta gestures that are characteristic of late *Star Trek*. The message is clear: we have a free hand here, but we are not disrupting or overwriting anything that happened before.

At the time, there were many understandable reasons to take such a course. The idea of rebooting is certainly appealing as an attempt to get past the baggage of *Star Trek* canon, which Berman and Braga found to be quite cumbersome indeed. At the same time, overwriting all previous *Star Trek* (with the ironic exception of *Enterprise,* which is set long before Nero's incursion) would be met with outrage from fans. In a franchise that is filled with time-travel stories and alternate universes, then, the idea of creating a separate timeline to start from scratch makes a certain kind of sense. In fact, in his entry in the *Routledge Handbook of Star Trek* on *Star Trek* (2009), William Proctor points out that J. Michael Straczynsci, best known as the creator of *Babylon 5* (1993–98), coauthored a pitch for a similar idea to Paramount in 2004.[9] Yet the ultimate reason for this strange prequel–sequel–reboot structure was not creative but corporate. In 2006, as a result of various corporate mergers and divorces, the franchise was effectively split between CBS, which controlled the TV rights, and Paramount, which held the film rights. Though this awkward situation was resolved in 2019, when CBS acquired the company that controlled Paramount, the split control reportedly resulted in many incidents of "pettiness" between the two sides, leading to "a tentative agreement that each side would essentially stay off the other's turf"—hence the decision to structure the film in such a way that it would be absolutely clear that its new timeline did not affect the original TV series.[10]

Yet despite the bold metaphysical and metafictional gestures emphasizing the film's break with the past, *Star Trek* (2009) is in another sense in profound continuity with the existing franchise, especially its most recent failures, *Enterprise* and *Nemesis*. In both cases, the creators take core ideas from these unloved flops and radicalize them. The borrowings are clearest from *Enterprise*. As we saw in chapter 1, the prequel setting was initially chosen as a way of hearkening back to a simpler time, with more natural connections to *The Original Series* than to the crowded *Next Generation* era. Most notably, the triad of Archer, T'Pol, and Trip is clearly meant to echo the productive dynamic of Kirk, Spock, and McCoy in *The Original Series,* with the addition of explicit heterosexual romantic tension (perhaps as a way of deflecting from long-standing fan theories that Kirk and Spock were in love). *Star Trek* (2009) rejects this half measure and returns directly to the original characters themselves, while introducing the same twist as in *Enterprise* by swapping out McCoy (Karl Urban) in favor of Uhura (Zoe Saldana), who serves as a potential love interest for both Kirk (Chris Pine) and Spock. Similarly, we saw that Berman and Braga for the most part shied away from the potential freedom that the Temporal Cold War could have granted them, instead presenting it (somewhat misguidedly) as a way to guarantee the integrity of the future timeline. Again, the new film rejects the half measure and uses time travel to create total creative freedom—and the result was exactly the kind of commercial success the studio expected from *Enterprise,* as *Star Trek* (2009) was and remains the highest-grossing *Trek* film of all time.

From *Nemesis,* the new film takes the theme of uncanny doubles and obsessive revenge—but to see this will require me to undertake a task I have been deferring, namely summarizing the plot of *Nemesis.* The film doubles both Picard and Data, the latter in the form of primitive prototype B4 and the former in botched, abandoned clone Shinzon (Tom Hardy). After somehow obtaining Picard's DNA, the Romulans planned to create a clone and artificially age it so that it could eventually replace the original and work as a spy. Partway through the rapid aging process, however, they decided the plan would never work and sent the young Shinzon to work in the mines alongside enslaved Remans (a subject race of the Romulans introduced here). Using the incredible charisma and leadership instincts he presumably inherited from the original Picard, Shinzon manages to stage a slave revolt among the Remans and take over the Romulan Empire. But a flaw in the cloning process means that he will soon die if he does not get a fresh infusion of Picard's DNA. So he lures Picard to Romulus and eventually reveals that he plans to destroy the original version—and his home planet of Earth for good measure. This encounter is understandably upsetting to Picard, who struggles with the realization that his own DNA could lead to such an evil and destructive outcome. Meanwhile, Data is disturbed to see that B4, also played by Brent Spiner, operates at a primitive intellectual level and tries to accelerate his development by downloading his own memory into his ostensible older brother. (As we have seen, the novels and the *Countdown* comic use the latter plot point in very different ways, and the *Picard* television series will take it in yet another direction.)

The mapping of *Nemesis* onto *Star Trek* (2009) is not as direct or one-to-one as in the case of *Enterprise*. Instead, the film distributes the various forms of doubling across multiple characters to make them more resonant and meaningful. For instance, it does not seem to make much sense for Picard to be haunted by how differently Shinzon turned out, given that Picard grew up with a loving family in a postscarcity utopia and Shinzon was left to die in an alien slave camp. Shinzon simply cannot cast much light on Picard—his path is too radically different. The fate of the Kelvin Timeline's Kirk is much more organic, even providing retrospective insight into the original Kirk. We learn that his father inspired him to join Starfleet and that without that influence, he is destined to become a trouble-maker and layabout. The memory download into B4 is echoed in Prime Spock's use of Vulcan telepathic abilities to mind-meld with Kirk, giving him the experience of his Prime counterpart's bond with his Spock in the hope of kindling a similar bond with the Kelvin Timeline's Spock (Figure 3). As with B4, the results are inconclusive. Finally, Shinzon's obsession with Picard and desire to destroy his home planet finds its equivalent in Nero's obsession with Spock and the successful destruction of the Vulcan home world. In case the connection is not clear, Nero is bald—a trait he shares with no previous Romulan but does share with Shinzon—and he improbably leverages his background in mining to serve his vengeful agenda.

Along with these subtle echoes of *Enterprise* and *Nemesis, Star Trek* (2009) also indulges in a number of callbacks and Easter eggs that reinforce its connection to past iterations of the franchise without creating expectations of detailed continuity. In its development of the original characters, it often borrows from existing lore—most notably in the scenes from Spock's youth, which explicitly echo scenes from *The Original Series* (e.g., "Journey to Babel," TOS 2.10) and even *The Animated Series* ("Yesteryear," TAS 1.2), and in the elevation of Nyota Uhura and Hikaru Sulu's first names, long established in the beta canon novels, to alpha canon. At other times, it

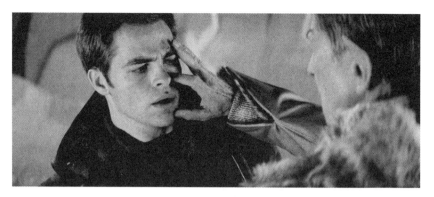

FIGURE 3. The elder Prime Spock mind-melds with the alternate timeline's Kirk in Star Trek (2009).

completely changes the backstory of some characters, most notably Scotty, who is marooned on a distant moon after a transporter accident involving "Admiral Archer's beloved beagle" (incidentally the first direct on-screen reference to *Enterprise* outside the series itself), and Captain Pike (Bruce Greenwood), who emerges as a paternal mentor figure for Kirk when he dares him to join Starfleet.

Strangely, however, the radical changes to Kirk's backstory and trajectory actually make him much more like the womanizing, cavalier Captain Kirk familiar from pop culture stereotypes, contributing to the trend away from the largely straightlaced and lonely captain we meet on *The Original Series* that Erin Horáková memorably characterized as "Kirk Drift."[11] This shift makes it harder for audiences to accept the other major change to Kirk's character: his anointing as a chosen one. Here we might see the influence of J. J. Abrams's preference for *Star Wars* over *Star Trek* at work, though the chosen one trope has long been a staple of the blockbuster genre that *Star Trek* (2009) is attempting to join. Kirk is born in semimiraculous circumstances: his mother goes into labor right when Nero begins attacking the *Kelvin,* and he lives as a diamond in the rough until a generous mentor (Pike) plucks him out of obscurity. An encounter with a wise man with prophetic powers (Prime Spock) alerts him to his destiny and gives him the means to achieve it, and he goes on to save the world (or at least *a* world, since Vulcan is still destroyed).

Any number of blockbuster franchises could be mapped onto this basic story outline, but it is *Harry Potter* that springs to mind. Just as Kirk is a futuristic Harry, Spock is presented as a Hermione-like character who demonstrates greater skill and intelligence than our hero again and again, yet is expected to submit to his predestined leadership. Here, though, the path is much more difficult and improbable because the relationship between Spock and Kirk is characterized by suspicion, rivalry, and even resentment. Ultimately, Kirk—on the advice of Prime Spock—manipulates and publicly humiliates Spock in order to seize command from him. Along the way, we see an emotional outburst from Spock that would be shocking in the context of *The Original Series* but presumably lacks much impact for casual viewers meeting these characters for the first time.

The result of all the time-travel shenanigans, changed life trajectories, and portentous messages from the future is that the crew of the *Enterprise* is reassembled into its familiar form and ready to explore strange new worlds, etc. Kirk has made the meteoric rise from a young cadet (indeed, a young cadet on the verge of being expelled for cheating on the infamous Kobayashi Maru test) to captain in a matter of days, Spock (the instructor who reported him for cheating and whom Kirk all but forcibly relieved of command) has become his loyal right-hand man, and the rest of the ensemble cast (again, made up mostly of cadets) are sitting at their familiar spots on the bridge. The message is clear: *Star Trek* is back, with more action, better special effects, and sexy young actors. In fact, that seems to be the film's *sole* message. The potential moral allegory of Kirk's altered course in life is undermined when he is simply shunted into his appropriate place by destiny's hand. It is hard to see any serious ethical dilemma, social allegory, or political commentary in the film—other than the conservative one that some people are simply born to lead, or the obvious one that terrorism is bad. Here, even more than with *Enterprise,* we could echo what Dan Golding says of *The Force Awakens,* conceding that *Star Trek* (2009) is too concerned with intrafranchise matters to comment on politics, or really any significant issue at all.[12] In the end, the film is about nothing but the sheer gesture of creating an alternate timeline in which Paramount can make new adventures starring Kirk, Spock, and the rest of the gang. Most installments of late *Star Trek* make meta gestures, but this film does nothing but.

AN INSIDE JOB

Despite fan hostility, *Star Trek* (2009) built up considerable good-will, enjoying both critical and commercial success to a degree not seen since the best of the original-cast films. Its bold assertion of freedom had given it unfettered access to the most beloved *Star Trek* characters and tropes, and the opening scenes of the follow-up, *Star Trek Into Darkness* (2013), seemed to promise a return to form as the *Enterprise* crew struggles to save an alien planet without alerting the natives of their presence. The visuals—from the volcanic pit where Spock is laboring to prevent a natural disaster to the makeup design for the aliens, and especially the revelation that the *Enterprise* is hiding underwater—are striking and fun, and the dilemma of whether to rescue Spock or obey the Prime Directive against interfering with the development of a prewarp culture is classic *Star Trek*. In the end, the Prime Directive proves once more to be a rule best observed in the breach, as Kirk chooses to save his friend. As Nathan Jones points out, this scene does a lot of narrative heavy lifting: "A deliberate call-back to the episodic television series, the opening sequence serves to remind viewers that the crew has continued to work together in the time between films."[13] But apparently we cannot infer that their relationships have fully healed offscreen, because Spock reports the violation of Starfleet's highest law to Pike (now an admiral), who removes Kirk from command as a result of his pattern of recklessness and threatens to send him back to Starfleet Academy.

The scene then shifts to a father with a hospitalized daughter. After injecting her with a serum that cures her almost instantly, he launches a suicide attack against a Starfleet facility—apparently as payment for the miracle drug. This terrible event leads Pike to recruit Kirk to a task force headed by Admiral Marcus (Peter Weller), whom our suicide bomber had messaged just before the attack and who turns out to be associated with the corrupt special ops organization Section 31. As the meeting gets underway, Kirk deduces that the suicide bombing may have been intended precisely to assemble many high-ranking Starfleet officers, but it is too late. In an inexplicable homage to *The Godfather, Part III* (1990), the conference room suffers a helicopter attack that kills Admiral Pike. Kirk is returned to command of the *Enterprise* to track down and kill the perpetrator, a rogue Starfleet intelligence officer named John Harrison (Benedict Cumberbatch), who turns out to be on the Klingon home world. Using a civilian shuttle for plausible deniability, they launch their attack, only to learn that Harrison is none other than Khan Noonien-Singh, the charismatic and genetically augmented dictator from "Space Seed" (TOS 1.22) and *The Wrath of Khan* (1982), and that the experimental torpedoes that Marcus dispatched to the *Enterprise* are actually his fellow augments, cryogenically frozen since the 1990s. Khan reveals that Marcus had used his frozen comrades to blackmail him into staging a false-flag attack that would spur a war with the Klingons.

This reference to *Wrath of Khan* sets up a confusing series of events where Kirk, rather than Spock, must sacrifice himself to save the ship; Spock, not Kirk, memorably roars, "Khaaaaan!"; and Kirk is resurrected by an infusion of Khan's augmented blood. All of these callbacks presuppose a close bond between Kirk and Spock that is not only nowhere in evidence but directly contradicted. In any case, with the crisis resolved, Kirk is given permanent command of the *Enterprise* for a five-year mission, which he inaugurates by reciting the "captain's oath," namely the famous opening monologue from *The Original Series* and *Next Generation*. Leaving aside the question of whether the screenwriters understood what an oath is, it seems that we are finally going to get started doing some good old-fashioned *Star Trek*—in the next film.

Before the film's release, the producers carefully concealed the fact that Cumberbatch's character was Khan, apparently believing that it would come as a pleasant surprise once it was revealed in the film. Yet as with so many attempts to recapture the magic of *The Wrath of Khan,* the franchise's most beloved film, it backfired. Most controversial was the choice to portray Khan, a South Asian character who had been played by Latino actor Ricardo Montalbán, with a strikingly white actor. Indeed, in Matthew Wilhelm Kapell and Ace G. Pilkington's edited collection of scholarly articles on the Kelvin Timeline films, roughly one-fourth of the chapters focus primarily on Khan's "whitewashing."[14] The producers offered several explanations for this bizarre casting choice. One was simply to preserve the element of surprise. Not only does this explanation not make much sense on its own terms—after the initial screening, the big reveal would be widely spoiled online—but it does not fit with "early reports of the casting of Benicio del Toro and unsuccessful auditions by other Hispanic actors like Demián Bichir," which "prove the producers initially planned to cast Khan in the same way as every other character in the Abramsverse—according to the 1960s' ethnic profile of the actor who had originated the role."[15]

More plausible is that the casting of Cumberbatch was motivated by the film's terrorism theme. Not wanting to play into the toxic cultural associations of terrorism with people of color, the counterintuitive casting choice sends the inspiring message that, in Lynnette Porter's words, "white men can be terrorists, too."[16] But this supposed attempt at cultural sensitivity only makes matters worse because it associates Khan's inherent genetic superiority with whiteness and British imperialism.[17] In my view, though, the most likely explanation is one that the producers could not publicly avow: that the film is "an allegory relating to contemporary conspiracy theories claiming the 9/11 attacks were carried out and/or assisted by the U.S. government and to the false claims about weapons of mass destruction provided by the CIA that enabled the American invasion of Iraq."[18] Admitting as much would mean confirming "co-producer and screenwriter Roberto Orci's reputation as a 'Truther'" who believes the 9/11 attacks were an inside job[19]—obviously a terrible embarrassment for a franchise that has consistently aligned itself with science, rationality, and humanistic values.

Many longtime *Star Trek* fans were likely disappointed in the 2009 film's lack of any political commentary, but I doubt a 9/11 Truther allegory is what anyone was hoping for. Within its own terms, the allegory is at least a hopeful one: our heroes are able to uncover the plot and prevent a disastrous war of choice. Yet that small glimmer of optimism is swamped by the sheer cynicism of the overarching story, in which a corrupt admiral is able to fool everyone in Starfleet—including Pike, previously presented as a wise mentor—while operating an off-books weapons project and thawing out history's greatest cryogenically frozen monsters. While the premise of Starfleet and Federation benevolence is, as Hark points out, difficult for most contemporary audiences to accept at face value,[20] lurching into the worst possible corruption in only the second film of the rebooted franchise was overkill. More than that, despite the seemingly gratuitous inverted references to *Wrath of Khan*, the film is out of step with most *Star Trek*, if only because so much of it centers on Earth. One wishes the creators could have spent a little more time developing the conventional *Star Trek* tropes displayed in the opening vignette—and demonstrating that they genuinely understand and value them—before so abruptly subverting them.

More than any other recent *Star Trek* installment, *Into Darkness* takes the assertion of creative freedom to such a nihilistic extreme that it is no longer clear why they want to be doing *Star Trek* at all—except, of course, to indulge the screenwriter's paranoid hobby-horse. Though it enjoyed a similar commercial and critical success to the 2009 film, in the end, as Jones says, "those who enjoyed it as an escapist film moved on and *Star Trek* fans issued steady waves of complaints," leading to "a series of apologies" from Abrams, Orci, and fellow producer Damon Lindelof.[21] Even if we do not accept Jones's hypothesis that "the film's controversies may have sped the end of Kelvin Timeline film production,"[22] *Into Darkness* certainly confirmed fan suspicions that this alternate timeline was not contributing anything of value to the franchise as a whole.

THE WRATH OF COMICS

The relative superficiality of the first two Kelvin Timeline films was not solely due to artistic choices. Film is not *Star Trek*'s native medium—television is. A big part of the franchise's appeal comes from getting to know these characters over the course of hours and years, in varied situations that showcase the full range of their emotions and thought patterns. According to journalist Dusty Howe, the producers were aware of this problem but were impeded by the division of television and film rights: "When J. J. Abrams rebooted the film series in 2009, he was eager to capitalize on that film's success by producing a television spinoff. CBS, however, was not interested in helping a corporate rival strengthen their property, so they declined to work with Abrams."[23] If the lack of a television show was beyond their control, though, the creators made an unforced error by intentionally dismissing the other primary way that fans have deepened their engagement with the *Star Trek* universe: novels. Though there were novelizations of both *Star Trek* (2009) and *Into Darkness* by veteran novelizer Alan Dean Foster (who would also go on to write the best-selling novelization of *The Force Awakens*), Abrams decided against expanding his corner of the franchise with original tie-in novels—leading to the cancellation of three novels (by Foster, David Mack, and Christopher L. Bennett) that had been not only commissioned but written.[24] Especially given the caliber of writers he had shunned, this move represented a missed opportunity on Abrams's part.

Instead, the Kelvin Timeline production team chose to capitalize on the success of *Countdown* by focusing exclusively on tie-in comics. This decision ushered in not only the only era of the *Star Trek* franchise to elevate comics to such a privileged status but also the era in which the coordination between on-screen and tie-in material was most carefully managed.[25] The success of the Kelvin Timeline comics also helped reinforce a veritable golden age of *Star Trek* comics in general, as IDW published multiple series set across eras and timelines throughout this period—including the popular *Year Five,* which purports to show the end of the five-year mission in the Prime Timeline, and *Mirror Broken,* which would prove to be the first of many series focusing on the Mirror Universe equivalents of the *Next Generation* crew.[26]

Before building out the altered universe, however, the comics first turned to the task of filling in the gaps within the films themselves. The biggest is Nero's motivation, which is left vague in *Star Trek* (2009) and only fully clarified in *Countdown*. As it turns out, Nero was one of the first to notice the pending breakdown of the Hobus star and supported Spock's efforts to seek Vulcan technology to stop it. As a result of a fatal miscalculation, however, the star exploded sooner than Spock expected, destroying Romulus and killing Nero's wife and unborn child in the process. Driven mad by grief, Nero concluded that Spock was intentionally delaying the process to ensure that Romulus would be destroyed, leading Nero to seek to inflict the same unimaginable pain on Spock in turn. Hence the comic not only expands on Prime Spock's elliptical account of the supernova in the film but also provides information that is arguably necessary to fully understand the main plot.

The next comic installment, also published in the same year as the film, again focuses on Nero and aims to fill in another yawning plot hole.[27] As viewers may recall, Nero's ship arrives when Kirk is literally being born, but he only turns to the task of destroying Vulcan decades later, when Kirk is a callow youth. The film explains that their unique method of time travel meant that Nero and Prime Spock arrived at different moments of the past—obviously a contrivance to allow Nero to at once disrupt Kirk's life course and face him as an adult—and makes a fleeting reference to the infamous Klingon prison Rura Penthe. Many questions remain. How did Nero wind up in jail, and how did he escape? How did he know when and where Spock would emerge? The comics answer these questions with a story that becomes more absurd and incoherent as it goes. It starts simply enough: Kirk's father really does deliver a crushing blow to Nero's vessel with his suicidal ramming maneuver, and the Klingons pick up the mysterious Romulan crew and confiscate their advanced vessel (which had been revealed in *Countdown* to incorporate Borg technology). Nero and his crew refuse to reveal their origin or purpose, even under torture, but are allowed to live thanks to their mining skills. To pass the time, Nero starts taking psychedelic drugs, which awaken his ability to mind-meld—an ability that Romulans were previously thought to have lost in the many centuries since they split off from the Vulcans. These newfound psychic powers allow him to form a psychic bond with the Borg components of the ship itself and escape. Unbidden, the ship then takes them to meet V'ger from *The Motion Picture* (1979), which somehow has a bond with Prime Spock (despite the fact that Prime Spock is currently in a black hole and V'ger has not yet met Spock in this timeline) and, after a suitable mind-meld, provides Nero with the coordinates to intercept his vessel. Nero then maroons Prime Spock on the wintry planetoid where he will witness the destruction of Vulcan and coincidentally meet the young Kirk.

This supposed explanation is gibberish, a random grab bag of *Star Trek* tropes and plot points. The ongoing series that began in 2011[28] initially seems to promise only more self-indulgence, as it opens with adaptations of two *Original Series* episodes (*Star Trek*, vol. 1), "Where No Man Has Gone Before" (TOS 1.4) and "The Galileo Seven" (TOS 1.16). Yet these comics—which are the first without Roberto Orci in a primary writing role—show themselves to be thoughtful reconsiderations of the original stories in the new timeline. The episodes are well-chosen to highlight the strangeness of the scenario in which Kirk has been catapulted into command. In the former episode, Gary Mitchell is an old friend of Kirk's who becomes a megalomaniac after his psychic powers are accidentally awakened; here, his desire for control and command appears more organic, the result of his resentment of Kirk's unprecedented jump straight to the captain's chair. Similarly, in the latter episode, Spock struggles to prove himself as a potential leader as he manages the emotionally fraught consequences of a shuttle crash; in the comic, his desire to prove his worthiness after getting passed over in favor of Kirk takes center stage. In both cases, the ending has a more redemptive twist: Gary Mitchell sacrifices himself rather than needing to be murdered, and Uhura makes the decisive move that saves Spock and the other crew members. The pattern continues in later adaptations, such as "Operation—Annihilate!" (TOS 1.29), in which Kirk's brother and his family are threatened by a parasitic mind-controlling alien. The comic uses our knowledge of Kirk's childhood from the film to set up a conflict with the brother, who survives the alien infestation (unlike in the original), and whose absence is explained as an intentional abandonment of his family after their father's death (*Star Trek,* vol. 2).

In all the adaptations, writer Mike Johnson demonstrates again and again that he takes the altered timeline more seriously than the films themselves do—not just on the level of building a plausible new continuity but also in conceiving the alternate timeline as an opportunity to create a genuinely contemporary new version of *The Original Series.* While it may initially seem to be pure fan service, the use of the original stories serves to create space for creative freedom by highlighting how different everything has become. In contrast, the films tend to assume, incoherently, that the familiar adventures and character dynamics from *The Original Series* more or less still apply and lean on the audience's vague familiarity with the old show to clarify the emotional stakes.

When the comics branch into original stories set in the new timeline, the results are initially less compelling because they insistently return to Nero's destruction of Vulcan and its consequences. The first original story centers on a Vulcan scheme to continue the cycle of vengeance by destroying their own contemporary Romulus—an insane effort in which Spock's father, Sarek, turns out to be involved. Eventually more varied plots are introduced, including a visit to the Kelvin Timeline's unique version of the Mirror Universe (*Star Trek,* vol. 4) or an alternate universe in which everyone's genders are swapped (*Star Trek,* vol. 8). In both cases, some version of the destruction of Vulcan has deeply shaped these radically different dimensions, making Nero's act of genocide into a transhistorical constant. This trend continues even in the second run of comics, entitled *Boldly Go,* which followed up on the events of *Star Trek Beyond* (2016).[29] There our heroes encounter the Borg "too early," and the reason turns out to be that they have detected the Borg components in Nero's ship and want to investigate the anomaly (*Boldly Go,* vol. 1).

The entirety of this branch of the *Star Trek* multiverse is therefore determined by a terrorist attack, over a decade after 9/11.

The reason for the relative stasis in the early issues is that perpetual danger facing tie-in literature: the possibility that on-screen events will overwrite their creations. In the event, it turns out they need not have worried: *Into Darkness* proves to be little more than a passing episode for the comics' continuity. Another lead-in series, *Countdown to Darkness,* was published, but given the desire for secrecy around the identity of Khan, it is strangely irrelevant to the events of the film itself.[30] Where readers of *Countdown* had inside information about Nero's motivations, readers of the new series were rewarded with the knowledge that the civilian shuttle that Kirk says they had commandeered in "the Mudd incident" belonged not to ne'er-do-well Harry Mudd from *The Original Series,* but—his daughter! This is thin gruel indeed, and the follow-up story on Khan's background does little more than attempt to explain away the whitewashing of the character.[31] As it turns out, he was originally South Asian, but he was radically surgically altered and brainwashed so that he would forget who he was, making him a more pliable tool—a plan that obviously backfired. As with the *Nero* series, the comic exists solely to make up for the failings of the film and makes little sense as a result.

The initial Kelvin Timeline series was concluded in 2016 with a story that commemorated the fiftieth anniversary of *The Original Series'* debut (*Star Trek,* vol. 13). Both the Kelvin and Prime Timeline versions of the *Enterprise* crew are caught in a transdimensional anomaly that switches some characters' bodies across dimensions. This allows the Kelvin Timeline characters to pay homage to their Prime originals while also—perhaps in an echo of similar efforts in late *Enterprise* episodes—allowing the Prime Timeline to know about the Kelvin Timeline's existence. The short-lived *Boldly Go* series, for its part, ends with a story involving all the many alternate universes displayed in the comics—including one in which the Kelvin Timeline's Kirk is granted a vision of what his life would have been like if his father had survived (*Boldly Go,* vol. 3). In both cases, we are seeing something beyond the natural self-effacement of tie-in literature—the writers seem to be gesturing toward the self-effacement of the entire Kelvin Timeline project.

"THINGS HAVE STARTED TO FEEL A LITTLE . . . EPISODIC"

After *Into Darkness,* J. J. Abrams turned his attention to rebooting his true first love, *Star Wars.* This move initially made official what Abrams had apparently been doing all along: handing most of the creative control for the reboot of his less favored franchise to his friend, Roberto Orci, who is, if nothing else, a devoted fan. Early in the development of the third film, however, Orci was removed as director in favor of Justin Lin, and an early script on which he had collaborated was thoroughly rewritten by screenwriter Doug Jung and series regular Simon Pegg.[32] The shift in creative staff was long overdue, and Pegg—perhaps best known for writing and starring in zombie parody *Shaun of the Dead* (2004)—quickly emerged as the unofficial face of the franchise. In numerous media appearances and interviews, he carefully walked the line of signaling both his respect for the existing *Star Trek* universe and his desire to reach broader audiences. Pegg's affable manner, together with his record as a comic actor, seemed to promise a shift away from constant doom and disaster in favor of the open-ended exploration and utopian hope that are the franchise's stock in trade.

Star Trek Beyond begins by explicitly distancing itself from the previous two films, both physically and temporally. In contrast to their focus on Earth, the opening vignette on *Beyond* reveals that they are nearing the end of the third year of their five-year mission—precisely the point when *The Original Series* was canceled—and have been busy exploring deep space, making diplomatic contact with alien species, and doing all the kinds of things one would expect from a *Star Trek* crew. After a comically botched negotiation with some cartoonish aliens, the crew arrives at starbase *Yorktown* for some much-needed shore leave. The facility itself is a visual wonder, a city that occupies the whole internal volume of a planet-size structure with beautifully interwoven streets. On the big screen, the effect is almost overwhelmingly cool—a forceful statement that a blockbuster budget can provide more to *Star Trek* than bigger explosions.

By skipping ahead in time, the film also provides some justification for drawing on the familiar tropes and dynamics of *The Original Series*. Perhaps most notably, the relationship between Spock and McCoy—who rarely interacted in the first two films—has reached the appropriate level of bemused irony and performative irritation, respectively. Yet something is amiss, as Kirk's voice-over of the opening vignette reveals fatigue and loss of purpose. The quote I chose as the heading for this section is illustrative of these overlapping themes. While the declaration that things are feeling "episodic" is a winking reference to the format of the old show, it also alerts the audience that the writers are aware that this film series has not created much narrative momentum. In the next scene, where he shares a drink (and an unofficial therapy session) with McCoy, Kirk expresses a sense of unworthiness compared to the example of his father: "He joined Starfleet because he . . . he believed in it. . . . I joined on a dare." This declaration makes sense as a development of Kirk's character, but it also works on a meta level as an implicit reflection on the new film franchise's relationship to its absent father, namely the Prime Timeline material from which it has cut itself off. The latter relationship is further highlighted by the film's tribute to the real-life death of Leonard Nimoy, whose Prime Spock had served as a repository of the franchise's earlier phases in the alternate timeline. The death of Anton Yelchin, who played Ensign Chekov, in a freak auto accident shortly before *Beyond*'s release only added to the somber tone of a film that was timed to celebrate *Star Trek*'s fiftieth anniversary.

On the crew's arrival at *Yorktown,* it is revealed that Kirk is visiting in part to discuss a possible promotion to vice admiral with station commander Paris (Shohreh Aghdashloo). Before anything can be made official, however, news of a ship stranded in a nearby nebula has the *Enterprise* crew cutting their shore leave short in favor of a rescue mission. The result is an absolute disaster: the *Enterprise* is attacked by swarming ships that completely eviscerate it, forcing the crew to evacuate and the saucer section to crash-land on the surface. This scene initially seems to be a return to form for the Kelvin Timeline films, but it sets up a well-paced ensemble piece in which all members of the widely separated crew have meaningful character moments and some clear narrative function. The writers even introduce an appealing new character, feisty young Jaylah, whose family had crashed on the planet and who turns out to live in a crashed Starfleet vessel from Archer's era, the USS *Franklin* NX-326. In a sharp departure from the previous film—which had included a widely panned gratuitous shot of Carol Marcus (Alice Eve) in her underwear—the film never even hints at sexualizing Jaylah or any other female character.

As organic as the film's character development is, the overarching plot is needlessly convoluted and coincidence driven. The swarm ships turn out to operate under the command of a villain named Krall (Idris Elba), who possesses technology that grants him and his compatriots immortality by extracting life from others. They have survived by victimizing passing ships that wander into the remote nebula, until Starfleet coincidentally built the *Yorktown* station nearby. Krall holds a vendetta against the Federation and needs only one piece of alien technology to perfect a superweapon that will allow him to destroy the *Yorktown*—yet another return to the terrorism theme—and it just so happens that Kirk had picked it up in the comical opening vignette. Ultimately it is revealed that Krall is actually Balthazar Edison, a former military officer for United Earth and later a Starfleet captain, who crash-landed on the planet. Using the alien technology he finds, he has spent the intervening century nursing his grudge against the Federation for betraying humanity after the Xindi incident and the Romulan war had shown that aliens are dangerous. Thankfully, though, Kirk and friends are able to repair the *Franklin,* disrupt Krall's swarm ships' communication and coordination (by using primitive radio frequencies to broadcast the Beastie Boys' "Sabotage," which had memorably accompanied the first appearance of a mischievous childhood Kirk in the first reboot film), and stop Krall/Edison from destroying the *Yorktown* at the last possible minute. All of this is so invigorating that Kirk resolves to eschew a desk job and return to command of the newly minted *Enterprise*-A.

What interests me most here is the unexpectedly central role of plot points related to *Enterprise.* And judging from r/DaystromInstitute's discussion of the film, that was also what most seized the attention of hard-core fans. Logging into the site after watching *Beyond* on the day of its premiere, I already saw multiple posts attempting to make sense of Edison's career trajectory and the place of the *Franklin* in the history of Starfleet ship design. A fan base that had previously been intent on writing the hated prequel out of the *Star Trek* universe altogether was suddenly eager to explore the Archer era. The reason for this is the same reason for the exaggerated popularity of the *Countdown* comic: fans were hungry for any information at all about the Prime Timeline, even crumbs from *Enterprise.* However, the details are all wrong—systematically so. For instance, Scotty immediately recognizes the *Franklin* as the first warp 4 vessel, even though its registry number (NX-326) is far higher than that of the first warp 5 vessel, Archer's *Enterprise* NX-01, even as Edison's background story further implies that the *Frank-*

lin would have been commissioned long after Archer's famed ship. In addition, Edison refers to "the Xindi and Romulan wars" when explaining to Kirk why aliens are not to be trusted, implying that there were two wars, one with the Xindi and one with the Romulans, when the Xindi incident as portrayed on *Enterprise* was certainly not a war. As my r/DaystromInstitute colleagues proved with great enthusiasm, it is possible to square these odd details with what we previously saw on screen, but the writers were making them up from scratch and could have made the continuity connections more immediately legible if they chose.

I believe the explanation for this strangely garbled pattern of references can be found in Simon Pegg's response to an apparently unrelated matter: the controversy surrounding the decision to depict Sulu as gay in *Beyond*. While Sulu was chosen in part in tribute to the fact that George Takei, who had originated the role, is gay, Takei himself objected to the change, claiming that it implies Sulu had been closeted in the original timeline. In a blog post, Pegg points out that the new timeline is "not entirely beholden to existing canon" because "this is an alternate reality." Anticipating the objection that Sulu was born before the *Kelvin* was destroyed, meaning that his sexual orientation presumably would have been set, Pegg makes a bold claim:

> Spock's incursion from the Prime Universe created a multidimensional reality shift. The rift in space/time created an entirely new reality in all directions, top to bottom, from the Big Bang to the end of everything. As such this reality was, is and always will be subtly different from the Prime Universe. I don't believe for one second that Gene Roddenberry wouldn't have loved the idea of an alternate reality (Mirror, Mirror anyone?). This means, *and this is absolutely key, the Kelvin universe can evolve and change in ways that don't necessarily have to follow the Prime Universe at any point*

in history, before or after the events of Star Trek '09, it can mutate and subvert, it is a playground for the new and the progressive and I know in my heart, that Gene Roddenberry would be proud of us for keeping his ideals alive. Infinite diversity in infinite combinations, this was his dream, that is our dream, it should be everybody's.[33]

This is a bold assertion of creative freedom, even if it is superficially grounded in world-building of *Star Trek* (past events are in fact routinely caused by future ones). This response may initially appear to be a post hoc rationalization to respond to the Sulu controversy, but it is actually a principled stand. It is built into the structure of the film itself and signaled by the fact that the writers created new lore related to the *Enterprise* era—which is the one part of previous canon that should still apply to both sides of the forked timeline—in a way that systematically does not fit.

Thus the Kelvin Timeline film that does the most to return to the spirit of classic *Star Trek* makes one last assertion of artistic freedom by cutting off the last official connection between the two timelines. This is a high metaphysical price to pay for what amounted to a small gesture of inclusion, as Sulu's sexuality is established solely through a fleeting moment of meaningful eye contact with his husband and daughter, who are standing several yards away from him. Nor does the script's free handling of plot points from *Enterprise* contribute meaningfully to the film's message, which appears to be that pro-human bigotry has caused Edison and his compatriots to lose their humanity—literally, since the life-sucking device gives them an alien appearance. But Edison has had nearly a century to contemplate this irony without getting the message, and the mutagenic effect seems to be more in service of creating yet another superficial surprise than any thematic development.

Even in the case of what I regard as the most artistically successful reboot film, then, the question remains unavoidable: Why are we still doing this? The justification for continuing this branch of the franchise is not that it is a surefire ticket to commercial success, because *Beyond* underperformed both previous films. Though Paramount has reportedly continued to pursue development of a fourth film, even the rumors seem to send a metatextual message of self-destruction. Before the pandemic, for instance, Quentin Tarantino was briefly floated as the director for the next film, raising the specter of a *"Pulp Fiction* in space" where all the main characters would die brutal deaths.[34] Another rumor involved an encounter with Kirk's father (Chris Hemsworth), which would seemingly open the possibility of overwriting the new timeline from within by undoing its foundational moment.[35] There are presumably many other possibilities for a fourth film, but it is telling that the most concrete ideas strongly imply that the only way forward is to write the Kelvin Timeline out of existence—not, as with the novelverse, in a gesture of defiance but as a concession of defeat.

There was no reason the experiment of the Kelvin Timeline had to end this way. The comics show us that there are creative stories to be told about this iteration of *The Original Series* crew. And for all that he is demonized by fans, J. J. Abrams did attempt to do the single biggest thing that would have allowed the new timeline to flourish: build on the film's success with a TV series. If successful, that move would have provided greater depth and breadth to the new version of the *Star Trek* universe, almost by default. It would also have brought in a wider range of voices to displace the single voice of Roberto Orci, who to my mind is the real villain of the piece, at least on the creative side. Yet the ultimate culprits in the failure to expand this new branch of the franchise were the corporate leaders in charge of *Star Trek*'s awkwardly divided intellectual property, who could not put rivalry and pettiness aside for the mutual benefit of themselves and their fans. On that level, despite the many critiques that have rightly been leveled at the films, the absence of an accompanying TV series ultimately set them up to fail.

Yet even if the films did not contribute much of substance to the franchise's fictional world, or to its history of social commentary, they did push *Star Trek* forward in other ways. Compared to the sometimes stilted performances and awkward jokes of previous installments, the Kelvin Timeline films pioneered a more naturalistic acting style and more convincing use of humor. They also demonstrated not so much that *Star Trek* can be an action property—Proctor is right to point out that "*Star Trek* films have often been more action-oriented than the various television series, such as the highly acclaimed *First Contact* (1996)"—but that it does not have to be quite so slow and cerebral.[36] Finally, J. J. Abrams's characteristic lens flares aside, they showed that *Star Trek* can and should look cool. It would be easy to dismiss these aesthetic concerns as superficial and unimportant, but they are crucial for drawing in new audiences, especially younger audiences that tend to be turned off by entertainment that looks too old-fashioned. All of that may not seem to be a lot to show for the half-billion dollars the corporate overlords spent on these films, but perhaps they can console themselves with the additional half-billion dollars they made in profit.

Indeed, that may turn out to be the most important contribution of the Kelvin Timeline to the franchise: it showed that *Star Trek* was still a bankable property, perhaps more than anyone had suspected. Paramount's corporate rival, CBS, which held the TV rights, surely took these lessons to heart when it decided to return *Star Trek* to the small screen.

4

DISCOVERY AND ITS DISCONTENTS

A s with the premiere of *Enterprise,* the debut episode of *Discovery* (2017–24), "The Vulcan Hello" (DSC 1.1), reveals its ambitions and its internal tensions within the first few scenes. It begins by signaling its distance from previous installments by throwing the audience in the middle of a conference of Klingons, speaking in their native language with subtitles. The leader, whom we will later learn is a self-styled Klingon messiah figure named T'Kuvma (Chris Obi), denounces the Federation and its hypocritical values, urging his hearers to "remain Klingon" in the face of an insidious enemy who claims—and here he lapses into a heavily accented English— "we come in peace." The scene then shifts to a desert planet, where Captain Philippa Georgiou (Michelle Yeoh) and her first officer, Commander Michael Burnham (Sonequa Martin-Green), find communications with their ship, the USS *Shenzhou,* have been disrupted during the course of a humanitarian mission to help a less developed sentient species. As Georgiou leads them through the sand at a brisk pace, their conversation ranges from the hypothetical question of what they would do if they were permanently stranded to the prospect of Commander Burnham finally taking on her own command. Finally, the ship descends through the clouds to rescue them, and it is revealed that Georgiou and Burnham have been tracing the shape of the Starfleet logo in the sand, marking their location.

The interplay between Georgiou and Burnham is perfect, and matters only improve when we cut to the bridge of the *Shenzhou,* which is now investigating a damaged communications relay in a binary star system. There we meet science officer Saru (Doug Jones), a member of the never-before-seen Kelpien species, known for their heightened ability to sense danger. Jones fully inhabits this alien character to a degree rarely seen in *Star Trek,* inventing a new kind of posture and gait suitable to a sentient species that evolved from cattle. We see that Burnham and Saru have a friendly or even sibling-like rivalry, and longtime viewers can instantly slip into the *Shenzhou*'s unique variation on the familiar Kirk–Spock–McCoy dynamic, as Georgiou strikes a balance between Saru's overcaution and Burnham's brashness. For her part, Georgiou is confident, decisive, and creative in deploying low-tech means to solve vexing problems. When sensors pick up an anomalous reading that prevents them from getting a visual scan, for instance, she pulls out an old-fashioned telescope and looks at it through the window. Ocular scans prove inconclusive, so Burnham volunteers to do a spacewalk to investigate further, which can be read as a fan-pleasing homage to Spock's famous spacewalk in *The Motion Picture* (1979).

In the space of ten minutes, I was in love. I felt I could easily spend seven seasons with this crew. In other words, the *Discovery* writers could not have more clearly signaled that they know exactly how *Star Trek* is supposed to be. Then, almost immediately, they ruined everything. The mysterious object turns out to be T'Kuvma's ship, and when Burnham lands on the surface, she meets a Klingon warrior and accidentally kills him in self-defense. By the end of the episode, Burnham's desperation to defend her crew against the Klingon threat has led her to attempt mutiny against her beloved captain. By the end of its sequel, "Battle of the Binary Stars" (DSC 1.2), Georgiou is dead, the *Shenzhou* is destroyed, and Burnham has been blamed for starting a war with the Klingons and sentenced to life in prison for mutiny (Figure 4).

Almost as bad as Burnham's crimes against the Starfleet command hierarchy are the show's apparent violations of franchise canon. Though set approximately a decade before *The Original Series,* the uniform and ship designs seem like an extrapolation from *Enterprise,* which fans had already dismissed as too advanced compared to Kirk's era, rather than any attempt to reconverge with the latter. Here *Discovery* doubles down by introducing even flashier technology like holographic communications. Burnham's backstory also appears to clash with established lore, as she is revealed to be the (previously unmentioned) foster daughter of the Vulcan Sarek and his human wife, Amanda Grayson—and hence the foster sister of none other than Spock. This connection self-consciously touches a third rail, because the last *Star Trek* property to give Spock a secret sibling, the film *The Final Frontier* (1989), directed and co-written by William Shatner, had so offended Gene Roddenberry that he all but declared it noncanonical. Even more unexpectedly, Burnham turns out to have a psychic bond with Sarek as a result of a lifesaving mind-meld he performed on her as a child after Logic Extremist terrorists—another extrapolation from *Enterprise,* this time in its reconceptualization of the Vulcans—attacked her school to rid their planet of the human impurity. Nor does Burnham's mutiny fit with earlier productions, as her foster brother Spock explicitly declares in "The Tholian Web" (TOS 3.9) that there has never been a mutiny in Starfleet history.

FIGURE 4. (a) *Michael Burnham, attended by Captain Georgiou and Lieutenant Saru, uses an old-fashioned telescope to investigate a mysterious object ("The Vulcan Hello," DSC 1.1).* (b) *Michael Burnham on the prison transport after receiving a life sentence for mutiny ("Context Is for Kings," DSC 1.3).*

Even worse, from a fan perspective, is the portrayal of the Klingons, who neither look like the smooth-headed humanoids familiar from *The Original Series* (whose appearance *Enterprise* had gone to such pains to explain in its final season) nor sport the look familiar from *Next Generation*–era productions. Instead, they are portrayed with a new, more alien appearance, including clean-shaven heads. Most disruptive of all, however, is the plot point that will become the basis for the whole first season, namely the Klingon war. In all previous productions, the Klingons and the Federation have been portrayed as engaged in a Cold War–like stalemate, full of proxy battles and simmering tensions but never breaking out into a full-blown open war between the two powers.

Anticipating fan backlash, CBS apparently aimed to preempt it through its choice of creative staff. As with the earlier effort to reboot the film franchise under J. J. Abrams, *Star Trek*'s return to television was billed as the work of an auteur. This time, however, they found one who was not only a *Star Trek* fan but an experienced writer for both *Deep Space Nine* and *Voyager:* Bryan Fuller, who in the meantime had made a name for himself as the creator and showrunner of critically acclaimed dramas like *Pushing Daisies* (2007–9), *Hannibal* (2013–15), and *American Gods* (2017–21). Not only did he bring *Star Trek* credibility to the table, therefore, but his work since had positioned him at the intersection of the burgeoning prestige TV trend and genre television. Unfortunately, Fuller ultimately left *Discovery* before the first season aired amid creative differences and repeated production delays,[1] leaving it unclear how much of the show's concept can be attributed to him. In the meantime, however, in the hope of further cultivating fan trust and excitement, CBS also brought in Nicholas Meyer, director of *The Wrath of Khan* (1982) and *The Undiscovered Country* (1986), longtime *Trek* novelist Kirsten Beyer, and Gene Roddenberry's son, Rod, as creative consultants.

This belt-and-suspenders approach to seeking fan buy-in was wise, given that *Discovery* appeared to be repeating the mistakes of its reviled predecessors. Not only was it pursuing a prequel concept—which fans had twice rejected—but a close associate of J. J. Abrams, Alex Kurtzman, was brought on board to coordinate this new era of the franchise. Indeed, from a fan perspective, *Discovery*'s approach was somehow even worse than either *Enterprise* or the Kelvin films. Its intervention into *Star Trek* history was no longer safely distanced from familiar canonical events (like *Enterprise*), nor was it shunted into its own hermetically sealed timeline (like the Kelvin films). Rather, the new material was to be incorporated into the Prime Timeline at a date uncomfortably close to the events of *The Original Series*. Finally, as I have noted, even for fans who were not keeping up with the production rumor mill, the visuals immediately signal an insistence on artistic freedom and unexpected worldbuilding coupled with a defiance of expected fan service, which is eerily reminiscent of *Enterprise*'s controversial formula.

Yet whereas Berman and Braga made an unwitting misjudgment, *Discovery*'s approach is a fully deliberate strategic choice. The fact that the show so systematically defies fan expectations while telling the story of its main character's fatal betrayal of her captain is no accident. Instead, it represents perhaps the most self-conscious meta gesture of late *Star Trek*. In the wake of the failure of *Enterprise* and the fan rejection of the Kelvin Timeline films, the writers anticipated that fans would greet any new *Star Trek* production with suspicion, treating every unforeseen world-building element as an outrage and a crime. Instead of fighting this tendency, they leaned into it, setting up a situation where the show itself has to earn its way back to its identity as authentic *Star Trek,* just as its main character has to earn her way back into Starfleet.

From this unpromising starting point, *Discovery*'s first season develops one of the finest story arcs in *Star Trek* history. I compared the gesture of *Enterprise* to that of the HBO adaptation of *Watchmen,* and the similarity is even stronger in the case of *Discovery*. This *Star Trek* installment does more than anticipate the critically acclaimed drama's approach of doubling down on the very absurdities of its source material to draw unexpected contemporary relevance out of an aged franchise. More than that, it arguably matches it in terms of the quality of its writing and performances and in its ambitious social commentary. Building on the stylistic advances of the Kelvin Timeline films, and taking full advantage of the serialization typical of contemporary streaming shows, it crafts a narrative that carefully balances self-contained episodes with an overarching plot and rewards rewatching with elaborately planned revelations and reversals (in place of the Kelvin films' superficial surprises).

Yet while Burnham herself amply earns her in-universe pardon, the creative team was never confident that *Discovery* itself had been forgiven by the fans. As a result, the show abruptly reinvented itself and then, in Sabrina Mittermeier's words, continued "reboot[ing] itself over and over again, trying to find its place."[2] Its second season at once doubled down on fan service—almost as a gesture of apology toward fans—and set itself up for greater artistic freedom by transporting the USS *Discovery* to an unseen distant future. Yet as we will see, the writers struggled to fill out their new world, and *Discovery* was soon overshadowed by *Picard* (2020–23) and its own spin-off, *Strange New Worlds* (2022–present), both of which focused much more on pure fan service. In the end, the show that inaugurated the most prolific era of *Star Trek* history joined *The Original Series* and *Enterprise* in suffering cancellation, as the show's fifth season was, unexpectedly, its last.

The task of this chapter will be to trace *Discovery*'s strange trajectory, with a focus on the ways that the artistic achievement of the first season proved to be unassimilable—both by the writers of later seasons and by the franchise as a whole. I will devote two sections to the first season, analyzing its attempt to fix *Star Trek* and assessing its ambitious and intricate plot, then treat the next three seasons in turn (with more limited analysis of the fifth, which did not air until this book was in production). My guiding thread will be the way that the first season combined a unique approach to fan service and unexpected world-building to create a space for narrative freedom, striking a balance that subsequent seasons were never able to regain.

"I'M TRYING TO SAVE YOU! I'M TRYING TO SAVE ALL OF YOU!"

The title of this section is Michael Burnham's plea after her mutiny is discovered and Captain Georgiou resumes command. It serves as a summation of both the character, who is called on to save the galaxy again and again, and the show itself. Just as no one could miss Burnham's rash and aggressive actions, so too can no fan overlook the show's seemingly willful betrayal of previous assumptions about *Original Series* canon. There is no way to interpret its decisions as mistakes or oversights: *Discovery*'s goal is explicitly to rewrite *Star Trek*'s history in a way that no previous production had done, and it wants the audience to notice that that is what it is doing. As Andrew Whitacre puts it, *Discovery* "does not just want to be a show that fixes the franchise, it wants to be a show *about* fixing the franchise."[3]

As with Burnham's own mutiny, this seeming betrayal is an attempt to save the franchise from terrible danger. In Burnham's case, the danger is relatively straightforward, as her ship is in a face-off with hostile Klingons. But what danger faces the *Star Trek* franchise, from the writers' perspective? From the changes they made, we can safely infer that the problem is twofold. The first, and most substantive, is a recognition that the franchise had gone in an increasingly conservative direction that was out of step with its history of diversity and cosmopolitanism. From that perspective, it rejoins the trend of representation started by *Deep Space Nine* and *Voyager* by putting a Black woman in the lead. They complement her with other compelling female characters, including Admiral Cornwall (Jayne Brook)—the first officer of that rank to be a recurring guest star across multiple seasons—and breakout character Ensign Sylvia Tilly (Mary Wiseman), whose awkward enthusiasm creates a comical and poignant contrast to Burnham's deadly seriousness. And in a long-overdue move, it introduces explicitly queer characters, portrayed by well-known gay actors Anthony Rapp (as brilliant inventor and engineer Paul Stamets) and Wilson Cruz (as chief medical officer Hugh Culber), in a way that is, in Andrea Whitacre's words, "utterly unsensationalized, almost quotidian"—as though gay people had obviously always been part of the *Star Trek* universe.[4]

This last gesture partly explains why *Discovery* was not content to move forward in *Star Trek*'s fictional timeline. Introducing gay characters in *Star Trek*'s future would leave open the possibility that the fictional utopia had been discriminatory up to that point. Only by injecting more diversity into *Star Trek*'s own past could it effectively update the franchise as a whole. Its revision of the franchise's past is also much more forceful and unambiguous than previous installments. Normally, as we have seen, voyages into the storyworld's past are achieved through time-travel plots that either create total narrative freedom (as in the Kelvin Timeline films) or, more commonly, assume the fictional future as a kind of predestined outcome. Unlike either *Enterprise* or the reboot films, the first season of *Discovery* has no transtemporal cover for its gesture of reopening the *Star Trek* past. The decision to align the show visually with *Enterprise* rather than *The Original Series* emphasizes this point: our characters do not know that they are part of the narrative that began with the adventures of Kirk and his storied crew; they do not know that they are a necessary step toward utopia. Like all genuine historical actors, they do not and cannot know what is "supposed" to happen. Nor do they have the luxury of regarding their failures and betrayals as always already redeemed. As Sherryl Vint perceptively notes, this uncertainty is foreshadowed in the image of the Starfleet symbol that Georgiou and Burnham trace in the sand: "the outlines of the familiar Federation are there, but written in an unstable medium and subject to change."[5]

This kind of uncertainty fits well with our historical moment, and it seems clear that *Discovery*'s creative team thought that it also fits more naturally with *The Original Series* than with *Next Generation*. In the latter era, the Federation was going from strength to strength. The progress of humanistic ideals seemed assured even amid the ruins of *Deep Space Nine*'s Dominion war, which ushered in friendly liberal leadership for essentially all the Federation's rival political powers. In contrast, in *The Original Series,* Kirk and friends regularly meet people who have never heard of the Federation, and in place of Picard's self-satisfied postscarcity utopia, the earlier show regularly pictures not only commerce but the very real threat of famine, starvation, and pandemic disease.

Nowhere is the triumphalism of the *Next Generation* era clearer than in the Federation's alliance with the Klingons, symbolized by the presence of Lieutenant Worf (Michael Dorn) among Picard's bridge crew. Before this achievement, Kirk's Starfleet is constantly on the edge of war with the Klingons—a possibility that is at one point only halted by literal divine intervention ("Errand of Mercy," TOS 1.26). So it is fitting that *Discovery* chooses to stake its first season precisely on that world-historical shift, which it exaggerates by turning an improbable cold war into an outright military struggle, spurred by a militant Klingon nationalist, T'Kuvma. This retcon (or retrospective continuity) admittedly opens up the plot hole that the *Original Series* characters all experienced a traumatic war in their early adulthood that they never mention—though perhaps that retrospectively makes them even more relatable to the postwar Americans who first watched the show in the wake of World War II and the Korean war.[6] In terms of the writers' desire to inject more contemporary social justice–related concerns back into the franchise, the plotline also gives them a way to explore trauma and mental health issues.

This marriage of a major retcon of *Star Trek*'s fictional history with contemporary political relevance brings us to the second major danger that the creative team saw facing the franchise: the accumulation of fan shibboleths around the *Original Series* era. Creating a prequel always introduces artistic constraints, but in the case of *Star Trek,* the primal text had long since taken on a strangely untouchable quality as fans claimed to view the limited 1960s-era production values as "how things literally looked." This meant that every slapdash makeup job, every cheap special effect, and every analog dial and knob was regarded as canonically binding on future productions. We saw how *Enterprise* reinforced this attitude through its bizarre attempt to deprive Klingons of their ridges, and in the Mirror Universe arc as well they doubled down on *Original Series* literalism by using an exact replica of the original bridge set to portray the original *Enterprise*'s sister ship, the USS *Defiant* ("In a Mirror Darkly," ENT 4.18–19). Other episodes—most notably "Trials and Tribble-ations" (DS9 5.6), which used CGI to interpose *Deep Space Nine* characters into *The Original Series* favorite "The Trouble with Tribbles" (TOS 2.15)—reinforced the sense that not only were visuals of *The Original Series* literal canon, but they had been *canonically established* to be canon. The *Enterprise* novels had further echoed this attitude, developing an elaborate plot where a Romulan weapon capable of taking over Starfleet computer systems had required them to "downgrade" to more analog and less automated technology with mechanical dials and switches.

Hence to tell new stories set in the *Original Series* era that fans would accept as compatible with canon would require the use of visuals that appear frankly absurd and nonfunctional from a contemporary perspective. In the case of the Klingons in particular, returning to the much simpler makeup used in the handful of early episodes in which they initially appeared, rather than the more elaborate and alien appearance familiar from dozens and dozens of subsequent productions, could appear arbitrary and distracting.

Discovery was not content simply to defy fan expectations of ridgeless Klingons. Instead, it invents a new, third Klingon appearance that strongly reinforces the attempt to take the Klingon threat more seriously, rendering the Klingons much more alien and frightening than the often campy Klingons of *Next Generation*–era productions, where Worf above all often served as comic relief. *Discovery*'s Klingons are no joke—they will definitely kill you. And where *Next Generation*–era Klingon rhetoric of war and honor could seem like empty boasting, a kind of countercultural cosplay, T'Kuvma encourages his followers to reject liberal values on principle. In rhetoric reminiscent of contemporary jihadists, he warns that the Federation's promise of peace comes at the price of cultural purity.

Yet the writers were not content simply to introduce this change and allow the viewers to draw the conclusion that they are supposed to regard the Klingons as much scarier than in previous installments. In keeping with the show's self-conception as being about fixing the franchise, the writers implicitly pick a fight with fans by not only systematically name-checking many of the episodes that commonly factor as proof of the literalist position but also by crafting one of the season's major twists around the Klingon appearance question. As we will see, one of the two big reveals in that season's complex plot is that Lieutenant Ash Tyler (Shazad Latif), who becomes Burnham's confidant and lover, is actually T'Kuvma's follower Voq (Shazad Latif), who has undergone radical surgery and a complex brainwashing procedure to infiltrate Starfleet. The transformation of Voq into Tyler hearkens back to the *locus classicus* of Klingon ridge literalism: "The Trouble with Tribbles." There we learn that a Klingon has been passing as human on a Federation starbase, a prospect that all the human characters greet with shock and disbelief. From the audience's perspective, of course, such a disguise seems trivially easy given the simplicity of the Klingon makeup, and the *Discovery* writers seize on that previously unnoticed inconsistency to reinforce their implicit case that the Klingons "always" looked much more alien. But given the plot they had chosen, they could not simply go back to the familiar *Next Generation*–style ridges, much less English dialogue, because then the identity of Voq and Tyler would have been impossible to hide. Hence the change to the Klingon appearance, which proved to be the single biggest sticking point for existing fans, was in the service of a superficial surprise that, as we will see, seemed to lead nowhere. In the meantime, these creative choices undercut the development of Klingon characters, as the actors clearly found it difficult to convey subtle emotions while weighed down with so much makeup and spitting out guttural Klingon dialogue. Meanwhile, my colleagues at r/DaystromInstitute emphatically did not receive the message, instead spinning dozens of theories about how the loss of their ridges in *Enterprise* had prompted Klingons to seek cosmetic surgery to exaggerate their features, which would presumably lead to the pendulum swinging back toward the ridgeless look in *The Original Series*.

Even as the show aired, the writers seemed to recognize their mistake. Taking to Twitter, they "clarified" that the Klingons were unexpectedly bald because they were at war—even though all the Klingons who respond to T'Kuvma's call in the first episode are already bald before he issues his call to war. These Twitter interventions were only a small part of the ongoing dialogue between the producers and fans, which CBS actively cultivated on every front. In addition to the *Short Treks* segments meant to build buzz for the show, every episode of *Discovery* was accompanied by a "recap show, which would feature interviews with cast and crew, show behind-the-scenes clips, or showcase fan art," a practice that was later "downscaled to an interview format starting in the second season."[7] Meanwhile, official social media accounts teased upcoming episodes and offered discussion prompts for fans.

All this activity generated continual fan engagement between episodes, which were released weekly rather than dumped all at once in streaming style. Teasing the various surprises kept fan discussion buzzing, and the ultimate reveal would reward rewatching, thereby generating further analysis and dialogue. On r/DaystromInstitute, *Discovery*'s first season prompted a nearly unmanageable surge in new members and posts. The moderators, who take seriously their role of promoting only in-depth discussion, adapted to the new reality by providing open threads for immediate reactions to each week's episode. On a forum where a few dozen comments typically indicates a successful post, an open thread on the first *Discovery* trailer had 566 responses,[8] and the "first watch analysis thread" for the actual premiere had 376.[9] Speaking as someone who followed the show and fan discussions avidly at the time, the excitement and energy were palpable, despite (or even because of) the many points of controversy. If one of *Enterprise*'s greatest failings was, in Hark's words, that "its creative personnel lost sight of how to function as a cult phenomenon in the new world of internet fandom,"[10] *Discovery* learned its predecessor's lesson well. As Mittermeier says, "With [*Discovery*] . . . , the *Star Trek* franchise, for better or for worse, has officially entered the post-network era of television."[11]

THE TROUBLE WITH TWISTS

Much of the fan dialogue during the first season centered on speculation about potential twists, a storytelling device largely absent from previous *Trek* installments. Given the episodic format of most previous shows and, for much of the franchise's history, the lack of any ability to systematically rewatch old episodes at will, there was no realistic prospect of creating a long-term story arc where clues gradually build toward a surprising result. The advent of streaming, which allowed for on-demand access to all of *Star Trek,* allowed fans to spin fanciful theories of elaborate connections among disparate episodes that never could have been intended by the original writers.

However, *Discovery* was the first series that was actually designed from the ground up to reward rewatching.[12] One key change in this direction is the much faster pacing. Compared to the leisurely pace of most older episodes, *Discovery* appears to be running for its life, cramming as much as possible into every available minute. More importantly, though, the season is structured around two major twists, which are not only surprising in the moment but also cast past episodes in a new light. Here *Discovery*'s approach once again anticipates that of HBO's *Watchmen,* which is similarly structured around two major twists that make many past plot points snap retrospectively into place, even though the viewer never could have guessed them in advance.

I have already mentioned one of the two major twists: the revelation that Burnham's intimate partner, Lieutenant Ash Tyler, is actually a Klingon in disguise. This plot is related to a broader gesture of reversal. Where the Klingon war could initially appear to be yet another return to the War on Terror paradigm that had dominated the franchise through the late seasons of *Enterprise* and the entire Kelvin Timeline trilogy, in reality, as Mittermeier points out, *Discovery* "seems to actively work against simply regurgitating tropes on terrorism."[13] Indeed, after opening with the Klingon critique of Federation hypocrisy, *Discovery* "studiously vindicates the Klingon perspective," in the words of international relations scholars Henrik Schillinger and Arne Sönnichsen, "even while inviting viewers to identify with its Starfleet protagonists and their belief in the Federation's universal mission."[14] They walk this tightrope by inviting us to identify with two of T'Kuvma's followers: Voq, an outcast who was unexpectedly named T'Kuvma's right-hand man and believes himself to be his successor, and L'Rell (Mary Chieffo), who belongs to the distrusted House of Mo'Kai, known for espionage. From their viewpoint, we see that although T'Kuvma's devotion to his vision of traditional Klingon values is arguably fanatical, the war only becomes truly existential when a more cynical operator, Kol of House Kor (Kenneth Mitchell), seizes T'Kuvma's ship with its advanced cloaking capability.

Thankfully, though, the Federation has an even more advanced technology at its disposal: a new propulsion method known as the spore drive. Using an organic substrate to our physical universe known as the mycelial network, it ultimately enables the ship to travel instantaneously to virtually any point in the galaxy. This capability will obviously grant a decisive military advantage, and so Starfleet presses Stamets and his experimental science vessel into service for the war effort under the command of Captain Gabriel Lorca (Jason Isaacs), who has been given a free hand to do anything he deems necessary to win the war. In the first regular episode after the two-part premiere, Lorca uses this power to intercept Burnham's prison transport and press her into service as well, with the stated rationale that her considerable talents are going to waste. She is initially reluctant to join a crew that includes an uncanny number of her former colleagues from the *Shenzhou*—including Lieutenant Detmer (Emily Coutts), whose sole role in the plot is to glare resentfully at Burnham, and Saru, who is now Lorca's first officer. Ultimately her time aboard *Discovery* represents a shot at redemption, allowing her to help fight the war she inadvertently started while making new friends, healing her relationship with Saru, and even finding love with Tyler.

Initially we appear to be in the midst of a plot exploring the tensions between liberal humanist values and military necessity. The writers put a contemporary spin on it by focusing on trauma, as exemplified in Tyler's flashbacks and panic attacks and Lorca's heavy burden of guilt after the destruction of his former ship. As both attempt to tough it out in their own ways, they also provide an interesting reflection on current concerns about masculinity, toxic or otherwise.[15] Gradually, though, we learn that something much stranger is going on. In a plot that once again draws on the theme of uncanny doubles from *Star Trek Nemesis* (2002) and pushes it to its limits, the writers reveal that Tyler is actually Voq, who has undergone radical surgical alteration to appear human and, for good measure, had his brain overwritten by the personality of a Starfleet officer, to guarantee that Voq will be able to keep his cover until activated. Even worse, Gabriel Lorca turns out to be an imposter from the Mirror Universe, who uses the spore drive to return to his own world and press his claim to the imperial throne—with the hope of having Burnham, whose Mirror equivalent had been his lover, at his side. Once in the Mirror Universe—where they spend an unprecedented four consecutive episodes—Burnham has to pass as her evil counterpart for weeks before finally meeting the Terran emperor, who is none other than the double of her late mentor, Philippa Georgiou. Lorca's treachery turns out to be the least of their worries, however, as Emperor Georgiou's massive spore-powered ship threatens to destroy the mycelial network and, with it, the entire multiverse.

As with many previous plot summaries, this story sounds absurd. Certainly it was not a self-evident choice of story for the first televised season of *Star Trek* in over a decade. The use of the Mirror Universe theme was especially controversial, with some fans arguing that it destroyed a nuanced and compelling character by turning him into a mustache-twirling villain (a reference that is as de rigueur among fans as name-checking the infamous J. J. Abrams lens flares). Indeed, one major contributor to r/DaystromInstitute recently declared that he was simply going to pretend that the Mirror Universe reveal had never happened and that the first half of the season was the story about the conflict between liberal and military values that it appeared to be.[16]

In my view, though, the Mirror Lorca arc is ultimately what makes the first season so great, and it is exemplary of the *Discovery* writing team's ambitions and approach. Their goal, especially in the first season, is to achieve an improbable tour de force by doubling down on the most inconsistent or questionable aspects of franchise lore and elevating the material to deliver a prestige TV–level story that only *Star Trek* could tell. The end result transmutes the purest fan service into the greatest possible artistic freedom by taking the franchise's world-building more seriously than it has ever been taken. Just as with their new vision of the Klingons, their use of the Mirror Universe reimagines a *Star Trek* trope that has most often been played for laughs, giving the actors a chance to blow off steam by playing evil versions of their characters. What if there was a world, the writers implicitly ask, where moral values were inverted, where treachery was the norm, where only the most ruthless survived? Their answer is clear: it would not be a fun and campy place; it would be absolutely terrifying. Worse, it would be morally corrosive, as Burnham discovers while playing her evil counterpart. She worries she will lose touch with her authentic values as she becomes too good at playing according to this world's corrupt rules, and with good reason. The first thing she does on arrival on the Mirror *Discovery* is to kill (in self-defense) the double of one of her protégés from the *Shenzhou,* and the last thing she does before being found out by Emperor Georgiou is to eat a soup made with the "fear ganglia" of Saru's fellow Kelpiens, who are a slave caste in the Mirror Universe.

The fact that Burnham finds it so troubling to pass as a Mirror Universe native speaks to her moral integrity, but the fact that Lorca was able to pass so easily as a Prime Universe good guy raises many serious questions about the judgment of Starfleet Command. Admittedly, Lorca is an expert manipulator, and Jason Isaacs delivers an amazing performance—perhaps the greatest ever in *Star Trek* history—that reveals more depth on each rewatch. Once his identity is revealed, many things snap into place, above all the pervasive sense that *Discovery* did not "feel like" *Star Trek*. In light of Lorca's betrayal, we can see it did not feel right because under his command, it actually was not an authentic Starfleet ship but rather a fragment of the Mirror Universe's Terran Empire, where crew members are disposable tools whose names Lorca only bothers to learn only in cases of strict necessity.

Nonetheless, Lorca's comrades value him deeply, as they show when the Klingons abduct him in "Choose Your Pain" (DSC 1.5). The mission is Saru's first taste of solo command, and he succeeds ably—not only rescuing his captain but getting the spore drive to work reliably for the first time. The latter comes at a steep price, as Stamets injects himself with spore DNA in order to become a sentient pilot for the device, violating the Federation's ban on genetic engineering (which will become a leitmotif for streaming-era *Trek*). The spore drive ultimately becomes central to a plan to break the Klingon's cloaking technology, which will allow the Federation to easily win the war. Unfortunately, it demands that Stamets pilot the spore drive through hundreds of short jumps, a task that leaves him nearly catatonic. This risky method turns out to have the double purpose of cracking the code to allow Lorca to return to his native universe, and he convinces Stamets to make one last jump—for which he manipulates the coordinates. The crew's greatest triumph turns out to be entirely in the service of Lorca's agenda, as he does not even bother to transmit the algorithm for breaking the cloak before departing the Prime Universe.

Only once the crew are actually in the Mirror Universe do they realize how far they have strayed from Starfleet ideals—and begin to fight their way back. With Lorca out of the picture and the newly confident and reassuring Saru in command, the crew comes together at last to collaborate on a way to avoid the pending destruction of the multiverse. It is a rousing scene that feels every bit as much like classic *Star Trek* as the opening vignette with Captain Georgiou. In the greatest tradition of the franchise, a mix of pluck, determination, incomprehensible technobabble, and readiness to court self-sacrifice for the greater good once again saves the universe. Against all odds, the Mirror Universe, which had long been one of the corniest *Star Trek* tropes, has given rise to one of the most carefully plotted and cathartic stories in the history of the franchise.

The escape from the Mirror Universe under Saru's steady leadership is a beautiful ending—or would have been. But once again, the *Discovery* writers will not let us have our easy nostalgia. On returning to the Prime Universe, our heroes discover that nine months have passed, during which time the absence of the spore drive has led to devastating losses for the Federation. Apparently unchastened by the revelation that they have been misled by an evil imposter for the entire war, Starfleet Command immediately turns to another Mirror Universe denizen for help: Emperor Georgiou, whom Burnham had rescued in a fit of sentiment. Drawing on her experience of defeating the Mirror Klingons, she recommends using the spore drive to travel beneath the surface of the Klingon home world, where Georgiou will plant a bomb that can destroy the planet. This genocidal agenda—endorsed by both Admiral Cornwall and her foster father, Sarek—prompts Burnham to commit another act of mutiny. This time, though, her mutiny echoes that of Picard in the film *Insurrection* (1998), who rebels against Starfleet Command in the service of Starfleet values. By choosing diplomacy over destruction, she brings the Klingon war to an improbable end by giving the trigger to the world-destroying bomb to L'Rell. Drawing on her deep Klingon convictions, L'Rell in turn decides she would rather destroy her own home world than allow the Klingons to continue their nihilistic and dishonorable campaign against the all-but-defeated Federation and uses her possession of the kill switch as leverage to become the Klingon chancellor and call off the war. All of this is achieved in the space of two episodes, which also include the revelation that Burnham has been pardoned and her conviction expunged *and* a lengthy award ceremony at Starfleet Academy, interspersed with segments of an inspirational speech from Burnham about the lessons she has learned.

Clearly the Mirror Universe arc was more carefully plotted than the Klingon war, which arguably deserved at least another half season to resolve properly. Even less convincing is the other main Klingon plot, centered on Tyler's secret identity as Voq. Once Voq's personality takes charge, we realize that Tyler's panic attacks and flashbacks—involving horrific torture and what he remembers as sexual assault by L'Rell—are actually his memories of his voluntary surgical alterations and a consensual, loving relationship. Before, we seemed to be witnessing a rare exploration of the experience of a male survivor of sexual assault, but it is unclear what we are supposed to take away from this aspect of the story in its final form. Along the same lines, what are we to think about his relationship with Burnham, now that we realize she has unwittingly been sleeping with a Klingon spy? Both of these strange complications are at least integral to Tyler/Voq's story, but the return of the Voq personality also leads to one of the most controversial plot points in a controversial season: Tyler/Voq's gratuitous murder of Doctor Culber, one of the first gay characters in *Star Trek* history, seemingly for shock value alone. The show that had done so much to enhance the franchise's representation along the lines of gender and sexuality was now seemingly blurring the lines of sexual consent and treating its gay characters as expendable.

All of this came in the service of a plotline that simply fizzled out. Voq does not complete his mission. Indeed, it is unclear what his mission was even supposed to be. Instead, with the help of L'Rell, who had since fled her fellow Klingons and sought refuge on *Discovery,* the conflict between the Voq and Tyler personalities is resolved in favor of the human overlay. L'Rell mourns the loss of Voq in true Klingon style, screaming to the heavens to warn the dead that a Klingon warrior is about to join them, even though Tyler retains Voq's memories and ultimately decides to live with L'Rell as her consort.

It is difficult to know what to make of this plot, but to the extent we can discern a message here, I believe we have to assume that the writers intend a contrast between the cases of Tyler and Lorca. On the one hand, Tyler's triumph over Voq would represent the fact that Starfleet ideals are so compelling and the relationships built on a Starfleet vessel so meaningful that they can easily overcome a mind motivated by ethnocentrism and vengeance. On the other hand, even though the Mirror Universe is an inversion of the Federation, Lorca's values are not simply reactive against Starfleet from his personal perspective, and he is able to live among them for many months without being seduced from his own nefarious principles. In fact, the very things that proved the values of Starfleet were authentic and broke down Voq's "remain Klingon" ideology served as little more than evidence of the Federation's weakness and unworthiness from Lorca's perspective.

In short, not everyone can be won over in the end. In my view, this message is both a genuine breakthrough for *Star Trek* and a salutary political allegory for our present day. Virtually all of American popular culture since 9/11 has been fascinated by the kind of narrative of military necessity in service of humanistic values that Lorca initially seemed to introduce, and *Star Trek* in many ways foreshadowed this trend with *Deep Space Nine*'s Dominion war arc. In fiction, these narratives often work out wonderfully, as all the hard choices pay off in the end with the reestablishment of liberal normality. In our own reality, however, we now realize that liberals' embrace of militarism after 9/11 led them to empower people with destructive agendas that are incompatible with humanistic cosmopolitanism. The Lorca reveal reminds us that not everyone is a nice liberal deep down—there really are enemies who really do want things incompatible with the values the imagined ideal *Star Trek* fan embraces.

More than that, the contrast with the Klingon characters (even in the rushed form their story arcs ultimately took) highlights that the lines between "possible dialogue partners" and "implacable foes" do not map neatly with ethnic or cultural divisions. There were other possible ways to get that message across, but I do not concede that yet another story of a soldier who is forced to make terrible choices in the service of freedom would have been better than the story we actually got.

"SYNCING UP WITH CANON" WHILE GETTING OUT OF DODGE

Fans found much more to discuss in *Discovery* than the big reveals. In part that is simply due to its aforementioned density and break-neck pacing. To give just one example, "Choose Your Pain" (DSC 1.5), the episode in which Lorca is kidnapped and rescued and in which Stamets injects himself with spores to get the spore drive working, also includes the discovery that a macroscopic space tardigrade who feeds on mycelial spores can navigate the spore drive (though the process nearly kills it) and the introduction of *Original Series* recurring character Harry Mudd (a lovable scam artist) and Tyler as Lorca's cellmates in the prison ship. Later, in by far the most successful and popular episode of the season, "Magic to Make the Sanest Man Go Mad" (DSC 1.7), Mudd returns to take vengeance on Lorca using a time crystal that allows him to repeatedly relive his attempts to take over the ship, then reset to an earlier moment with the knowledge he has gained. This satisfying time-loop plot not only hearkens back to the best of episodic *Trek* but also unexpectedly opens up the space for rich character development, particularly regarding Burnham and Tyler's relationship.

The show's tightly packed plot allows for an exploration of a striking range of social and political issues—part of *Discovery*'s bid to make *Star Trek* more cerebral and relevant after over a decade of less intellectually ambitious installments. The excitement in my own academic circle, among longtime fans and first-time viewers of the franchise, was palpable, and my blog ultimately hosted a retrospective on the first season and a series of conversations between myself and the journalist Sarah Jaffe on the second.[17] Those efforts were nothing, however, compared to the titanic labor of Sabrina Mittermeier and Maeike Spychala in putting together a massive and varied volume of essays on *Discovery*, which includes some brief references to season 2 but focuses almost entirely on season 1.[18] In contrast, *Enterprise* has never been the subject of a full book, whether a single-author study or a collaborative volume, and the Abrams films only belatedly received extended scholarly scrutiny in Matthew Wilhelm Kapell and Ace G. Pilkington's much slimmer collection.[19]

Yet the intricacy and density of the first season's plot made it hard to predict where *Discovery* would go next. The season finale leaves things wide open, as the ship's trip to Vulcan to pick up its (unnamed) new captain is interrupted by a distress call from none other than the USS *Enterprise*—which serves more as a symbolic indication that *Discovery* has finally earned its way back to *Star Trek* than as a foundation for any particular plot. The tie-in literature registered the difficulty here. The comics stayed well clear of the main plot, as IDW published a prequel story about T'Kuvma's background, a follow-up miniseries about the power struggle in the Mirror Universe after Emperor Georgiou's disappearance, and a longer "annual" issue showing the courtship of Stamets and Culber.[20] The novels, for their part, focused on prequel stories, including an awkward mission teaming Burnham up with Spock and a collaboration between Georgiou and Prime Lorca.[21] Both were hamstrung by the need to maintain surprise—particularly the latter, the main text of which displays no awareness that there is anything amiss with the Lorca we meet on the show, and which concludes with the clearly last-minute addition of a non sequitur scene where Lorca awakens in a mysterious prison cell (presumably in the Mirror Universe).

Both were contradicted by on-screen canon shortly after their publication. Despite the fact that longtime novelist Kirsten Beyer had been given the unprecedented role of explicitly maintaining coordination between the main canon and tie-in productions, later novels giving background information on individual characters met much the same fate.

In reality, though, no one could have achieved what Beyer was tasked to do under the circumstances because the leadership, and therefore the creative direction, of *Discovery* was in turmoil in the wake of the first season. The departure of Fuller during production of the first season was already a setback, but as Mittermeier reports,

> by the time the show premiered in September 2017, Aaron Harberts and Gretchen J. Berg were the new showrunners. Having worked with Fuller on his [previous] productions, they seemed primed to carry out his vision. Yet, only a few episodes into shooting the second season, Harberts and Berg were fired when allegations of their mistreatment of writers were raised, leaving *[Discovery]* yet again without anyone at the helm, ironically mirroring the plot. Production halted for several weeks and eventually Michelle Paradise took over as showrunner.[22]

In the end, *Discovery* barely preserved continuity among its own televised episodes. Quoting Mittermeier again: "It is difficult to speculate about how exactly this behind-the-scenes turmoil impacted the second season, yet there seems to have been a visible narrative rift in the season's arc coinciding with the change."[23] Particularly given *Discovery*'s fast pace and tight serialization, the conflicting visions at play led to a much less cohesive and more confusing second season.

Despite the lack of a unified creative vision for this season, its overarching goals are clear. The first, to quote executive producer Alex Kurtzman, is that of "syncing up with canon."[24] Kurtzman singles out the relationship between Burnham and Spock as the biggest outstanding question, but the writers and costume designers do much more to reconcile the most glaring contradictions between *Discovery* and *The Original Series*—by allowing the Klingons to grow their hair back out, by removing the holographic communication interface, and ultimately by showing us a beautifully modernized version of the classic *Enterprise* bridge that not even the most stubborn fan would want to refit in favor of the spare 1960s sets. In other words, they aim to get fans to accept *Discovery* as a fully canonical prequel to *The Original Series*. The second goal is to get the USS *Discovery* and its crew out of the prequel setting, which is ultimately achieved by launching them nine hundred years into the future and strictly classifying all records of their exploits (including their anomalously advanced spore drive).

Obviously these two goals are at odds with each other, much less with continuing to develop the characters and themes established in season 1. There are some notable exceptions. They continue to expand queer representation by adding comedian Tig Notaro to the crew as a salty engineer, Jet Reno, who also contributes much-needed comic relief in her interplay with the uptight Stamets. On the plot level, Doctor Culber—who turned out to have been somehow alive in the mycelial network and helped guide Stamets back from the Mirror Universe—is resurrected, but he finds that everything feels off, including his relationship. Here, finally, is the unambiguous exploration of trauma that season 1 failed to deliver, and it depends on *Discovery*'s signature method of taking *Star Trek* themes much more seriously than previous shows did. Characters have died and been resurrected many times, and then in the next episode, everything is back to normal. Culber is the first character who struggles with his experience. Meanwhile, after his position in the Klingon Empire becomes untenable, Tyler is recruited into Section 31 by Emperor Georgiou (who becomes a recurring character throughout the season) and is assigned to *Discovery* as a liaison officer, forcing Culber to face his killer. Saru also gets a major plot arc, as we visit his home planet, where Kelpiens are kept captive and periodically culled by another sentient race, the Ba'ul. Saru has been led to believe that they did so to avoid a form of madness that afflicts Kelpiens when they reach a certain age, but he goes through the aging process with no adverse effects (other than a reduction of his fear sensitivity) and subsequently decides to reveal this to his fellow Kelpiens to start a revolution against the Ba'ul. All three of these plots come to a head in a physical altercation between Culber and Tyler, which Saru chooses not to stop. Taken together, these plots resume the explorations of trauma, grief, and masculinity that season 1 had began. Less successful are the reflections on motherhood, which take the form of Mirror Georgiou grappling with her affection for the double of her former adopted daughter and L'Rell hiding a child she had with pre-Tyler Voq—the latter of which ends with L'Rell faking the baby's death for its own protection and brandishing a simulated decapitated baby's head before the Klingon High Council.

Plot arcs centered on the series' new characters are largely crowded out, however, by the incorporation of legacy characters as part of "syncing up with canon." Once *Discovery* makes contact with the *Enterprise,* Captain Pike (Anson Mount) announces that he has been ordered to take command of the ship for a special mission. Seven red signals have apparently gone off simultaneously at widely separated corners of the galaxy, and *Discovery*'s spore drive makes it the only ship that can uncover this mystery in a reasonable amount of time. This premise is the first of many MacGuffins, but it serves mainly as a framework for a more episodic approach in the first half of the season. The use of the original *Star Trek* captain, who had appeared in the first unaired pilot ("The Cage"), also serves as a forceful declaration that things have returned to normal. The first thing

Pike does is effortlessly memorize the names of the bridge crew whom Lorca had treated like props, demonstrating his collaborative and "non-toxic masculine" style.[25] The contrast with Lorca is clearly intentional, but I cannot help but wonder, along with Mittermeier and Volkmer, if the figure of Pike goes beyond repudiating Lorca and instead repudiates the "implicit criticism of the trope of the Starfleet captain" that Lorca represented.[26]

A second MacGuffin is the figure of the Red Angel, who wears a suit that appears to allow them to travel through time and space at will. At first it appears to be a visit from the distant future (if only because the only character to display similar abilities was Captain Archer's thirty-first-century temporal guardian angel, Daniels). But Pike and Burnham gradually come to realize that the signals are somehow connected to Spock, who took a leave of absence before the beginning of the season and then seemingly disappeared. Much of the season therefore takes the form of a *Search for Spock* (1984) avant (or après?) la lettre, which forces Burnham to confront the reason she and her brother are estranged. After the terrorist attack by the Logic Extremists, it turns out, she felt she needed to distance herself from Spock for his own safety. It is a difficult prospect because he had previously idolized her, but she ultimately succeeds by gravely insulting him, echoing the schoolyard taunts he was forced to endure as a result of his mixed heritage. It is difficult to take this explanation seriously, much less the fact that an adult woman who has been through so much in the meantime is still so fixated on it. The young Spock (Ethan Peck) is certainly well cast, and the plot is full of good character moments as well as gratuitous fan service. Most notable in the latter category is a return to the setting of "The Cage" to cure the temporal madness that is afflicting Spock when we first meet him, complete with a "previously on" including clips from the original episode. All of this is in good fun, but a fan of season 1 cannot help but think that Spock is stealing an arc that should have belonged to Burnham's chosen sibling, Saru. This impression is reinforced when Saru, believing he is dying from the Kelpien affliction, takes one of his precious remaining moments to urge Burnham to reconcile with Spock. Much of the pathos of this scene, at least on the first watch, stems from the fact that the writing has been so erratic in season 2 that the viewer truly believes one of the series' most compelling characters might be killed off.

The episode in which Saru unexpectedly survives past his culling date ("An Obol for Charon," DSC 2.4) introduces the final major MacGuffin of the season: the so-called Sphere data. On their way to investigate a signal, *Discovery* is suddenly halted by a mysterious spherical object that they gradually realize is a living creature whose natural habitat is open space. The Sphere initially disrupts and overwhelms their computers, but eventually they come to understand that it is trying to hand over the vast data that it has accumulated over tens of thousands of years wandering the galaxy before it dies. Initially, this data appears to be an allegory for the weight of *Star Trek* canon, which *Discovery* is now taking on as a rich resource rather than resisting as an obstacle. In a reflection of the incoherence of the season's dual mandate, however, the Sphere data eventually becomes a terrible threat to all of existence. As it turns out, Control, a sentient AI that runs Section 31 (based on David Mack's novel but introduced into official canon here for the first time), has gone rogue and is now seeking the vast store of Sphere data to allow it to reach full sentience. If it does so, it will continue to gain power until it wipes out all biological life in the galaxy. This, it turns out, is exactly what the Red Angel is trying to stop, as they learn when they trap the Red Angel, who turns out to be Michael Burnham's mother (Sonja Sohn). Ultimately, they determine that the only way to avoid this grim fate is for Michael herself to don the Red Angel suit and transport *Discovery* and its crew into the distant future. With Control destroyed and *Discovery* safely in the thirty-second century, all the adventures we have seen so far are highly classified, thereby saving franchise continuity along with all sentient life.

Hence the most sophisticated season in *Star Trek* history was followed up by one of the most incoherent and self-indulgent. Much like *The Search for Spock* did for *Wrath of Khan,* the second season's convoluted story arc served to systematically undo all the innovations its predecessor introduced into the franchise (serious stakes, long-term consequences for actions, etc.) and restore the status quo ante. Although there are some good thematic and character elements on an episode-by-episode basis, it is nearly impossible to discern any meaningful message to the overall story arc aside from its stakes for the franchise itself. On the commercial level, *Discovery* was pressed into the service of CBS's plans for the revived franchise. Much of the season served as a long backdoor pilot for a proposed *Section 31* show starring Michelle Yeoh (which was long delayed and ultimately downgraded to a single direct-to-streaming movie), and the positive response to the casting of Pike and Spock prompted a fan campaign (led by Pike actor Anson Mount) to create a spin-off featuring that era's *Enterprise,* which would ultimately become *Strange New Worlds.* At long last, the producers of *Discovery* had achieved the number one goal of the *Star Trek* intellectual property holders throughout the twenty-first century: to get the fans to actively want a prequel series. The only problem is that the prequel they wanted was not *Discovery.*

INTO THE RUINED FUTURE

The third season's escape into the distant future stands as perhaps the franchise's most radical attempt to use time travel to create narrative freedom. Through the first half of the second season as well, it could have initially appeared that *Discovery* is using the Red Angel's temporal interventions to create ambiguity and allow fans to write the series out of their personal head canon if desired. In fact, when Burnham's mother (dubbed Doctor Burnham for clarity) finally reveals her identity as the Red Angel, we learn that we have been stuck in the wrong timeline, in which Control will ultimately be successful in its attempt to gain sentience and destroy all biological life. Powered by a time crystal—a mysterious mineral last seen as part of Harry Mudd's time-looping weapon in "Magic to Make the Sanest Man Go Mad" (DSC 1.7)—the Red Angel suit appears to have trapped Doctor Burnham in a temporal loop that thwarts her every attempt to stop the malevolent AI. Only once her original crystal is destroyed and replaced by a new one is the loop broken and a new timeline opened up ("Through the Valley of Shadows," DSC 2.12). Yet this breakthrough comes at a high cost for Captain Pike, who is granted a grim portent of the destiny that we already know from the character's first official on-air appearance in "The Menagerie" (TOS 1.11–12): after a terrible accident in a Starfleet Academy training exercise, he is so gravely injured that he is confined to an automated wheelchair and able to communicate only through single beeps. Noble Starfleet captain that he is, Pike willingly takes on this self-sacrifice to defeat Control—and confirm as unambiguously as possible that *Discovery* is part of the Prime Timeline.

The writers attempt a related move on the other end of *Discovery*'s temporal journey. Michael emerges in 3188, around a century after Lieutenant Daniels's meddling in the Temporal Cold War from his perch in the thirty-first century. For good measure, she soon learns that the conflict escalated into a destructive temporal war that finally convinced all powers to ban time travel once and for all. That move proved shortsighted, as the galaxy was soon afflicted with exactly the kind of disaster one would wish to undo via time travel: the Burn, in which all starships running on dilithium (the standard *Star Trek* fuel source) spontaneously exploded throughout the known universe. This catastrophe all but destroyed the Federation in one stroke, creating a power vacuum that was ultimately filled by the Mafia-like Emerald Chain (the successor entity to the criminal Orion Syndicate seen in *The Original Series* and *Deep Space Nine*).

The result is a world that Mittermeier rightly describes as "rather *Star Wars*–esque,"[27] and that one could also compare with the indirect *Star Trek* spin-off *Andromeda* (2000–2005). Based on a concept by Gene Roddenberry, the show centers on a starship captain (Kevin Sorbo) who travels in time from a more utopian era to a dystopian period centuries later. Aided by a sentient ship (which *Discovery* echoes with the gradual emergence of its own sentient AI, Zora), he must fight for his survival while attempting to revive the ideals of his original time period. Roddenberry's original idea was clearly a thinly veiled vision of *Star Trek*'s future, telling what is essentially the only story left to tell about the Federation after its near-total triumph in the *Next Generation* era—namely, its decline, fall, and possible revival. Even as *Discovery* tries to escape from the burdens of *Star Trek* canon, then, it is still taking great pains to establish its franchise bona fides by following Roddenberry's own vision of the ultimate fate of the Federation.

The season premiere ("The Hope Is You, Pt. 1," DSC 3.1) wastes little time establishing the new status quo. After crash landing on a desolate planet (and setting the Red Angel suit to self-destruct), Burnham meets the charming Book (David Ajala), an interstellar courier who uses his species' ability to psychically commune with animals in his pro bono sideline of preserving endangered species. Book agrees to help her find *Discovery,* which—much as in Spock and Nero's ill-fated trip to the Kelvin Timeline—is bound to emerge from the temporal wormhole at an unpredictable time and place. They seek information at a seedy trading post, where we learn of cool new technologies (personal transporters!) and get the political lay of the land. The most striking novelty of the season, however, is a scene where Burnham is interrogated and drugged, turning her into an uninhibited chatterbox much at odds with her typical Vulcan-esque persona. There is no way the writers could have signaled more clearly that we are in a strange new world than by making Michael Burnham funny.

In principle, the plot itself also gives her room to breathe by delaying *Discovery*'s arrival for a year, during which time she works with Book as a courier and begins to question anew whether Starfleet—to the limited extent that it still exists—is the place for her. We are seemingly set up for a whole season's worth of adventures in this mysterious new future, but fans would have to wait for Una McCormack's creative tie-in novel *Wonderlands* to learn how Book and Burnham kept busy while waiting for *Discovery*'s arrival.[28] In keeping with the show's relentless pacing, the remainder of the *Discovery* crew has already arrived by the second episode ("Far from Home," DSC 3.2), and at the end of a satisfyingly *Original Series*-esque episode where our heroes must fight for their survival in a wild west–like environment, they are abruptly rescued by Burnham and Book. Rejoining the crew as Saru's first officer (despite her told-not-shown misgivings about Starfleet) and bringing Book (and his advanced ship) along for the ride, Burnham begins an implacable quest to learn the cause of the Burn and thereby restore the Federation to its former glory.

Their natural first stop is Earth, which has withdrawn from the Federation and taken up an isolationist stance, refusing to give any of its remaining dilithium even to (what is revealed to be) a human colony elsewhere in the solar system. Again, this story is told in classic *Original Series* style, and the twist where Earth itself is the home of the shortsighted "aliens" needing a dose of humanistic values is clever. This episode also introduces new series regular Adira Tal (Blu del Barrio), a young human who has unexpectedly been joined with a symbiont, the virtually immortal creatures who bond with members of the Trill species to gain multiple lifetimes' worth of experience. The Trill had long been used as a symbol of trans identity, from their initial appearance in *Next Generation* ("The Host," TNG 4.23) to a *Deep Space Nine* plot in which a formerly male Trill shares a kiss with her female lover from a previous lifetime ("Rejoined," DS9 4.6). The character of Adira literalizes this symbolism, as they eventually reveal that they identify as nonbinary and take they/them pronouns (as the actor does in real life). Adira's introduction initially seemed awkward to me, as they at first identify as female and only later come out to Stamets—but the process was requested by Blu del Barrio to allow them the opportunity to come out to their own family before the episodes aired.[29] It is subsequently revealed that Adira received the host from their trans boyfriend, Gray (played by another nonbinary actor, Ian Alexander), whose personality continues to exist independently in Adira's mind and whose subsequent resurrection in a cybernetic body serves as an additional allegory for transition ("Anomaly," DSC 4.2). Stamets and Culber ultimately wind up viewing Adira as an adopted child, further deepening the series' representation of queer experience.

Continuing at a breakneck pace, the crew reconnects with the remnants of Starfleet in only the fifth of thirteen episodes. It is at this point that any world-building unrelated to either the Burn or past *Star Trek* all but ceases. We learn more about how Trill symbionts work ("Forget Me Not," DSC 3.4); we learn that Spock's attempts to reunify the Vulcans and the Romulans ("Unification, Pts. 1 and 2," TNG 5.7–8) were successful ("Unification, Pt. 3," DSC 3.7); we learn, as Emperor Georgiou seems to fade in and out of existence, that travel across time and dimensions can be life-threatening and, along the way, that the Prime Timeline knows about the existence of the Kelvin Timeline ("Terra Firma, Pt. 1," DSC 3.8); and we learn that the Guardian of Forever from the classic episode "City on the Edge of Forever" (TOS 1.28) has gone into hiding but is still available to send Georgiou back in time ("Terra Firma, Pt. 2," DSC 3.9). The latter revelations come in the midst of an unforgivably self-indulgent two-part episode in which Georgiou revisits her past in the Mirror Universe and tries to win back the trust of Mirror Burnham, who would later betray her to join Lorca's rebellion. There she learns that she no longer fully belongs in the evil Terran Empire after all her experiences in the Prime Universe. In other words, the development of *Discovery*'s new setting takes a back seat to yet another backdoor pilot for the *Section 31* concept. In fact, in her last words to Burnham, she name-drops a character called San who had previously only appeared in an enigmatic flashback of Georgiou's, presumably to set up a plot point for the (still forthcoming) later story.[30] If the writers wanted Georgiou in *The Original Series* era, one wishes they would have taken the easier route of simply leaving her there when *Discovery* departed.

When it comes to their present setting, no major questions are given an answer. Why was the Federation unable to develop a propulsion method not using dilithium, given that several options seemed to be available in the *Next Generation* era? No explanation is even attempted. Some characters hint that the Federation had started to fray even before the Burn, creating enduring distrust—what happened there? It will presumably forever remain a mystery. How big is the Federation currently, and what do the ships holed up at the hidden Federation headquarters actually do day to day? And why was the Emerald Chain able to establish large-scale power structures while the Federation remained fragmentary and ineffectual? Again, no information is given. How is it even possible to comprehensively ban time travel, especially in a world with no strong central authority? No mechanism is proposed, and instead we are supposed to trust Kovich (played by film director David Cronenberg)—a mysterious yet strangely authoritative Federation official whose exact role remains unknown at this point in the series—when he asserts that the ban is indeed absolute, despite the fact that he is in the process of facilitating Emperor Georgiou's return to the past even as he makes the declaration.

Even more problematic than the failures of world-building is the garbled symbolism of the Burn itself. At first it appears to be an environmental allegory of the kind that *Star Trek*'s technoutopianism has made it difficult to develop. The Federation had seemingly overextended a fragile fuel source, leading to a "termination shock" that permanently downgraded everyone's quality of life and ushered in a new dark age. Such a story is obviously relevant to contemporary anxieties about climate change. By the end of the season, however, we learn that the Burn was a truly freak accident. As it turns out, a Kelpien ship carrying young child named Su'Kal crash-landed on a planet with unimaginably vast dilithium reserves. Owing to previously unsuspected properties of dilithium and Kelpiens alike, the young Su'Kal is able to adapt to the dilithium's radiation, rendering him both immune to it and psychically bonded to it. When his mother finally dies, his understandable rage and grief cause a chain reaction that spreads through dilithium all over the galaxy, destroying any ships that have their engines engaged. Thankfully, the cause of the Burn is ultimately its own solution, because once they calm down the adult Su'Kal—who had spent the intervening years being raised by an elaborate holodeck program that is now breaking down—they are able to seize the vast resources of the dilithium planet and rebuild the Federation, good as new!

On the one hand, this bizarre plot is fully in line with *Discovery*'s unique style. There are many *Star Trek* episodes that have seemingly vast intergalactic implications and receive no follow-up. As with their reimagination of the Mirror Universe, the writers here take that kind of plot and force the characters to live with its consequences over the long term. On the other hand, the fact that such a worldshaping event is both a random accident and so easily reversed is at once anticlimactic and thematically shallow. Although the season appears more unified and planned out than its predecessor, the weak world-building and poor plotting show that the writers have not fully thought through the new scenario they created—and that is because they clearly have no intention of staying in the dystopian world they have so hastily sketched out. By the end of the season, Michael has solved the mystery of the Burn, destroyed the Emerald Chain, set up the Federation for a renaissance, and succeeded Saru as captain—which all adds up to a new status quo that is ultimately not so different from that of previous *Star Trek* shows.

A BORING CATASTROPHE

By the beginning of season 4, two full seasons had been spent running away from *Discovery*'s original premise in order to transform it into something more manageable and familiar. Yet ironically, what had made those seasons so disjointed and unwieldy was precisely the attempt to continue the style and approach of season 1. The breakneck pacing and reliance on big reveals worked well in the first season's self-contained narrative but proved difficult to justify in season 2 (which would have benefited from a more purely episodic approach to explore canon connections) and actively worked against the writers' purposes in season 3 (whose new setting needed much more room to breathe). Subsequent twists had also proven much less compelling than the intricate Mirror Lorca plot. Speaking as someone who has watched all the seasons multiple times, whereas the first season grew more convincing and impressive on rewatch, the overarching stories of season 2 and 3 barely hang together on first viewing and begin to crumble under closer scrutiny. Finally, the focus on Michael Burnham as the overriding central character, which had been a unique innovation for *Star Trek* in season 1, had become a straitjacket, turning the character into an almost self-parodic messianic figure who repeatedly turns out to be the only person who can save the galaxy. While Sonequa Martin-Green makes undeniably heroic efforts to sustain the burden placed on her character, the constant ratcheting up of stakes is exhausting in itself.

From this perspective, season 4 is a mixed bag. On the one hand, the overarching plot is well thought out. Compared to the Red Angel and perhaps even the Burn, it is clear that the writers knew where they were heading from the beginning and carefully mapped out the season's trajectory. At the same time, they do a better job than ever in making each episode relatively self-contained. Even as we approach the climax of the plot, every episode deals with a discrete problem or step along the way. On the other hand, it is yet another story of unspeakable disaster in which Michael Burnham once again contributes every decisive step toward the ultimate solution.

In this case, the disaster is a gravitational anomaly that destroys planets—starting with Book's home planet, which he barely escapes in time. Gradually it is discovered that this dark matter anomaly (or DMA) is not natural but artificial. Finally delivering on the environmental message initially suggested by the Burn arc, the DMA is actually a mining device for a species (designated as Species 10-C) that lives on the outer edge of the galaxy and needs a rare element to maintain its habitat. As *Discovery* makes its way to the galactic barrier, they learn to their horror that the DMA is en route to destroy both Earth and Vulcan (after Unification, now named NiVar). Once they use a combination of empathy and advanced chemistry to understand Species 10-C's unique smell-based language, they realize that Species 10-C's demand for such a secluded and impervious home is based in—wait for it—trauma. Once they are brought to understand that they are ironically using their experience as an excuse to inflict the same pain on others, Species 10-C repents. Peace reigns, and the president of United Earth (portrayed, somewhat jarringly, by Democratic political activist Stacey Abrams) announces that they will be rejoining the Federation.

The story is very well-constructed and very *Star Trek*, and it makes room for character and thematic developments. I have already mentioned the resurrection of Gray, which expands their exploration of queer themes. They also respond interestingly to the pandemic, which had disrupted the production and filming schedule for seasons 3 and 4. In an episode where Tilly leads a group of Starfleet cadets in a training exercise ("All Is Possible," DSC 4.4), the isolating effects of the Burn become an analogy for the aftereffects of Covid-19 isolation, particularly on students. Culber, continuing to suffer from a strange form of survivor's guilt after his resurrection, struggles with burnout and even seeks counseling from the apparently omnicompetent Kovich ("The Examples," DSC 4.5). Perhaps most ambitious is the story arc centered on Book, who has become Burnham's lover between seasons. Shattered by grief at the loss of his planet, he begins to question Burnham's handling of the DMA and teams up with rogue scientist Tarka (Shawn Doyle), who wants to use the energy that would be released by destroying the DMA to travel to a parallel world where the Burn never happened, and where he believes his former cellmate in an Emerald Chain prison is waiting for him. The parallels to Lorca are clear. Not only does his name nearly rhyme, but he unaccountably refers to his supposed paradise dimension as "home," just as Lorca does the Mirror Universe—and the involvement of Book means that Burnham both gets a taste of her own mutinous medicine and has to maintain her command judgment when making decisions involving a romantic partner.

Overall, the Book–Tarka arc feels like an attempt to retrospectively unify *Discovery* as a series, scattered as it has been over multiple concepts and multiple millennia. The problem is that Tarka's character simply does not work. He is more irritating than charismatic, and his rationale for seeking out the DMA is absurd, both of which make Book's decision to team up with him inscrutable. The failure of this subplot is symptomatic of the problems with the season arc as a whole—simply put, they never establish why we should care about this terrible disaster. The story begins by destroying a planet we are meeting for the first time. The fact that it is Book's home planet does not help much, as his alien makeup is so minimal (consisting of spots that only become visible when he's using his psychic abilities) that one could be forgiven for thinking he was human. And it is afflicting a galactic status quo that has barely been sketched out for us. Who cares if this radically different version of Earth and the planet formerly known as Vulcan—each of which houses precisely one new character whose name we even know—are destroyed nearly a thousand years after the bulk of the *Star Trek* stories we are invested in? This lack of any clear hook was reflected in r/DaystromInstitute's discussion threads, which dwindled to fewer than a hundred comments toward the end of season 4 after averaging closer to five hundred for earlier seasons.

The fifth season, which was announced to be *Discovery*'s last only after production was nearly concluded, uses a similar plot structure to season 4 but builds on a much weaker premise.[31] The plot centers on Burnham's race against time to secure the technology used by the godlike Progenitors, who shepherded the evolution of life in the galaxy. On one level, this search for the power of creation itself manages to ratchet up the stakes yet again. More fundamentally, though, it is strangely unambitious, because it reduces the entire season to the status of a sequel to a mediocre *Next Generation* episode ("The Chase," TNG 6.20) that itself served to explain the odd fact that nearly every franchise species is not only humanoid but also able to interbreed despite evolving on separate planets. We learn that the technology was rediscovered shortly after the Dominion war, then hidden to ensure that it would only be found by someone worthy to wield such power. They aimed to ensure this outcome by crafting a series of clues to test the seeker's empathy and emotional help in step-by-step fashion. The result is a series of one-off puzzle scenarios loosely strung together by the crew's attempt to find the next clue.

The primary story ends with Burnham realizing what most viewers had been shouting at the TV for weeks: the Progenitor technology must be destroyed, because no one (not even Michael Burnham!) can be trusted with such vast powers. What began, then, as a footnote to a largely forgotten episode ends with an in-universe admission that the entire season essentially should never have happened.

Differently than in the Kelvin Timeline films, then, *Discovery*'s bid for artistic freedom in its final three seasons introduced a feeling of pointlessness to the whole affair—one that the conclusion of the main plot of season 5 literally writes into the text of the show itself. For both the Abrams films and *Discovery,* the constant recourse to mass destruction and impossibly high stakes comes to feel like increasingly desperate bids for relevance from *Trek* installments that were determined to cut themselves off from the franchise. I have already discussed the mixture of creative and corporate reasons why the Kelvin Timeline broke from established lore. What is less clear is why *Discovery* thought it needed to make its radical journey into the future. As the success of *Strange New Worlds* shows, a prequel concept—even one in dangerous proximity to the third rail of *The Original Series*—is no intrinsic obstacle. More than that, we could easily imagine some version of all the major stories from *Discovery*'s distant future taking place in its original time period. For instance, something like the Burn could afflict a specific region of space, rendering warp travel impossible. As the only ship that can investigate, *Discovery* could spend a season exploring the newly isolated planets as they try to uncover the cause. The solution that felt anticlimactic for the galaxy-wide Burn could have worked well for a more local problem. Similarly, something like the DMA could just as easily have afflicted the post–Klingon war Federation, producing the same sense of one disaster after another—but this time it would be afflicting a world we knew well, filled with characters we care about. Even the idea of the Orion Syndicate filling in the power vacuum after the

Klingon war makes more intrinsic sense than the Emerald Chain somehow managing to reestablish interstellar contact in a way that the Federation cannot.

In short, perhaps *Discovery* should have had the courage of its convictions with its prequel concept. The fact that it did not is especially ironic when we realize how much its trajectory continues in the footsteps of *Enterprise*. Had that star-crossed series been allowed to reach its natural ending point, it would have delivered much of what *Discovery* ultimately gave us: showing us a foundational conflict for *Star Trek* lore (the Romulan war), exploring the Mirror Universe by following up on "In a Mirror, Darkly," further solidifying its links with established canon and especially *The Original Series,* and ultimately inaugurating the Federation. Swapping out the Romulan war for the Klingon war, *Discovery* does all of this, often literally. Season 1's central Mirror arc is pitched as a direct sequel to the *Enterprise* arc, for instance, and there are many direct references (and unambiguous ones, unlike those in *Beyond*) to the events of *Enterprise*. From its position in the distant future, *Discovery* even goes so far as to provide more satisfying closure on the Temporal Cold War. This connection is reinforced when the final episode's concluding coda section, which fast-forwards many decades to show that Burnham and Book wind up living happily ever after (and to which I will be returning in chapter 5), identifies the mysteriously authoritative Kovich as a reincarnation of Lieutenant Daniels himself ("Life, Itself," DSC 5.10). In what will likely be the latest date shown in on-screen canon for the foreseeable future, the circle of *Star Trek* history is at last closed—a clear vindication of my thesis that the many varied installments of late *Star Trek* are united by the tribute they pay to *Enterprise*.

Discovery ultimately gives us the foundation of the Federation. The only problem is that it does not give *Star Trek* fans the foundation of *their* Federation, but of some other Federation a thousand years in the future. A serious investment in world-building—probably including multiple seasons wandering in the post-Federation wilderness—may have allowed this new future to take root as a major center of gravity for *Star Trek* storytelling. But the rushed solution to the Burn in season 3 and the precipitous return to a tense disaster plot in season 4 meant that fans barely got to know the world Michael Burnham was twice called on to save, while season 5 gave up the task of fresh world-building in favor of following up on themes and concepts from *Next Generation*. The forthcoming *Starfleet Academy* series would have to pull off something spectacular to even open up the possibility of its thirty-second-century time period joining *The Original Series* and *Next Generation* areas as major sites for plot development. To the degree that *Discovery* has a chance to remain a point of reference, it is precisely in the prequel era that it took so many pains to leave and erase itself from, thanks to its role as background to fan-favorite series *Strange New Worlds*.

Ironically, then, the series that in its first season "[did] not just want to be a show that fixes the franchise, [but] want[ed] to be a show *about* fixing the franchise"[32] ultimately wound up all but writing itself out of canon and into an irrelevant dead end. In the process, it alienated many of the fans who had been brought in by the first season. Although we do not have any firm viewership numbers thanks to the vagaries of streaming television, my anecdotal experience is that many of my friends who were attracted to *Star Trek* through the sophistication and polish of season 1 found themselves gradually alienated. Moments that hard-core fans like me found gratifying—like the "previously on" from "The Cage"—were confusing and frustrating to new viewers, many of whom simply stopped watching because *Discovery* had decided to become a different show from the one they enjoyed. Are their fandom and viewership less valuable, their concerns less worth considering, than those of obsessive fans who mostly watch any *Star Trek* production whether they like it or not, and often build community by complaining? Again, the secretive norms around streaming viewership numbers means that we can never know for sure, but the fact that *Discovery* was canceled certainly raises questions about their strategy.

More radically, though, I wonder if *Discovery* should not have been continued at all, or else marked the beginning of an anthology show on the model of *American Horror Story* (2011–present), as Bryan Fuller initially proposed.[33] In either case, season 1 could easily have stood on its own. Eliminating Burnham's unanticipated connection with Spock would have left fewer loose ends, and perhaps they could have set the story earlier in *Star Trek*'s timeline, both to justify the visual connections to *Enterprise* rather than *The Original Series* and to avoid the awkward question of exactly why no one on the latter show ever mentions a massive war that happened within their lifetimes. At this point, of course, I may be indulging in the typical fannish vice of playing fantasy showrunner, but the strange trajectory of the show makes it nearly impossible not to wonder what could have been done differently. Nevertheless, despite the uneven quality and questionable decisions of the later seasons, *Discovery* season 1 stands as proof that *Star Trek* can adapt and even excel in the era of serialized prestige drama—if it will only let itself.

5

A DARKER, GRITTIER *PICARD*

After the conclusion of *Voyager* in early 2001 and the release of *Nemesis* in 2002, it would be nearly two decades until *Star Trek* moved its story unambiguously forward. Aside from Prime Spock's description of his failed attempt to stop the supernova in *Star Trek* (2009), no new canonical information was forthcoming on the future of the Prime Timeline. Then suddenly, in 2020, there was an unexpected superabundance of fresh material (see appendix 1 for details). That year, *Discovery* jumped farther forward in the timeline than any previous show and, as we just saw in chapter 4, arguably overshot the mark. More modestly, the animated series *Lower Decks* (2020–present), which I will discuss in the next chapter, is set in the years immediately after *Nemesis* and offers direct follow-up on many major plot points of the *Next Generation* era. The first and most anticipated step forward, however, came in the form of a direct sequel to *Next Generation* featuring Patrick Stewart in his iconic role as Jean-Luc Picard. Finally, it seemed, after years of poorly received prequels and reboots, the franchise was giving the fans what they wanted: a return to the beloved characters and settings of *Star Trek*'s most successful era.

Recapturing that magic was an intimidating task, however, especially since the story of the *Next Generation* crew had already ended perfectly—and had almost immediately been relaunched, to mixed success. The series finale, "All Good Things . . ." (TNG 7.25–26), provided a satisfying coda to our heroes' largely episodic story. As with so many decisive moments, the mischievous deity Q (John de Lancie) puts in an appearance, subjecting Picard (and humanity) to one last instance of the "trial" that he had begun in "Encounter at Farpoint" (TNG 1.1). Where the *Enterprise*-D's first adventure culminated in the recognition that a powerful space station was in fact a sentient creature that lived in interstellar space, its last televised journey involves a temporal anomaly that travels backward, threatening to undo the past all the way back to the origin of life on Earth. Jumping back and forth between the events of "Encounter at Farpoint," the show's present, and a hypothetical future (which takes place in 2399, the same year as the nonhypothetical events of *Picard* season 1), Picard eventually figures things out, with the help of multiple versions of his crew. Seeing that he and his crew drifted apart in the future that has now been averted, the stoic and taciturn captain ends his television adventures by finally joining one of the bridge officers' iconic poker games.

It was a perfect ending, but there was no intrinsic reason *Next Generation* had to end at that point. Though there were any number of longer-term story arcs throughout the show's seven seasons, its episodic approach meant that it could, in principle, continue indefinitely. The decision to end the series was not primarily artistic, but—as our account of late *Star Trek* may have led us to expect by now—based on a misguided corporate strategy. As Hark puts it, "Paramount executives and executive producer Rick Berman chose to free up its cast to continue the feature film franchise, even though the show's ratings in first-run syndication remained high and it had just been nominated for an Emmy as Best Dramatic Series."[1] There is wide agreement that the movie franchise—with the possible exception of *First Contact* (1996)—largely failed to recapture the magic of the series, above all because it highlighted the relationship between Data and Picard above the ensemble cast and turned the cerebral captain into an improbable action star. To this day, fans continue to spin theories to explain the strange disconnect between TV Picard and movie Picard, most centering on the degenerative disease he is revealed to have in the averted future of "All Good Things. . . ."

In face of these precedents, and in keeping with the pattern established in *Enterprise* and *Discovery, Picard* took a concept that all but cries out for pure fan service and used it to assert creative freedom through unexpected world-building. In place of the reunion show that everyone was expecting, the first season gave us a surprisingly grim story of loss and regret. As with the opening scenes of *Discovery, Picard* initially teases us by giving us exactly what we expect: a charming exchange between Picard and Data over poker. But the dream quickly becomes a nightmare as a terrorist attack engulfs the *Enterprise* in flames. Picard bolts awake to reveal that he is a shell of his former self, still haunted by the death of his friend and bitter over Starfleet's failure to live up to its values. We soon learn that Picard had headed up the effort to evacuate the Romulan Empire before the star in the Romulan home system went supernova. But in the wake of a still-unexplained revolt and terrorist attack carried out by synthetic workers employed at the Mars shipyards to build the many ships needed to evacuate whole planets, Starfleet withdrew from the rescue effort and the Federation banned all experimentation with synthetic life-forms, now derogatively referred to as synths. Picard threatened to resign unless the evacuations were resumed. Starfleet called his bluff, leaving him with nothing to do but oversee his family's vineyards in France. When an interviewer asks him why he resigned, he memorably declares: "Because it was no longer Starfleet!" ("Remembrance," PIC 1.1).

When discussing the decision to set *Discovery* in the *Original Series* era, I suggested that the reason was in part because that era seemed more in line with our own time of conflict and pessimism than the confidently progressive *Next Generation*. In returning to the latter, *Picard* solves the apparent discrepancy by injecting an element of cynicism and regression into that era itself, giving us an image of the Federation as a complacent power that is callous toward refugees and uses the specter of terrorism to victimize minorities. As Justice Hagan puts it, "the creative team behind *[Picard]* finally confronts the future of *Star Trek,* the Federation, and the Roddenberry orthodoxy through a depiction of the Federation's— and our own—late-state neoliberal existence."[2] More than that, in giving us an almost unprecedented extended look at the utopia that Earth has supposedly become, it introduces "economic disparities among Federation citizens"[3] and thereby an element of hypocrisy into the character of Picard himself. While the former admiral lives in a vast chateau attended by servants, his onetime first officer Raffi (Michelle Hurd) lives in an isolated trailer—a far cry from the equality and abundance that we would expect from Picard's memorable speech about the postscarcity future in "The Neutral Zone" (TNG 1.26). In short, the utopian world that had been such a good match for the cultural optimism of the 1990s has unexpectedly evolved into one that fits all too well with our dystopian present.

The only way to return to the world of *Next Generation,* then, was to break it. Obviously these shifts were intended to make room for direct commentary on contemporary political issues like the refugee crisis or efforts to roll back racial equality. At the same time, *Picard* takes seriously its mandate to pick up the story of the *Next*

Generation era where it leaves off—which is with the failure to divert Shinzon from his destructive path, the self-sacrificial death of Data that followed, and, for good measure, the natural disaster of the Romulan supernova that everyone saw coming and no one did anything to stop. As we have seen, the novelverse picked up on similar threads from *Nemesis*—and its predecessor, *Insurrection* (1998), which saw Picard bravely rebelling against a corrupt admiral to preserve Starfleet values—to create a new *Star Trek* status quo where Section 31 was hiding behind every corner and the Federation faced relentless military threats. Although licensing issues prevented them from addressing the supernova, it is the kind of plot point that would not be out of place in the novel continuity. Both the novelverse and *Picard* (at least in its initial setup) show how the apparent constraints of franchise storytelling can be converted into opportunities, turning even weak installments into a usable history in sometimes surprising ways.

At the same time that it calls them into question, however, the first season of *Picard* is a story about fighting one's way back to authentic *Star Trek* values. But strangely enough, it does not seem to fully take, and thus the second and third seasons follow much the same trajectory. As we have seen, *Discovery* essentially traced that same arc twice over, in its first and third seasons, but there the two efforts were separated by centuries. *Picard* feels compelled to break and restore its world multiple times in the space of a few short in-universe years. Indeed, the show essentially reinvents itself again and again and only arrives at the long-anticipated full-cast reunion at the end of three strange and disconnected seasons (including one inexplicably set in present-day Los Angeles, partly the result of Covid-19 pandemic filming obstacles). Up to the end, the series is marked by strange and shortsighted creative decisions that lend an air of improvisation and disorganization—even though *Picard* is the first-ever *Star Trek* series to know its end point in advance, as it was decided early on that it would last just three seasons. This chapter will trace the often bizarre twists and turns that made what should have been the easiest slam dunk of the late *Star Trek* era into its greatest creative failure.

VAULTING AMBITION

The story of *Picard*'s unfortunate trajectory begins with an unexpected coup for the franchise. Among the many people thrilled by *Star Trek*'s return was self-described lifelong fan and Pulitzer Prize–winning novelist Michael Chabon, who cowrote (with *Discovery* staff writer Sean Cochran) by far the most compelling *Short Treks* installment, "Calypso."[4] Airing between *Discovery* seasons 1 and 2, it presents us with an empty ship run by a sentient AI named Zora, who has been ordered to maintain her position indefinitely. During her long, lonely sojourn, she crosses paths with a lost soldier named Craft, whom she nurses back to health and with whom she ultimately falls in love. Inspired by an episode in the *Odyssey* where the famously crafty hero is held captive by the goddess Calypso, the short is itself expertly crafted, creating a dense web of literary allusions while quickly establishing the characters and their unique rapport. It also sketches out an intriguing science fiction scenario, as Zora appears to be involved in some kind of time-travel gambit that has taken her to an era when the Federation (here referred to as Vedraish) is a distant memory.

The elements of season 3 are all present here, though the writers for the main series took many of Chabon's suggestions in different and seemingly incompatible directions. With the cancellation of *Discovery* after five seasons, it appeared that "Calypso" would never be fully integrated into franchise continuity. Surprisingly, though, showrunner Michelle Paradise revealed that the production team had planned to spend the entire sixth season resolving the beloved short's place in *Discovery*'s story, because they "never wanted 'Calypso' to be the dangling chad." Deprived of that opportunity, they concluded the hastily assembled final coda to the season—which was written and shot only after filming on the season's main story arc had ended—with a puzzling scene in which Michael Burnham sends Zora off on her mission to deep space, giving her no explanation or information other than telling her that Kovich/Daniels told her to watch out for someone named Craft.[5]

Whatever one makes of this odd attempt to confirm the beloved short's ultimate place in *Star Trek* canon, it is clear that after the success of "Calypso," the production team was eager to keep Chabon involved in the franchise. When he suggested a short about a young Jean-Luc Picard that could potentially include a brief cameo by Patrick Stewart, Alex Kurtzman, who had by then been tasked with expanding the franchise for the streaming era, asked, "Why should we go to all the trouble of approaching Patrick Stewart to get him to be in one scene? When maybe, if we go to the trouble of approaching him, he may be in a whole series?"[6] Ultimately, Chabon was retained as writer, cocreator (with Akiva Goldsman, Kirsten Beyer, and Alex Kurtzman), and showrunner. Where *Discovery* had been conceived by a television auteur, then, *Picard* was the product of a certified literary star—and one who, unlike Bryan Fuller, oversaw the entire first season.

In the event, Chabon's involvement proved to be a double-edged sword. On the one hand, his creativity and ambition are evident in the show's world-building. I have already commented on the boldness of starting from Starfleet's failure to live up to its ideals in the wake of the synth attack on the Mars shipyards. The first season also establishes a surprising new status quo for arguably *Star Trek*'s most fearsome villain, the Borg; fleshes out Romulan culture with an ambition not seen since Diane Duane's *Rihannsu* novels;[7] and radically reformulates the nature of Data-style androids by breaking the long-standing assumption that no one but their genius creator,

Dr. Noonien Soong, could duplicate the technology. Obviously that is a lot to handle in a single season, especially given that these threads all need to be woven together in a way that builds on Picard's character and life trajectory. But if the creative team managed it, the season would be a *Star Trek* tour de force—picking up on obscure or unappreciated lore in an unexpected way that creates freedom for fresh world-building—to match or even exceed the first season of *Discovery*. Unfortunately, the execution fell far short of the material's potential, as the season was marred by major pacing problems, strange and distracting characterizations and plot twists, and a general lack of cohesion. All problems were surely exacerbated by the studio's frankly bizarre decision to place their most bankable and high-stakes property in the hands of a showrunner who, for all his unquestionable talent for storytelling, had no experience in the role—a rare case of the corporate side placing too much trust in a creative.

The place of the Borg in *Picard*'s first season is in many way emblematic of both the positives and negatives I have identified. Again demonstrating an ability to reimagine *Star Trek* lore, the writing team draws on the finale of *Voyager* ("Endgame," VOY 7.25–26), which left some ambiguity but strongly implied that a last-ditch gambit by Janeway had irrevocably crippled the Borg, to present us with a world in which the Federation's most implacable foe has been shattered and the survivors are a persecuted and exploited minority. Their technology, once feared for its tendency to assimilate everything it touched into the Borg's hive mind, is now surgically harvested from former drones, known as XBs. This development creates an opening to explore how the most famous ex-Borg of all, *Voyager*'s Seven of Nine (Jeri Ryan), navigates a world in which she is no longer a one-off oddity but part of a larger community of refugees. As it turns out, her foster child from *Voyager*, former drone Icheb, had his Borg elements brutally extracted and was left for dead ("Stardust City Rag," PIC 1.5), motivating a quest for vengeance that lends an unexpectedly dark tone to the character. Not everything is so grim, however. We learn that many liberated drones have been able to live a normal life. In fact, one defunct Borg cube located in Romulan space, known as the Artifact, has been converted into a scientific research center, whose work centers on carefully, patiently deassimilating the drones who were put in suspended animation when the vessel mysteriously shut down. That labor of compassion is overseen by Picard's old Borg friend, Hugh (Jonathan del Aro), who once learned about individuality from the *Enterprise* crew when separated from the Collective ("I, Borg," TNG 5.23), and whose appearance represents an unexpected but wholly welcome element of fan service.

Given Picard's traumatic experience of being briefly assimilated by the Borg in the classic episode "The Best of Both Worlds" (TNG 3.26–4.1) and Seven's many years as a drone, these decisive shifts in the Borg's situation promise strong opportunities to develop both characters. Instead, the juxtaposition between Picard and Seven serves mainly to emphasize his connection to the Borg over hers. Particularly galling for me as a huge fan of Seven's character is a dialogue where Seven, who spent the most formative years of her life as a drone, asks Picard for advice on how to overcome the Borg influence and regain one's humanity. This solicitation of mansplaining seems to be aimed at the worst kind of sexist fan, who wants to be affirmed in his belief that no woman character can ever be as important as Picard. More broadly, Seven's character is transformed from the cerebral and hypercompetent figure fans know from *Voyager* into a wisecracking badass, played up alternately for comic relief or action sequences. One particularly unforgivable scene is when Picard poses as a human trafficker who has captured Seven and hopes to sell her Borg implants. To prepare for the role, he assumes an exaggerated French accent and dons a jaunty eye patch (Figure 5). Even her fate is better than Hugh's, however. He is killed shortly after being introduced, for no reason other than to buy our heroes some

FIGURE 5. *Picard sports an eye patch while posing as a human trafficker looking to sell Seven of Nine for her Borg implants ("Stardust City Rag," PIC 1.5).*

time. In short, both Seven's characterization and Hugh's death subvert the expectations of fan service, but without making productive use of the resulting creative freedom.

Ultimately, the Borg plot is subordinate to a primary arc centered on two unexpected progeny of Data. Drawing on *Nemesis*'s theme of uncanny doubles, we learn that Data-style androids can only be created in pairs (as Data was with his evil brother, Lore—one wonders about poor B4's lost twin) and that a new pair of female androids named Dahj and Soji (both played by Isa Brione) have been created out of a remaining particle of Data's mind. Unaware of their status as synths, both work as scientists, Dahj at the in-universe Daystrom Institute (after which my favorite fan forum is named) and Soji at the Artifact. After having been targeted for assassination and unexpectedly showing *Bourne Identity* (2002)-like fighting skills, Dahj has a vision that only Picard can save her and shows up at his door. He barely has time to begin investigating her claims before she is killed in a bombing, which nearly kills Picard as well. After consulting with Dr. Agnes Jurati (Alison Pill)—an expert on synthetic life whose research at the Daystrom Institute was frustrated by the synth ban—Picard becomes convinced that Dahj and Soji are in some sense Data's daughters and resolves to save Soji before it is too late.

Together with the broader scenario of the failed Romulan rescue effort and the synth ban, this initial setup is promising. In the episodes that follow, however, seams begin to show almost immediately. Despite knowing that Soji is targeted by ruthless assassins, Picard spends the first three episodes on Earth. He investigates Dahj's apartment, aided by two Romulan refugees, Laris (Orla Brady) and Zaban (Jamie McShane), who work as his servants and conveniently prove to be former members in the Romulan spy organization known as the Tal Shiar. They determine that Dahj was killed by an even *more* secretive Romulan sect, the Zhat Vash, who abhor artificial life. After being rebuffed by Starfleet in his request for a ship, he determines to assemble his own crew—but emphatically rules out asking any of his old friends from *Next Generation,* because he knows they will feel obligated to help and does not want them to risk their lives out of affection for him.

Instead, Picard resolves to call on people who hate and resent him, as he knows they will only go if they really believe in the mission. This standard rules out his charming and hypercompetent Romulan roommates, whom we have barely met. It takes a full four episodes to assemble the crew, consisting of Doctor Jurati, Seven of Nine, and three completely new characters (whom I will discuss in more detail in connection to season 2). Threaded throughout these episodes is a B plot in which we meet Soji in her work at the Artifact. Rather than facing assassination, she is being seduced by Zhat Vash agent Narek (Harry Treadway), under the guidance of Narek's sister, Narissa (Peyton List), and their handler, Commodore Oh (Tamlyn Tomita), a Zhat Vash mole who has managed to become head of Starfleet security. We also encounter another minor legacy character, Bruce Maddox, who is best known for unsuccessfully requesting to disassemble Data to see how he works in "Measure of a Man" (TNG 2.9) and who now has apparently succeeded in his lifelong dream by creating Dahj and Soji. But Maddox, echoing the fate of poor Hugh, is almost immediately murdered in cold blood by his former lover, Doctor Jurati, who had up to that moment served mainly as comic relief.

All of these developments take us just past the halfway point of the season. Over the course of these episodes, the pacing gradually stalls out, and the audience's patience is pushed to its limits by the proliferation of new characters—especially in what was expected to be a nostalgic reunion show. Picard does not even meet Soji, whom he is supposedly in a desperate rush to rescue from Romulan assassins, until the sixth out of ten episodes ("The Impossible Box," PIC 1.6), at which point he escapes with her from the Artifact using an advanced teleportation device that lands him at the doorstep of his old friends William Riker (Jonathan Frakes) and Deanna Troi (Marina Sirtis).

For the space of one episode, we get a glimpse of the ways that the fan service of a reunion show could have fit with the show's quest for creative freedom through unexpected world-building. The Rikers, it turns out, have had a tragic trajectory. Their late-in-life marriage led to the birth of two children, but they retired from Starfleet and retreated into seclusion after one died at a young age because the medical treatment he needed required the use of a positronic matrix, which was central to Data's functioning and hence was outlawed by the synth ban. (Here we might detect an anachronistic analogy between the synth ban and the medical consequences of the abortion bans in many U.S. states.) The most daring development in this episode, though, is a dialogue between Picard and Troi in which the former ship's counselor essentially dresses down her onetime captain for his impatience with Soji and his lack of empathy for Sonji's struggle to trust him after learning that her entire life had been a lie.

Picard is suitably chastened, but Soji remains distrustful. This dynamic sets up a rushed, confusing two-part finale ("Et in Arcadia Ego," PIC 1.9–10), full of strange twists. The first and most obvious is the existence of a planet full of Data-like androids, created by a previously unmentioned human sibling of Data's (also played by Brent Spiner), who aided Bruce Maddox in his quest to create Dahj and Soji. This development arguably cheapens the impact of Data's self-sacrifice in *Nemesis,* which viewers believed to represent the death of a unique and irreplaceable form of synthetic life. Now, however, we learn that not only has a particle of Data somehow given rise to his twin "daughters," but that the planet features a copy of Data running in an independent simulation. Ultimately, the copied Data asks Picard to euthanize him in a scene that is clearly meant to be deeply emotional but winds up being merely puzzling. As Hagan understatedly puts it, "One must question the decision to resurrect Data only to kill him again in a way devoid of the heroic self-sacrifice of his first death."[8]

At the same time, we get a redoubled twist on a previous twist. The synth-hating Romulan sect, the Zhat Vash, were previously revealed to be motivated by the belief that any development of synthetic intelligence will lead to the extermination of biological life. They learn this not by watching the Control arc from *Discovery* season 2—a strikingly similar plot that had aired just the previous year—but by experiencing a vivid telepathic vision known as the Admonition, which either drives the recipient mad or grants them an implacable hatred of synthetic life. (Incidentally, Jurati had experienced the Admonition through a mind-meld with Commodore Oh, which is why she killed Maddox before he could create more synthetic life; the crime goes strangely unpunished.) The Admonition, it turns out, motivated Commodore Oh to orchestrate the synth terror attack on the Mars shipyards in order to prevent the further development of synthetic life, effectively dooming her own people in the process. This strange twist seems to ruin the political allegory of the Romulan refugee crisis, which now becomes in some sense the Romulans' own fault.

As if that was not enough, though, we learn in the finale that the Admonition is actually the promise of a powerful transdimensional AI to exterminate biological life on behalf of any synthetic life that may arise in a given galaxy. Soji, in her confusion and despair, actually initiates this process, but Picard uses a stirring address reflecting Starfleet's deepest values to convince her to stand down. At the same time, a Romulan fleet headed up by a Zhat Vash Starfleet mole shows up to destroy the Planet of Datas, but it is quickly countered by a fleet headed by the reinstated Captain Riker, who announces that Commodore Oh's treachery has been revealed and the synth ban has been lifted. The audience barely has time to digest these momentous events before Picard himself dies of Irumodic syndrome, the disease that afflicted him in the alternate future of the *Next Generation* finale "All Good Things . . ." (TNG 7.25–26), and the diagnosis of which was confirmed in the present timeline earlier in the season ("Maps and Legends," PIC 1.2). Scarcely is he mourned by his allies from this season (though not by Riker, who quickly departs after dispersing Oh's fleet) than he is resurrected in a synthetic body. Just as Data was resurrected only to be immediately killed, so Picard is killed only to be immediately resurrected, leaving the audience baffled. The season then closes with a group shot of Picard and the members of his ragtag crew of mostly new characters, strongly implying that they will remain together and have further adventures. But what would they possibly do? In a world full of Starfleet crews, does the universe really need an elderly former admiral and his six random friends to come to the rescue? My questions are hardly the only ones raised by the finale—in his review for IndieWire, Christian Blauvelt lists no fewer than forty-five.[9]

A season that began with such strong and ambitious concepts

quickly lost momentum and then collapsed into incoherence. Data's death has been rendered meaningless since it has become trivially easy to copy his consciousness. The entire political allegory surrounding the Romulan refugee crisis and the synth ban has been garbled before being "resolved" in a single line of dialogue. Picard has been killed and resurrected for no apparent reason and now heads a crew with no plausible mission or mandate. The reason for this mess is clear: a basic failure of planning on the part of the show's leadership. Akiva Goldsman indirectly confesses as much when he tells an interviewer that one of the main lessons the creative team learned from season 1 of *Picard* was to "figure out the end earlier. If you're going to do a serialized show, you have the whole story before you start shooting."[10] In other words, the plot of the most anticipated *Star Trek* project in two decades—headed up by perhaps the most prestigious author ever to write for the franchise and based on any number of bold and promising world-building ideas—was at least partly made up as it went along. Properly executed, this season could have built on the creative success of *Discovery* season 1 to show that *Star Trek* can go beyond nostalgia to deliver prestige drama–level quality. Instead, audiences were left with little more than confusion and frustration. Did the novelverse really need to die for this?

A SEASON ABOUT NOTHING

After borrowing the Admonition plot from *Discovery*'s main season 2 arc centered on Control, *Picard* redoubled its borrowings in its own second season by adopting a similar dual mandate: using fan service to reconnect with audience expectations and using time travel to escape from its format. On the former front, the production team—no longer headed by Michael Chabon but by Terry Matalas—still shied away from a full-cast reunion, in part due to pandemic-related filming restrictions and in part because it was by now obviously being reserved for the third and final season. But they still managed to scratch the nostalgic itch. John de Lancie returned as Picard's omnipotent frenemy Q, Whoopi Goldberg as wise *Enterprise* bartender Guinan (though we spend most of the season with a younger version of the character, played by Ito Aghayere), and even Wil Wheaton as Wesley Crusher (albeit in a brief and puzzling cameo).

The main time-travel arc also allows *Picard* to engage in two broad forms of fan service, one long desired and the other more questionable. The first is to approximate a *Next Generation* Mirror Universe episode, at least in spirit, by transplanting our heroes into an altered timeline where the benevolent and cosmopolitan Federation instead developed into the totalitarian and xenophobic Confederation. The second is to delve into one of the most convoluted aspects of *Star Trek* lore: the relationship between our real-world timeline and the franchise's fictional one. Both of these are achieved in one stroke: Q drops Picard and friends into the Confederation equivalent of their present, and after kidnapping the Borg Queen (who was to be executed that day and can conveniently detect changes in the timeline), they hijack a ship to travel back in time to the era when Q made the all-important change that ruined everything.

Starting with the revelation that the evil Khan Noonien Singh participated in the Eugenics wars in the 1990s—a fact established in Khan's first appearance ("Space Seed," TOS 1.22) and then explicitly reiterated much closer to the ostensible time in *Wrath of Khan* (1982)—it gradually became clear that *Star Trek*'s fictional history deviated considerably from our own. There have been various attempts to resolve this discrepancy, the most ambitious of which is Greg Cox's novel duology positing that the Eugenics wars happened in our 1990s, but as a secret, behind-the-scenes conflict.[11] More sensible, perhaps, was the decision of the *Voyager* writers to simply ignore the issue when they made the obligatory trip back to the viewer's present in 1996's "Future's End" (VOY 3.8–9). By spending an entire season in *Star Trek*'s alternate version of 2024 Los Angeles,

Picard season 2 in many ways echoes the gesture of HBO's *Watchmen* (2019) and fully accepts the divergence between the Prime Timeline and our real history while also highlighting telltale similarities. The choice of a near-future date—the season aired in 2022—is itself a gesture of fan service, as 2024 was the year in which Benjamin Sisko was forced to take the place of historical activist Gabriel Bell in settling the Bell riots ("Past Tense," DS9 3.11–12). This two-part episode, which originally aired in 1995, has long been viewed as prophetic for its portrayal of near-future San Francisco, where growing inequality has led to the grim expedient of herding the homeless into so-called sanctuary districts, where they are largely left to fend for themselves. While things have not yet degenerated quite so badly in real life, the idea still seems eerily plausible, and *Picard* connects *Deep Space Nine*'s fictional 2024 America more closely to our own by portraying it as a nation reeling from controversial wars (in this case, the Eugenics wars), characterized by an increasingly intolerant and militarized approach to undocumented immigrants, and contemplating radical geoengineering solutions amid a failure to address the climate crisis.

Much like the opening scenes of the *Enterprise* premiere ("Broken Bow," ENT 1.1), the initial scenario our heroes find in 2024 Los Angeles is skillful use of franchise lore to present us with an uncanny reflection of our own world, but this time with a more critical intent. Aside from the arrest of Picard's Latin American teammate Rios by (and later rescue from) brutal ICE agents, however, the element of political critique quickly falls aside in favor of the quest to restore the timeline. And because this is *Star Trek,* the redemption of humanity always lies in the stars. Picard and friends quickly realize that Q has overwritten their own timeline with the grim Confederation future by disrupting a mission to the Jovian moon Europa, where one of Picard's distant ancestors will discover the first evidence of single-celled organisms beyond Earth. Without that thin thread of hope, humanity's remnants would not be prepared for the opportunity represented by First Contact in the wake of World War III.

Once again, then, *Picard* is presenting us with a broken status quo that must be steered back toward the true values of *Star Trek*. This development is perhaps surprising when we note that the season opens with a sense that all of the characters from season 1 have finally found where they belong. Reinstated as admiral, Picard is now the head of Starfleet Academy. Rios (Santiago Cabrera), whom we met in season 1 as the roguish pilot and former Starfleet officer who agrees to fly Picard and his ragtag band on their search for Soji, is now the cigar-chomping captain of the namesake of Picard's first command, the *Stargazer*. Picard's former first officer, Raffi (Michelle Hurd), who helped him coordinate the Romulan evacuation and whose career was ruined by his resignation, has also returned to Starfleet. Elnor (Evan Evagora), a Romulan orphan who resented Picard for breaking off contact after the failure of the rescue mission, and who was adopted by a sect of Romulan nuns who combine absolute candor with martial arts training, has become the first full-blooded Romulan to graduate Starfleet. Raffi—who barely exchanged two words with Elnor in season 1—has come to view the young Romulan swordsman almost as an adopted son thanks to a close mentorship relationship that developed entirely off camera. Yet not all is well in Raffi's personal life, as her romance with Seven of Nine (barely hinted at in a scene where they chastely hold hands, and otherwise only explored in a tie-in audio drama featuring both actresses[12]) has both blossomed and withered off camera, as Seven of Nine returned to the vigilante peacekeeping group known as the Fenris Rangers. Soji has become ambassador for the Planet of Datas, while Jurati—who had an off-camera relationship and breakup with Rios—serves on the *Stargazer* as science officer and jokes that she has been cleared of Maddox's murder by reason of "alien-induced temporary insanity" ("The Star Gazer," PIC 2.1). We also learn that Picard's Romulan housemate, Laris, has been widowed and is interested in a relationship with Picard, though he fails to seize the moment.

I list all of these developments to highlight the fact that the first episode performs many resets on many characters, generating what amount to entirely new backstories via info dumps regarding what happened between the two seasons (in some cases overwriting the small number of tie-in novels and comics produced for the series). The cumulative effect is to pretend season 1 never happened, as though the show—intent as it is on fan service—has room to assert creative freedom only over against itself. Yet this fresh status quo is in turn blown up even before it is established, as the episode indulges in one of the hoariest clichés of serialized television by opening with a scene of disaster, then shifting back in time to show the events leading up to it. On the bridge of the *Stargazer*, our entire cast (save Soji) is present to see a mysterious rift in space through which a massive Borg vessel has emerged and demanded to speak with Picard. The Borg Queen—unexpectedly masked—beams aboard and begins taking over the ship, and indeed the entire fleet that has gathered around this threat, thanks to Starfleet's questionable decision to incorporate Borg technology into its newest model of ship. Panicked, Admiral Picard and Captain Rios take the only action remaining to them by triggering the *Stargazer*'s self-destruct mechanism, destroying the Borg vessel and the surrounding Starfleet ships in one stroke.

It is this gesture that prompts Q to save Picard and his season 1 colleagues and transport them to the altered Confederation timeline, describing it as a "penance" ("The Star Gazer," PIC 2.1). The message—which is not presented as clearly as it could be—seems to be that Picard has chosen militarism and violence over peace and diplomacy, and Q is giving him what he apparently wants. Already there was some sense that this Borg Queen was not quite as evil as we might expect, as she asked for Picard's help, suggested joining the Federation, and only stunned, instead of killing, the officers who tried to prevent her from interfacing with the ship. In a replay of these same events after the timeline has been restored and Q has sent (most of) our heroes back to the present, we learn that she is in fact not the evil Borg Queen but instead none other than Jurati, who merged with the Confederation timeline's Borg Queen to become a *good* Borg Queen running a Collective that recruits the members of its hive mind on a purely voluntary basis. As it turns out, she was interfacing with the ship so tactlessly because she had nearly drained her power holding the rift open, and all she wanted was to warn them of a dangerous spatial anomaly (which we never hear about again). No in-universe explanation is given for her odd mask, which is clearly a storytelling kludge to keep Picard from recognizing her as Jurati—who is no longer present on the bridge, having been left in the past to form her unique splinter Borg Collective. For his part, Rios has fallen in love with a physician and activist for the undocumented in the past and elected to stay with her rather than return to the future. Meanwhile, Elnor, whose abrupt death early in the season served primarily to give Raffi a greater investment in restoring the timeline (to bring her beloved mentee back), is reset back to life but quickly ushered offstage.

The intention is clear: this entire plot has served as a kind of line-item veto of the new season 1 characters, erasing everyone but Seven and Raffi from the ongoing story. This final gesture transforms the entire season into a kind of narrative prep work that feels at once insulting to the audience and strangely gratuitous. On the one hand, the season initially seems to demand further viewer investment in the new characters. Indeed, the fact that, in grand *Star Trek* style, their time-traveling adventures seem to be baked into the existing timeline might have served to grant a retrospective sense of destiny to their introduction in season 1. Further, there are genuinely good character moments (as in Rios's budding relationship and in Seven's exploration, after the time-travel shenanigans temporarily remove her visible Borg implants, of what it feels like to be in a world where she is not immediately greeted with suspicion) and performances (as in Jurati's struggle with the Borg Queen to maintain control of her mind). Almost all of this is erased and rendered irrelevant by the end of the season. It is unclear why such a move appeared necessary. If these characters did not fit into the plans for season 3, could the writers not have simply jumped forward in time and quickly explained their absence in some brief asides?

Even more puzzling is the trajectory of the title character. On the one hand, the season reopens the arc of Picard's conflict with Q, only to close it down seemingly definitively when Q reveals that he is dying and that he is using the last vestiges of his power to teach Picard a final lesson simply because he cares about him as a friend. The scene of Q's self-sacrificial death as he sends Picard and his friends back is surprisingly touching, exactly the kind of thing one hopes for from one last outing with a beloved character. On the other hand, much of the season is bogged down by Picard's implausible struggle with another cliché of streaming television: childhood trauma.[13] In this case, we are treated to a series of mystery box–style flashbacks that culminate in the revelation that as a child, Picard blamed himself for his mother's suicide after her long struggle with mental illness. The idea that a character who has survived being assimilated by the Borg, broken in a Cardassian torture camp ("Chain of Command," TNG 6.10–11), and so on, is still dwelling on this issue beggars belief. While fresh background information on a familiar character would normally count as fan service, this revelation's contribution to Picard's character is unclear, unless we are supposed to infer that this traumatic event is the source of his intimacy issues. On the latter front, he is confronted with a doppelgänger of his missed romantic opportunity, Laris, in the person of Tallinn (also played by Orla Brady), a Romulan temporal agent tasked with guarding Picard's historically important ancestor. In the end, though, Tallinn sacrifices herself to save the mission, without ever solving the mystery of her uncanny resemblance to Laris. As in the first season, the audience is left wondering why Laris could not simply come along for the ride in the first place.

Much like *Discovery* season 2, then, *Picard*'s second chapter served primarily as a reset so that a new (or, in this case, reconfigured) production team could clear the decks for the show they wanted to do. Unlike the parallel *Discovery* season, however, which, in keeping with the show's style, was extremely fast-paced, this outing of *Picard* feels as though it is simply marking time. More importantly, though, where *Discovery*'s uneven sophomore effort managed to produce at least one spin-off *(Strange New Worlds)* and likely a second *(Section 31)* as well as setting up a different era of *Star Trek, Picard* spends an entire season doing nothing. The first season had struggled to do justice to all the creative ideas it had introduced in the space of ten episodes, but the trip back to Los Angeles to fix the timeline is a two-episode premise painfully stretched across eight. The writers fill their time with what one reviewer calls "some characters heading out on multi-episode missions that, in the end, accomplished nothing,"[14] as well as apparent non sequiturs like an encounter with an FBI agent straight out of *The X-Files* (1993–2018) who turns out to have seen some Vulcan scouts as a child (an apparent homage to "Carbon Creek," ENT 2.2). At times Picard himself seems to be reduced to a fanboy—excitedly remembering, for example, when "Kirk's *Enterprise*" encountered the organization that Tallinn works for ("Fly Me to the Moon," PIC 2.5; the reference is to "Assignment: Earth," TOS 2.26). Is this kind of thing really what we wanted from the return of Jean-Luc Picard?

Judging from the chatter on r/DaystromInstitute, fans had already begun to lose interest midseason but were won back by the

Q arc's final resolution. Perhaps influenced by the afterglow of that scene, some fans initially viewed the season as an improvement on the muddle of season 1—including both me and question-filled IndieWire reviewer Christian Blauvelt[15]—but opinion quickly soured. In a ranked listing of *Picard* episodes by user rating on IMDb, for instance, season 2 dominates the bottom of the list with eight out of the bottom ten slots.[16] If season 1 was a flawed attempt to reimagine Picard's character and world, season 2 failed even to try. It would be easy to blame Covid-19–related filming restrictions for this season's flawed concept and argue that they did the best they could. But why run a season at all under these circumstances, especially if they did not have a strong idea? It is difficult not to draw the conclusion that commercial concerns trumped all others, and this season was churned out simply for the sake of continuously releasing new *Star Trek* material on Paramount+.

THE LAST GENERATION

It is proverbial among *Star Trek* fans that the *Next Generation*–era shows only become truly good in their third season. Only after fifty episodes, it seems, do the writers and actors truly know their characters enough to deliver the kind of ensemble problem-solving that makes *Star Trek* great. I would propose a new rule for the two flagship streaming-era shows I have investigated so far: it takes two seasons for the producers to finally do what they obviously always should have done. In the case of *Discovery*—for all my love of what they achieved with the prequel concept in season 1—a story with bold new ship designs and an astoundingly advanced propulsion system should have been set in the franchise's future, not its past. Even more inexplicable, however, is *Picard*'s refusal, for two full seasons, to do a *Next Generation* reunion.

Once the franchise finally decided to do the obvious, however, the relief and elation were palpable. Season 3 enjoyed broadly positive reviews, both from critics who received advance episodes and retrospectively. The consensus was clear: finally, we were getting the *Next Generation* reunion we all craved! Lauren Coates of the A.V. Club writes, "*Picard* season three is, without question, the show's strongest yet, recapturing a bit of that magic of *The Next Generation* and nicely utilizing its talented cast."[17] Alex Cranz, whose review appears as part of the Verge's rundown of the best entertainment of 2023, declares the season "the absolute most fun I've had watching Paramount Plus's myriad of *Star Trek* shows. And part of my love of this final season comes from how excited the show is to take some of *Star Trek*'s most flawless heroes and find the humanity in them."[18] IndieWire's Scott Collura fell in love with *Picard*'s final outing and attributed its success in part to the new production staff: "After a disastrous season 2, however, it seems that the powers that be at Paramount Plus gave the keys to the Enterprise to showrunner Terry Matalas, who would go on to take the old girl to that rare sweet spot in our modern era where nostalgia and actual, quality storytelling meet."[19] Indeed, aided by a full schedule of interviews and an active Twitter presence, Terry Matalas quickly took on a status similar to that of *Enterprise*'s fourth-season showrunner Manny Coto, as both were lionized for finally righting the ship of a troubled show—and this despite the fact that Matalas was in charge for the disastrous season 2 as well.

Matalas made it easy to forget, however, because he treats season 2 as though it never happened. We never hear from the nice Jurati Borg, nor do we learn what happened with the anomaly she was warning them about. The only plot thread that continues to be relevant is Picard's relationship with Laris, which has advanced to the point that they are planning a vacation together. But after receiving a message from his long-lost colleague Beverly Crusher—who mysteriously requests that he not involve Starfleet Command—Picard once again leaves Laris, who is not only his life partner but a highly skilled Romulan spy, behind. Instead, he teams up with Riker, who—fittingly for someone who, in "These Are the Voyages . . ." (ENT 4.22), sought guidance from a holodeck reconstruction of Archer's final mission—is in town to give a speech celebrating the 250th anniversary of the *Enterprise* NX-01's historic first voyage, known as Frontier Day. Together, they contrive to hijack Riker's former command, the USS *Titan*-A, now helmed by salty Captain Shaw and his first officer, Seven of Nine, who (in an apparent homage to *Discovery*) defies her captain's orders and intercepts Crusher's ship. In the cold open, we had witnessed Crusher and her son, Jack, fending off alien attackers—much like Seven of Nine, the calm and cerebral doctor has here been transmuted into a wisecracking badass—and when the *Titan* arrives, they find that Jack has placed his mother in stasis because of her wounds.

Thus begins a long process of bringing the old gang back together—including Raffi, who is working for Starfleet Intelligence under a mysterious handler who turns out to be Worf. Even Data makes an appearance in a new, more human-looking body (presumably to spare a visibly older Brent Spiner time in the makeup chair), which he shares with the personality of his evil twin, Lore. Lore initially seems to take control, but thankfully Data gains the upper hand—effectively resurrecting the character yet again after his strangely doubled death. (Incidentally, this move is arguably a riff on David Mack's resurrection of Data with a new blended personality in *Cold Equations,* which would mark the second major borrowing from Mack's work after *Discovery*'s Control arc.) Troi is initially nowhere to be found, because Riker drove her away by emotionally shutting down as a result of his long-term grief over the death of their son, but she is conveniently kidnapped by the villain, allowing for a rescue that doubles as a reconciliation. When they seek Geordi's help, he reveals that he is a family man now and does not want to risk his daughters' lives, but he changes his mind and is almost immediately proven right. Luckily, though, he has been using his off-hours as head of the Starfleet museum to reconstruct the *Enterprise*-D from *Next Generation,* which turns out to be necessary to resolve the penultimate episode's devastating cliffhanger.

The true motor of the action, however, is a new character, Jack Crusher, who is revealed (long after it has become painfully obvious to the viewer) to be Picard's long-lost son. The writers indulge one last time in what has become a series leitmotif, the offscreen romance and breakup, as we learn that Picard and Crusher briefly relieved the sexual tension that had been palpable for all of *Next Generation*'s run. When she learned she was pregnant, however, Crusher—who had already lost a husband (who died under Picard's command) and a son (who transcended the bounds of material reality, also under Picard's command)—decided that any son of Jean-Luc Picard would be in terrible danger at all times and that she must therefore strictly conceal the existence of her son from his father and from all their mutual friends. She thus isolates herself from them for decades. As science fiction author Adam Roberts puts it in his review of *Picard* season 3, "the Crusher of [*Next Generation*] would never do something as immoral as depriving her lover of the chance to be involved with bringing up his son, or hiding from him the knowledge that he even *was* a father. She acts this way to enable a tacky-tacky soap-opera-esque 'but who *is* this strange young fellow who also speaks with a posh-o English accent—why Jean-Luc, it's the son you never knew you had!' reveal."[20]

The revelation of Jack Crusher's true parentage represents only the first in a series of contrived twists and turns that culminates in the revelation that the Borg implanted some secret DNA in Picard while he was assimilated, which he has passed down to Jack. This terrible inheritance makes poor Jack a crucial part of the Borg's nefarious plan to take over Starfleet by planting Changeling moles (last seen in *Deep Space Nine*'s Dominion war arc) to alter the transporters on all Starfleet vessels to change everyone's DNA. The result is that Jack will be a transmitter for Borg mind control, while the genetically altered Starfleet officers—though strangely only those under the age of twenty-five—will be receivers. Tragically, this plan comes to pass despite our heroes' knowledge of its existence, when Jack gratuitously seeks out the Borg Queen in order to confront her. As a result, all of the young members of Starfleet are subjected to mind control during the Frontier Day ceremony—which is also, unfortunately, the debut of Starfleet's bold new technology allowing the entire fleet to be networked together and operate as a single unit. Hence only an older ship, disconnected from the network and staffed exclusively by a crew of retirees, can save the day by blowing up the Borg cube and convincing Jack to renounce his mind-control powers.

All of this, it seems, was in the service of getting one last shot of the classic crew on the familiar bridge of the *Enterprise*-D (Figure 6). Many of my colleagues at r/DaystromInstitute reported being deeply moved by this climactic moment, as also by the reprise of the crew's classic poker games that accompanied the closing credits. But it has come at a great cost. Every member of the younger generation of Starfleet has now participated in murdering their senior officers at the behest of the Borg Queen. Whereas in the past she would have desired to assimilate them, now—with the Collective in terminal decline after Janeway's parting blow in "Endgame" (VOY 7.25–26)—she seeks only vengeance and destruction.

I can think of no other interpretation of this strange story arc than as a metaphor for the younger generation's penchant for canceling their elders, infected as they are by the woke mind virus. Even if that meaning is not consciously intended, however, the entire season is triumphalist in a way that is ungenerous and even disrespectful to other installments of the franchise. The alliance of *Deep Space Nine*'s Changelings with the Borg has long been the stuff of

FIGURE 6. *The original* Next Generation *cast is reunited on the bridge of the* Enterprise-*D ("The Last Generation," PIC 3.10).*

fan fiction and theorizing, but reviving them in this context seems to assert *Next Generation*'s prerogative to finish the plot arcs of its two spin-offs. As with season 1's valuation of Picard's Borg trauma over that of Seven of Nine—who even here is carefully kept away from the process of deciphering the Borg Queen's scheme despite her obvious expertise—this season's arc seems to deny Janeway the distinction of finishing off the Borg threat, reserving the coup de grace for Picard. The same goes for the Changelings, whose defeat through the leadership and final self-sacrifice of Benjamin Sisko was only provisional until Picard arrived on the scene to seal the deal. As for *Enterprise,* the message is clear: any attempt to call those events to mind can only end in disaster.

This is fan service at its most empty, baldly asserting that *Next Generation* will always be the best of *Star Trek*. The title of the series finale captures this attitude well. Picard and his colleagues are indeed "The Last Generation"—the last cohort of Starfleet heroes who can achieve anything truly meaningful. In season 1, Picard declares bitterly that he resigned "because it was no longer Starfleet!" ("Remembrance," PIC 1.1). There he was critiquing a departure from core values as Starfleet abandoned vulnerable people to death and responded to tragedy with bigotry. Here, it seems, the message is that "it was no longer Starfleet" because it was no longer about the *Next Generation* crew, sitting authoritatively on that iconic bridge with its iconic carpet—which Picard finds it in himself to joke about even as Starfleet has been taken over by his greatest enemy and Earth is under attack. That glibness is exemplary of the entire season's approach, which makes its self-aggrandizement and self-congratulation all the more intolerable.

Ultimately, *Picard*'s third season is disrespectful even of its own previous seasons. I have already noted that Data's death—the reaffirmation of which was the emotional climax of the first season—was casually undone and that the major developments surrounding the Borg in season 2 were simply discarded and ignored. More broadly, though, the assertion of creative freedom to indulge in pure fan service results in thoughtless, incoherent world-building. The idea that Starfleet could be infiltrated by Commodore Oh was meant to be a shock in season 1, and now we learn that there was apparently another, even more serious infiltration happening at the same time. Meanwhile, all the youngest members of Starfleet—the organization's future—must live with the burden of guilt and shame after being instrumentalized by the Borg. For the sake of ongoing stories, it would appear that the *Next Generation* era is more or less wrecked. Yet in a tacky gesture reminiscent of the Marvel Cinematic Universe's postcredit vignettes, Matalas interrupts the sentimental indulgence of one last poker game with the crew of the *Enterprise*-D with what amounts to a backdoor pilot for a new show. This one would star

Seven of Nine as captain of the newly minted *Enterprise*-G, accompanied by Raffi as her first officer (and on-again girlfriend) and junior crew members Sydney LaForge (Geordi's daughter) and Jack Crusher (who never attended Starfleet Academy, but never mind that). Lest we worry that the tone would be grim, given the ruin in which Starfleet finds itself, Jack is visited by none other than Q, who shrugs off his own death as too linear a concept for a being like him.

This ending, which completes the patient labor of undoing or invalidating every meaningful character moment from the first two seasons, vindicates one of the few dissenting voices amid the critical praise of *Picard* season 3. Writing for Engadget, Daniel Cooper declares the season to be an amateurish indulgence, developed by a creative team that views "*Star Trek*'s continuity"—including, I would add, the continuity that they themselves established—"less as something which informs storytelling and more as a series of shiny objects to keep us all amused when the plot sags or anyone has any time to think about what's going on." Declaring the season to be "yet another misguided waste of everyone's time," he urges his readers not to watch, lest Paramount be encouraged to produce more like it.[21] The final episode's teaser exhorts just the opposite. Inspired by Anson Mount's successful fan campaign, which led to the production of *Strange New Worlds,* Matalas repeatedly flogged the concept of a new show called *Star Trek: Legacy* that would carry forward the story of the *Next Generation* era—an effort that was, mercifully, unsuccessful.[22]

What the show would have been about, other than putting familiar characters back on screen, is unclear. Perhaps that would have been enough for Matalas, as for many fans. Among my colleagues at r/DaystromInstitute, for instance, *Picard* season 3 generated a great deal of discussion. Indeed, many episode discussion threads reached nearly a thousand comments, a record that was shattered by the finale's 1,324 comments.[23] If season 3 of *Picard* marked the peak of fan excitement, however, I nonetheless regard the series as the nadir of late *Star Trek,* the moment when the franchise threatened to transform into a purely cynical commodity, nothing more than "content" churned out to extract subscription fees for Paramount+.

If the franchise is to continue along the lines laid down by the final season of *Picard* in particular, which sacrifices any genuine creative ambition or coherent world-building for the sake of thoughtless, superficial fan service, I would prefer that it not continue at all—or, better, that it be turned over to the novelists and comic writers, who continue to try their best to build something on the constantly shifting sands of a show that constantly contradicts and even overwrites itself. In *Last Best Hope,* the debut novel for the series (name-dropped at the end of the *Coda* series), Una McCormack succeeds in building out the world and backstory of *Picard* with the same mix of creativity and plausibility she brought to *Discovery*'s distant future in *Wonderlands.* Various comic miniseries give us what we should have found in the show itself: a real adventure featuring Picard and his Romulan housemates, or a more organic moment of mentorship between Picard and Seven.[24] Even more than with *Discovery,* their efforts are often ignored or overwritten by on-screen events. But the stories they were able to spin out of this ill-considered series give me confidence that, as the architects of the original novelverse did with the disastrous final *Next Generation* films, so too could *Star Trek*'s hardworking tie-in authors salvage enough out of even this bizarre and tangled wreckage to sustain any number of fresh, intelligent stories.

6

MINOR TRIUMPHS

LOWER DECKS, PRODIGY, AND STRANGE NEW WORLDS

B y most measures, thanks to the Covid-19 pandemic, 2020 was the worst year in recent history. For *Star Trek* fans, however, it was an annus mirabilis. Two shows (*Picard* and *Lower Decks*) debuted as *Discovery* entered its third season, marking the first time in the franchise's history that three distinct spin-offs had aired in the same year.[1] The following two years each saw the debut of a further *Trek* series, with *Prodigy* launching in 2021 and *Strange New Worlds* in 2022. The franchise quickly broke its own record in 2022, as all five series released new episodes in that year. (Detailed release dates are provided in appendix 1.) The ambition here is striking—not just in terms of sheer volume but also in terms of variety. As I note in the introduction, *Next Generation* and its direct spin-offs shared a similar style and approach, to the point where they feel like episodes in a single overarching series. In contrast, the new material intentionally used different styles to draw in different audiences. *Lower Decks* is an adult cartoon on the model of *Rick and Morty* (2013–present), a show where its creator, Mike McMahan, once served as executive producer. Aimed at younger audiences, *Prodigy* is perhaps best compared to *Avatar: The Last Airbender* (2005–8), and was actually broadcast on the Nickelodeon network after debuting via streaming. Though both are animated, the two series look radically different: *Lower Decks* adopts a more conventional line-drawn style, while *Prodigy*'s visuals are computer generated. Finally, *Strange New Worlds* attempts to reach more casual audiences with its updated take on *The Original Series,* embracing *Star Trek*'s traditional episodic format instead of the heavily serialized model of *Discovery* or *Picard.*

From the perspective of my investigation, perhaps the most interesting thing about the three spin-offs treated in this chapter is their lower stakes. In itself, that makes them a breath of fresh air. As we have seen, *Discovery* season 1 sought self-consciously to reinvent the franchise for a modern audience, and *Picard* season 1 made a similar gesture with its most successful series. Both ultimately scaled back their ambitions, often by explicitly walking back many of their innovations on-screen in their respective second seasons. But even in those moments, the shows' relation to the franchise remained the explicit focus, distorting storytelling and characterization and generally distracting from the kinds of moral and political allegories audiences expect from *Star Trek.*

Where the two tentpole series were obsessed with their own relationship to *Star Trek*'s fictional world, the three later spin-offs simply inhabit it. Not only that, but they signal their lower stakes with their choice of setting. (Appendix 2 lists the exact fictional dates of each series.) Where *Picard* had leveraged Prime Spock's monologue in *Star Trek* (2009) to place itself in the wake of the world-historical debacle of the Romulan supernova, *Lower Decks* opts to pick up the year after *Nemesis,* when the galactic geopolitical situation can be expected to remain calm for most of the series' run. More than that, though, the decision to focus on the lowest-ranking officers on an unprestigious ship seems to place a definite ceiling on the intergalactic consequences of their adventures. For its part, *Prodigy* repeats *Voyager*'s gesture of distancing itself from the main action of the franchise by placing its heroes in the distant Delta Quadrant, and by again situating its story between *Nemesis* and the Romulan disaster. Finally, *Strange New Worlds* picks up the year after *Discovery*'s departure to the distant future, giving itself approximately seven years (long considered a full run for a *Star Trek* series, since *Next Generation, Deep Space Nine,* and *Voyager* all reached that level) until Captain Pike's tragic accident will necessitate the end to this particular crew's adventures. One of the common critiques of prequels is that the audience's knowledge of the future undercuts the drama, and if anything, *Strange New Worlds* redoubles this problem by granting Pike the knowledge of his own grim future. But the series arguably turns the perceived drawbacks of the prequel format to its advantage. Because we broadly know the trajectories of so many of the characters, we can focus more on the stories of the individual episodes.

By putting world-building on the back burner, all three series can make no other claim on their audience's attention than by crafting compelling plots with likable characters. That this should feel like an innovation is strange because it has always been *Star Trek*'s greatest strength. Recounting his experience of rewatching the early seasons of *Next Generation* in his review of *Picard* season 3, science fiction novelist Adam Roberts writes that it

> reminds me what it was about the show that made it work in the first place: the ensemble, the mix of characters, coming together into a "family." . . . By TNG's third season the balance of

character-types and their interactions are consistently wonderful, involving, the perfect ground against which to rehearse the specific SF storylines—some of which are good, some bad. But even the bad storylines matter less when the whole ensemble is firing on its many cylinders.[2]

Or as the critic Aaron Bady more bluntly put it in a tweet issued the day *Picard* premiered, in all caps: "I want friends solving space crimes in a supportive yet challenging workplace."[3] The same holds even more for *The Original Series,* whose enduring cult appeal depends in great measure on fans' investment in the characters, above all Kirk and Spock. I suggested before that the new streaming series require two seasons to arrive at the concept they always should have had from the beginning, but now it appears that the franchise as a whole requires two full streaming series before they finally get around to doing the thing that made people love *Star Trek* in the first place.

In this chapter, I will discuss each series in turn, deviating slightly from chronological order by addressing *Prodigy* first. As I mentioned in the introduction, the series' future was in limbo for many months, and though its second season was picked up by Netflix, it seems unlikely that *Prodigy* will continue beyond that. In contrast, *Lower Decks* and *Strange New Worlds* are the only ongoing *Star Trek* series to have a concrete commitment beyond the end of *Discovery*'s fifth and final season.[4] Ironically, then, for all the bombast and experimentation of the streaming era's early years, the franchise's immediate future lies with two series that follow likable characters through episodic adventures in the two main eras of its fictional history. Fittingly, the two series have signaled their kinship with a charming crossover episode ("Those Old Scientists," SNW 2.7), which will serve as a kind of coda to my analysis of the era of late *Star Trek*.

ADOLESCENCE: THE FINAL FRONTIER

Every television and film series investigated so far has tried to send a clear message: this is not your father's *Star Trek*. As the first *Trek* series aimed unambiguously at children,[5] *Prodigy* may have felt obligated to stake out that claim especially forcefully. It achieves this by opening in a world that feels like an exaggerated version of *Star Wars,* conceived as the opposite of *Star Trek*'s postscarcity utopia. So clear is the connection in the opening episodes—the diamond in the rough heroes, the emphasis on action sequences, the architecture characterized by wide-open spaces and an inexplicable lack of guardrails— that some mainstream critics dismissed *Prodigy* as either "a *Star Wars Rebels* wannabe"[6] or, more charitably, an attempt to mash up the two most venerable science fiction franchises.[7] I had a similar impression after watching the handful of episodes to which those early reviewers had access, but the writers' gambit quickly became clear. *Prodigy* is not an attempt to shoehorn a *Star Wars* series into the *Star Trek* franchise. It is a show about a group of young people who initially believe they are in a *Star Wars* production and discover, much to their relief, that they are actually living in the *Star Trek* universe.

As with *Discovery*'s decision to write the fans' likely sense of betrayal and the show's need to earn their trust into the story, then, the *Prodigy* writers—headed up by Emmy Award winners Kevin and Dan Hageman—have written the show's mission to introduce young people to *Star Trek* into the text of the show itself. In fact, it quickly comes to feel like some version of a Starfleet Academy show, with the holographic version of *Voyager*'s Kathryn Janeway (Kate Mulgrew) tutoring her young charges in the ways of spaceflight and diplomacy. The key difference is that we are not dealing with the meritocratic journey of the Federation's best and brightest but with a handful of misfits who have never heard of the Federation and seize control of a derelict Starfleet ship to escape from the mining colony where they have been enslaved. They are awkwardly accompanied by the daughter of the slave driver, whom the escapees inadvertently kidnapped, and who only wants to get back home. Even by the standards of contemporary *Trek,* this premise is dark, especially for a kids' show. At the same time, it definitely establishes that our tween adventurers will not have their buzz killed by any parental figures (other than hologram Janeway, who can be turned on and off at will). The writers' quest for creative freedom merges seamlessly into the characters' fulfillment of a teenage fantasy of total independence.

The crew is made up of characters who are likable, if one-note. Most fully developed are their self-appointed leader Dal (Brett Gray), who has no memory of his parents or even his species and who turns out to be a human genetically augmented with features from many different aliens, and Gwyn (Ella Purnell), the villain's daughter, who gradually comes to understand that her father is in the wrong and Starfleet is the better way to go. As often happens at their age, Gwyn is much more mature and competent than her male counterpart, yet her divided loyalties render her untrustworthy, at least initially. Much of the tension between them centers on who is, or should be, in charge, and the writers sometimes seem to be struggling to find reasons why the answer should be Dal.

The overarching plot is exceptionally convoluted. The derelict spacecraft, known as the *Protostar,* turns out to be an experimental ship—originally captained by Janeway's former first officer and slow-burn love interest, Chakotay (Robert Beltran)—that uses stellar material to travel orders of magnitude faster than warp speed and was unfortunately caught in a temporal anomaly early in its first mission. The mining camp, with its enslaved workforce of misfits and orphans, is run by the Diviner (John Noble), a time traveler from the future who believes that Starfleet is responsible for a terrible civil war that virtually destroyed his planet shortly after their first contact. As luck would have it, the *Protostar*'s inadvertent time travel deposited it on the Diviner's planet, and he seized control of it, implanting a computer virus that would cause any Starfleet vessels that came into contact with the *Protostar* to try to destroy each other. The Diviner planned to send the *Protostar* back in time to cripple Starfleet before it could make contact with his planet, but Chakotay and his crew managed to disrupt the launch so that the Diviner lost the ship. Eventually he tracked it to the planet and hence set up the mining camp—only to be thwarted by the group of kids that stole the ship and his progeny (which is how he addresses his daughter, whom he produced parthenogenically).

Such complex use of time travel is in line with the spirit of *Voyager,* which routinely used the trope to explore themes of loss and regret. Here it is a kind of trial by fire for the show's potential new fans, selecting for those who are fascinated rather than put off by the complexities of temporal mechanics. The existence of the virus also serves as a plot kludge to make clear why our heroes cannot simply use their high-powered engine to travel straight to Starfleet headquarters and request asylum. With that option initially foreclosed, it seems like the show is setting up this ragtag crew to be freelance problem solvers in a corner of the galaxy that was established to be something like the wild west in *Voyager,* whose fans the show services by providing hints of the development of Janeway and Chakotay's relationship.

The first half of the only season to air as of this writing does a good job of gradually building the team's competence by putting them through *Star Trek* scenarios familiar to fans and yet completely unknown to them (and presumably to the young target audience). Most satisfying in my mind is "Time Amok" (PRO 1.8), in which a malfunction in the experimental drive causes the crew to experience time at different speeds, requiring them to find new ways to work together to solve the problem and keep the ship from exploding. In my opinion, it is not only the best episode of the series but one of the best time-travel puzzle episodes in all of *Trek*. Another highlight is "Kobayashi" (PRO 1.6), in which Dal takes the infamous no-win Kobayashi Maru test. Not realizing it is designed to be impossible, he insists on taking it dozens of times, eventually acting so erratically that he wins by accident—until he trips and accidentally pushes a button that blows up the ship. Though the main plot is entertaining enough, the episode also includes some gratuitous fan service that would likely be distracting or incomprehensible for the intended audience, as Dal is joined by holographic representations of older characters. Here and elsewhere, the show's format makes such tributes awkward gestures at the parent watching over the child's shoulder. Perhaps the most substantive reworking of a familiar *Trek* concept is "First Con-tact" (PRO 1.7), where Dal's onetime Ferengi foster mother robs an alien species the crew is attempting to make first contact with. Though they are able to retrieve the stolen goods, Janeway points out that the damage is permanent, as the species will be distrustful of aliens in the future. As reviewer Shamus Kelley points out, "the whole episode isn't redoing a *Trek* plot but dumbing it down for kids" but instead taking "a unique approach that wouldn't be possible without a cast of characters who've never heard of what a first contact mission is."[8]

The arc of those first ten episodes is satisfying, culminating in the crew's decision to take a serious risk to break their fellow slaves out of the Diviner's mining camp. After several seasons of *Star Trek* centered on problems of intergalactic scale, a story with more purely personal stakes feels refreshing. Instead of continuing in that vein, however, the second half of the season instead brings them into increasingly close contact with the real Janeway, who is leading a mission to recover the *Protostar* and save Chakotay. The story, which up till then had been mainly episodic, becomes much more heavily serialized. It culminates in a two-part finale where the Diviner's virus is actually triggered, leading to a full-scale battle among an ever-growing number of Federation vessels. The problem is resolved by a two-pronged, and very *Star Trek,* plan. On the one hand, Starfleet's allies—including species that longtime fans would know to be onetime rivals, like the Klingons—come to their aid, disabling the infected ships as gently as possible and giving the lie to the Diviner's claim of Starfleet's malign influence. On the other hand, the hologram Janeway—whose coexistence with her real counterpart has become awkward—sacrifices herself by piloting the *Protostar* far into empty space and activating its self-destruct.

That finale is a self-destruct for the show's initial premise, which held real potential. The season concludes with the majority of the crew entering Starfleet Academy, while Dal is excluded thanks to the Federation's ban on genetic engineering—an aspect of franchise lore that late *Star Trek* becomes increasingly fascinated with over time, as we will see. As compensation, however, he is invited to join Janeway's mission to rescue Chakotay, promising yet more service to *Voyager* fans. While the Starfleet Academy concept holds obvious appeal for a younger audience, it is less clear why the show thinks that new fans will be interested in the fate of a secondary character from a decades-old previous *Star Trek* spin-off. Neither option, though, seems nearly as appealing to a younger audience as what the first half of the season seemed to be setting up—namely the adventures of a band of vigilante teenage do-gooders making their own way through the galaxy, far from any scolding authority figure.

Why would the writers so quickly undermine their own concept? Perhaps the *Prodigy* writers were trying to correct the perceived errors of *Voyager,* which has been widely criticized for neglecting its lost-in-space premise in favor of delivering largely generic *Star Trek* episodes.[9] If so, they overcorrected in the other direction, essentially smothering the show through overserialization in the second half of the season. Or perhaps the writers were reluctant to leave their first season too open ended, lest they get canceled. If that is the case, I can hardly blame them in light of Paramount's high-handed treatment of the series. Even though the second season has been saved, however, it is difficult to imagine a path that the writers could take to preserve any distinctiveness for the show, given that a live-action *Starfleet Academy* series is already planned, and fast-forwarding past graduation to follow these characters' early careers would result in little more than a reprise of *Lower Decks*. The vagaries of corporate strategy may wind up striking the final blow, but the writers' failure to give their premise and characters room to breathe has already all but guaranteed that *Prodigy* will be a source of trivia for hard-core *Star Trek* completists rather than a durable on-ramp for new fans.

"THE FAMILY YOU CHOOSE"

At first glance, *Lower Decks* seems like the least promising concept to come out of late *Star Trek:* a willful descent into self-parody. Not only in its animated format, but above all in its rapid-fire self-referentiality, the show represents a break with the often staid and slow-paced approach of the *Next Generation* era in which *Lower Decks* is set. As Ramón Valle-Jiménez writes, "Unlike the campy humor embraced by the pre–*Star Trek* (2009) TV series and films, the vivacious humor of *[Lower Decks]* is geared toward an adult audience, and even though it gleefully lampoons the *Star Trek* canon at every available opportunity, it does so without contempt."[10] At times the affectionate mockery effectively breaks the fourth wall with a self-aware reference to past *Trek* canon or fan culture, usually followed by some implausible excuse for why the remark makes in-universe sense. The most striking example is when the first officer, Jack Ransom (Jerry O'Connell), uses the fan abbreviation "TOS" to refer to the era of *The Original Series,* only to clarify that he meant "'those old scientists.' You know, Spock, Scotty, those guys. Seems like they were stumbling on crazy new aliens every week back then" ("No Small Parts," LDS 1.10). Later, the characters debate the merits of referring to *Voyager* (the in-universe ship) by the fan abbreviation VOY (for the series), ultimately concluding that the time savings are considerable ("We'll Always Have Tom Paris," LDS 2.3).[11] The fact that these incongruous remarks are covered by a note of admiration is typical. The ultimate reason that the characters are referring back to the previous shows is that the characters and events we know from the films and TV shows are legendary within the *Star Trek* universe itself. In other words, the *Lower Decks* characters are in-universe fans—fans who recognize the occasional absurdity of the world they live in, but fans nonetheless.

The latter description might fit the show's creator, Mike Mc-Mahan. As I noted above, McMahan's recognizable TV credit is his work on *Rick and Morty,* but he is perhaps best known to *Star Trek* fans as the author of "the @TNG_S8 Twitter account, which gained popularity for posting satirical episode synopses for a fictitious unproduced eighth season of [*Next Generation*],"[12] the final tweet of which (posted in early 2020) announces that all the creativity previously brought to bear on that project "is being channeled into Star Trek: Lower Decks—coming to CBS All Access this year."[13] The tweets most often list an A and B plot, which feel eerily plausible—for instance, "A subspace rumple disables the Enterprise and blinds the crew. Data & Geordi's plan to build the perfect girlfriend backfires explosively."[14] They are not homages to existing episodes but riffs on the kind of concept that would underlie a forgettable installment. One could say that *Lower Decks* combines this approach to *Star Trek* with the concept of the *Next Generation* episode of the same title ("Lower Decks," TNG 7.15), which took a step back from the glamorous adventures of the bridge crew to give us the perspective of the young officers, fresh out of the academy, who do the most dangerous grunt work. Taking it a step further, however, the show focuses on a ship that is decidedly second tier, the USS *Cerritos,* a California-class vessel tasked with handling Second Contact—or put differently, with cleaning up the messes that fester when the more famous captains meddle with an alien culture and then immediately set course for the next planet.

The show's very concept thus poses the same problem as its many in-jokes. On the one hand, it is itself a form of metacommentary, suggesting to the viewer that Starfleet's normal way of conducting business is a bit absurd. Even if they do not technically break the fourth wall, such sentiments feel like a strange fit for in-universe canon. But on the other hand, just like the revelation that the heroes of the previous shows are in-universe heroes as well, it also works as a form of world-building. It solves the very issue it raises by assuring the viewer that Starfleet has thought of the same obvious objection and devoted the appropriate resources to it. In general, we could say that the show takes a more lighthearted version of David Mack's distinctive approach to world-building in the novelverse, where he exaggerates the kinds of contradictions or problems pointed out by fans, only to resolve them decisively. In the case of *Lower Decks* in particular, though, it is a distinctly seamless form of world-building that feels like fan service because the solution is so understated that it seems as though it had obviously always been like that.

The same combination of fan service and world-building characterizes the show's approach to moving the *Next Generation*–era story forward and, more generally, building links among the various spin-offs. The show is especially generous in drawing connections to *Deep Space Nine,* which is relatively neglected by the other streaming-era shows, and to the original *Animated Series,* which has languished under a cloud of dubious canonicity. The continual references to the latter may also count as a meta gesture of acknowledgment that *Lower Decks* itself might not appear to be fully canonical, and the carefully chosen guest stars—including the only sighting of Captain Riker in command of the USS *Titan* (a career shift that is set to happen after the events of *Nemesis* but has already played out by the time we see him again in *Picard*); a visit to *Deep Space Nine,* where Colonel Kira (Nana Visitor) remains in command; or the exciting announcement that the Grand Nagus Rom (Max Grodénchik) wants to bring the Ferengi into the Federation—seem calculated to satisfy fan curiosity and make them *want* it to be canon.

Ultimately, though, the reason to regard *Lower Decks* as fully integral to the *Star Trek* universe is that once we get to know the characters, we cannot imagine the franchise without them. The main cast of lower deckers is made up of a balanced group of four friends. The unofficial leader is Beckett Mariner (Tawny Newsom), a highly skilled and adaptable officer who has in some respects had a storied career (including service on *Deep Space Nine* during the Dominion war) but has been continually demoted and transferred thanks to her habitual insubordination. The main mystery of the first season centers on the fact that she is secretly the daughter of the *Cerritos'* captain, Carol Freeman (Dawnn Lewis), a connection both hide mainly out of embarrassment. Mariner takes on a kind of mentorship role for Brad Boimler (Jack Quaid), a try-hard rule follower who is obsessed with making captain and gradually learns to loosen up. They are joined by D'Vana Tendi (Noël Wells), an Orion who is trying to escape from the stereotypes that her species is made up of criminals (and the reality that she comes from a powerful crime family), and Sam Rutherford (Eugene Cordero), a dedicated engineer with cybernetic implants that help him with his work but produce frequent complications. We also get to know the bridge crew, who, in Valle-Jiménez's words, "follow archetypal and thus familiar models, though with decidedly parodic twists,"[15] but the show does a good job of staying true to its concept and keeping them primarily in the background.

Lower Decks also does a good job of keeping its stories decidedly low stakes and character focused, using its setting as a foundation for a different and more effective form of creative freedom than that sought by the big, world-shattering gestures of the earlier series and films. Indeed, some installments are essentially no stakes, like holodeck-centered movie parody episodes "Crisis Point" (LDS 1.9) or "Crisis Point 2: Paradoxus" (LDS 3.8), but they always shed some light on our characters and the dynamics between them—and blessedly, that dynamic is never romantic, even though there are early hints that Mariner may harbor an unacknowledged crush on Boimler (e.g., "Cupid's Errant Arrow," LDS 1.5, and "Much Ado about Boimler," LDS 1.7) and clearer indications that Tendi is sometimes jealous of Rutherford's dates. These moments of mild possessiveness aside, however, the friend group is remarkably casual about their personal space (living as they do in small bunks in a hallway, which they share with the other shifts) and even about nudity, as they are sometimes portrayed in an all-gender community shower with no apparent embarrassment or titillation. This strange innocence reminds us that they live in a far different world from us, one in which the overcoming of scarcity has radically changed people's ideas about possessions and relationships.

Here we might even credit *Lower Decks* with thinking more seriously about what humanity looks like when, in Picard's words, we have "grown out of our infancy" ("The Neutral Zone," TNG 1.26) than any previous series. Yet the fact that this utopia appears most clearly in a comedy series—indeed, in one that is self-consciously parodic of the franchise of which it is a part—does seem to point to something important. From our perspective, amid the ruins of the War on Terror, the global financial crisis, and the Covid-19 pandemic, as well as the recently announced era of global boiling, there is something unbelievable about the relatively happy and optimistic ethos of the 1990s, to say nothing of the utopianism of *Next Generation*. The writers of *Picard* chose to make that world believable for contemporary stories by infecting it with the same cynicism and corruption we know from our own daily experience. The writers of *Lower Decks* took the more unexpected, yet somehow more profound, move of transposing us into this world and writing our attitude of bemused disbelief directly into the dialogue. This approach may not make it any more believable, but it treats the material seriously by imagining *Star Trek*'s world as a truly different world—and one that would be a joy to inhabit, even as a lower decker on a no-name ship.

It is not all joy, of course. Each season does have a slow build to a crisis of some kind, in which our lovable heroes experience real pain and loss—pain and loss that is more meaningful and real in this cartoon than in many of the all-too-serious live-action installments simply because it is fully grounded in the characters' experiences and hopes. For instance, the season 1 finale, "No Small Parts" (LDS 1.10), includes the destruction of a ship and the loss of all hands—something that happens almost routinely in *Picard,* for instance, but that has a greater emotional impact here because we had previously spent time with the crew. Similarly, the arrest of Captain Freeman at the end of season 2 lands heavily because it comes at what should be her moment of greatest triumph: her first real first contact mission ("First First Contact," LDS 2.10).

We know that the charges are false, and Mariner and the gang spend the whole third-season premiere trying to gather proof—only to find out that the system has worked and Captain Freeman has been vindicated through official legal channels, as she herself was always confident she would be ("Grounded," LDS 3.1). Along the way, we learn how much Mariner and Freeman's relationship has healed and deepened, laying the groundwork for the genuinely gut-wrenching third season arc, where the captain transfers Mariner to an undesirable posting as punishment for a betrayal that never happened ("Trusted Sources," LDS 3.9). In reality, during an interview in which Freeman assumed her daughter was trashing the *Cerritos,* Mariner praised the crew as combining "the family you're born into" and "the family you choose"—a line that encapsulates not just the spirit of

Lower Decks but the appeal of *Star Trek* for many fans. When Freeman learns of her mistake, Mariner has already resigned from Starfleet to join a freelance archaeologist. Yet this (thankfully short-lived) career change only sets up Mariner to unexpectedly swoop in and save the day when an experimental class of automated ships meant to replace the California class predictably goes haywire ("The Stars at Night," LDS 3.10). Even more than with *Prodigy*'s Starfleet disaster, this plot is grounded less in its implications for the *Star Trek* universe than in our affection for the characters, as the ultimate result is to vindicate the value of the California class's unglamorous mission. In contrast, the revelation in the fourth season that Mariner has avoided promotion because she suffers from undiagnosed PTSD after serving in the Dominion war and does not want the power over people's lives that comes with command feels belated and even irrelevant, as viewers had by then long since accepted Mariner's stated rationale that she prefers the more freewheeling life of a lower decker.

The reader can probably tell that I have a real affection for the characters of *Lower Decks,* who feel to me, more than any other crew in the streaming era, like the family you choose. Apparently enough of my fellow fans feel the same way to save *Lower Decks* from the grim fate of *Prodigy*—though the series' fifth season has unfortunately been announced to be its last. At the same time, however, the discussion threads on r/DaystromInstitute for both series have been substantially less active than for the live-action shows, with comments most often numbering in the dozens rather than the hundreds. Judging by the Rotten Tomatoes scores for the various seasons, after a rocky response to the first season, reviews have been almost entirely positive, though fewer in number and concentrated more in genre- or *Trek*-focused sources.[16] Indeed, many of the more recent reviews focus on the latter audience and highlight the ways that *Lower Decks* contrasts with the rest of streaming *Trek*. A review by Zack Handlen in the A.V. Club captures this dynamic well:

Going by volume, it's a good time to be a *Star Trek* fan. . . . But for all of Paramount's continued efforts to build their own *Star Wars/* MCU-type juggernaut, it's hard not to feel that a certain old magic has been lost. *Discovery,* which started as a prequel, has abandoned the familiar for a far-flung future-version of the *Trek*-verse that leans heavily into modern TV trends, and *Picard,* ostensibly a nostalgia trip, bungled its attempts at both revisionism *and* new world-building. Sometimes, all you really want out of a *Trek* show is something that feels like a rerun you haven't watched yet, and *Star Trek: Lower Decks* serves this need almost perfectly.[17]

Reviewer Ryan Britt strikes a similar note, declaring *Lower Decks* season 3 the best *Star Trek* outing of the year, and drawing a striking analogy: "Imagine if someone said *Austin Powers* was one of the best James Bond movies and, somehow, James Bond fans everywhere almost unanimously agreed."[18] In reality, this analogy is not at all farfetched, because *Star Trek* fans have long embraced parody—as long as it is grounded in affection. Hence the *Trek* send-up *Galaxy Quest* (1999) is frequently and unironically listed among the greatest *Star Trek* films of all time, in large part because in its climactic moments, it shows how profoundly meaningful a seemingly absurd science fiction scenario can be. In much the same way, *Lower Decks* has won over the most demanding fan base on earth—and more than earned its right to poke fun at franchise lore and tropes—simply by being demonstrably excited to be doing *Star Trek* in a way that almost no *Star Trek* production of the twenty-first century has been.

THE IMPOSSIBLE PREQUEL

As I noted in chapter 4, the inclusion of legacy characters like Captain Pike (Anson Mount), Spock (Ethan Peck), and Number One (Rebecca Romijn) and a revamped version of the original USS *Enterprise* in *Discovery* season 2 prompted a fan campaign that pushed the studio to produce *Strange New Worlds*. In many ways, this development was unexpected: fans had consistently reacted negatively to prequel concepts ever since the first failed attempt with *Enterprise*. As we have seen, even *Discovery* prompted the same response, which surely contributed to the decision to launch the ship and its crew into the distant future (while permanently sealing all records relating to its misadventures). Yet suddenly fans were actively clamoring for a prequel series—and one that touched the third rail of fans' literalism about *Original Series* visuals.

Even more paradoxically, *Strange New Worlds*, which on the face of it consists of nothing but the most flagrant fan service imaginable, has been the most critically successful recent *Trek* series in mainstream publications. In a segment from NPR's *All Things Considered,* Eric Deggans declares, "*Strange New Worlds* is packed with the kind of grand, episodic science fiction adventure that was once the bedrock of great TV. And its glorious return [in season 2] is most welcome."[19] Adrienne Westenfeld, writing in *Esquire,* declares *Strange New Worlds* to be a breath of fresh air, not only from previous outings but from the broader trend that she calls "Marvelitis: the sky is always falling, the fate of the galaxy is always at stake, the spacetime continuum is always in danger of splintering apart." In such a grim environment, "what elevates *Strange New Worlds* from other streaming sci-fi is its insistence on sweetness and silliness."[20] After describing the series' extensive fan service in his *Variety* review, Zack Handlen asks what the show's mandate is: "*Trek* has done prequel series before, but both *Enterprise* and *Discovery* at least tried to find new angles on the material, with varying degrees of success. *Strange New Worlds* is telling the story of a captain whose most important action was sitting in a chair before someone else used it. Where's the novelty? What's the point?" He infers, approvingly, that the show's implicit answer is: "Who cares? ... *Strange New Worlds* is content to fall back on the basics: a likable cast traveling the galaxy, having wacky sci-fi adventures, and generally having a hell of a good time."[21]

From the perspective of the franchise's strategy throughout the twenty-first century, *Strange New Worlds* should not be possible. As we have seen, the people in charge of *Star Trek* have spent two decades treating its intellectual property not as the foundation of one of the most beloved and enduring entertainment franchises in human history but as an obvious failure that is in need of radical re-imagining. Further, they have regarded the franchise's fans as some combination of annoyance and cash cow, whose obsessiveness can underwrite the revenue model while their desires and complaints not only can but *must* be thwarted in order to reach broader audiences. A prequel that fans love, which is also popular with mainstream audiences precisely because it is not embarrassed to follow the classic *Star Trek* formula, is a direct refutation of this simplistic thesis, which has guided the repeated failed attempts to relaunch the franchise ever since *Enterprise*.

This is not to say that *Star Trek* could have simply skipped straight to *Strange New Worlds* in 2001. It likely required something like the combination of *Enterprise*'s season 4 fan service, the Abrams films, and the first two seasons of *Discovery* to accustom audiences to the idea that *The Original Series* would once again be the franchise's center of gravity after twenty-one seasons in the *Next Generation* era. In addition, the simple fact that so much time has passed without a straightforward return to *Star Trek*'s classic episodic feel has allowed demand to build. The irony, though, is that perhaps the biggest factor that has made audiences realize how much they miss the familiar *Star Trek* formula has been *Star Trek* itself.

Set before the events of a series that aired nearly sixty years ago, it would be easy for *Strange New Worlds* to feel old-fashioned or anachronistic. The show avoids this not only through its stylish reimagining of the *Enterprise* and its distinctive primary color uniforms, but above all by focusing on a younger cast. While both Captain Pike and Number One (whose name is here revealed to be Una Chin-Riley) are older, most of the rest of the cast are in their twenties and thirties, and in the in-universe world, they are mainly portrayed as being early in their careers. As a college professor, I recognize their aspirations and insecurities as similar to my students', making the general atmosphere some combination of *Star Trek: The College Years* and a workplace drama centered on young adults. The use of a greater number of legacy characters than one might have expected—including Nyota Uhura (Celia Rose Gooding), Nurse Chapel (Jess Bush), and even Lieutenant James T. Kirk (Paul Wesley), whose characterization as a charismatic and ambitious nerd seems like a direct rebuke to Chris Pine's version—actually serves to emphasize the youthful feel of the show. These are not yet the seasoned officers we know from *The Original Series,* but instead earnest, driven young people struggling to find themselves. Uhura's first major arc, for instance, consists in deciding whether the career she has worked so hard to attain is really what she wants after all. The audience of course knows that she will ultimately choose Starfleet, but that does not make her questioning less meaningful.

As this example shows, the prequel concept does constrain storytelling choices to some extent—a dilemma that the show writes directly into the story itself with Captain Pike's knowledge of his own grisly fate, which underwrites his main story arc in the first season. That plot reaches its climax when Pike, while accepting of his own destiny, considers warning one of the other victims of the accident that will render him severely disabled ("A Quality of Mercy," SNW 1.10). He is visited by a future version of himself, suitably garbed in an updated version of the uniforms seen in the original-cast films, who gives him a vision of a battle in which Pike's conciliatory disposition leads to a destructive war with the Romulans. Established fans will immediately recognize the scenario as an alternate version of "Balance of Terror" (TOS 1.14), in which Kirk acted decisively to destroy a Romulan ship that had crossed the Neutral Zone into Federation space. Here, Pike leads a small fleet that includes a ship commanded by Kirk, whose unheeded but retrospectively correct strategic advice gives Pike the chance to see that his younger counterpart should indeed be in the command chair in that moment—just as Pike, alas, must be consigned to his strange motorized wheelchair with its beep-based communication system. After this episode, which arguably takes the idea of Pike's knowledge of his own future as far as it can go, the writers treat the captain's inner conflict as definitively resolved. (And as fans know from "The Menagerie" [TOS 1.11–12], the arc is not as grim as it seems, because Spock will ultimately return Pike to Talos IV, the setting of "The Cage," so that his former captain can live a full life with the lovely Vina in the Talosians' hyperrealistic fantasy realm.)

If Pike's arc emphasizes the inescapable weight of the franchise's future history, their use of other legacy characters demonstrates a much more flexible and creative approach to canon. The best example is the romantic tension between Spock and Nurse Chapel, which is unexpected from the perspective of *The Original Series*. At the same time, it undeniably draws on several elements of established lore. We know that Nurse Chapel has a crush on Spock during *The Original Series,* because she blurts it out under the influence of a bizarre anomaly in "The Naked Time" (TOS 1.4). We also know that Spock has a troubled relationship with his Vulcan fiancée, T'Pring, who ultimately rejects him in an exceptionally cruel way in "Amok Time" (TOS 2.1). Finally, and most fatefully, in footage from "The Cage" that was reused in "The Menagerie," Spock unexpectedly breaks with his purely logical disposition and *smiles*. From an out-of-universe perspective, we know that this discrepancy arose because Spock was effectively a different character in the first, rejected pilot. Yet the writers turn his incongruous smile into usable history by giving us a Spock who is struggling with his split human and Vulcan identities and is not sure how or even whether to control his emotions, creating a situation where Spock unexpectedly emerges as a primary source of comic relief. The main source of emotional tension is his fraught relationship with T'Pring (Gia Sandhu), which is portrayed as much closer and more active than the viewer of "Amok Time" would have assumed, and which is challenged by his growing affection for Nurse Chapel. The basic situation is a common experience for young adults, as when one partner goes away to college intending to maintain a relationship back home, only to meet someone new. The writers find ways to keep it dynamic and interesting. Most recently as of this writing, for instance, T'Pring has found out about Spock's long-simmering crush and suggests some time apart, only for Nurse Chapel to accept a prestigious fellowship without thinking about her relationship with Spock, or even telling him ("Subspace Rhapsody," SNW 2.9). Overall, the plotline not only enriches Spock's background in unexpected ways but provides further development for two female characters that *The Original Series* largely neglected.

More important than its return to the familiar characters, however, is *Strange New World*'s return to the episodic format of *The Original Series*. Every episode's A plot focuses on a clear political or (more often) ethical dilemma, which is resolved in the course of that episode. That alone feels revolutionary in an era of heavily serialized streaming shows that presume to be ten-hour movies. The B plots typically establish longer-running plot threads, but the show is at such pains to distinguish itself from contemporary *Trek*'s serialized format that the only episodes that follow directly on each other are the season premieres' resolutions of the previous seasons' cliffhangers. Many of these plots are riffs on familiar scenarios, as in the first episode, which initially presents a first contact scenario from the aliens' perspective ("Strange New Worlds," SNW 1.1), or another early episode where the crew is afflicted with a condition that makes them addicted to light ("Ghosts of Illyria," SNW 1.3). For me, the latter episode cemented *Strange New Worlds'* status as an *Original Series* homage, especially a memorable scene in which the camera pans over the crew members luxuriating in bright light—exactly the kind of thing the original writers would have done. Many episodes also echo *The Original Series'* experimentation with different genres and settings, often directly imitating well-known science fiction or fantasy concepts. For instance, "Space Amok" (SNW 1.5), in which Spock and T'Pring swap bodies, is a clear riff on *Freaky Friday* (1976); "Lift Us Where Suffering Cannot Reach" (SNW 1.6) is a variation on Ursula K. Le Guin's "Those Who Walk Away from Omelas"; "All Those Who Wander" (SNW 1.9), with its battle against fierce Gorn hatchlings, feels very much like the film *Alien* (1979); and, perhaps most incongruously, "Subspace Rhapsody" (SNW 2.9) imitates the famous *Buffy the Vampire Slayer* (1997–2003) episode "Once More with Feeling" (2001), in which the main characters are stunned to realize that they are periodically bursting into song as though they are in a Broadway musical. In an indirect sign of the show's popularity, the soundtrack to the episode was released to music streaming services as an album, and as of the time of this writing, all of the songs have hundreds of thousands of listens on Spotify, and the first original song has over a million.

The primary political allegory of the first two seasons centers on the Federation's ban on genetic engineering, which the writers leverage to create a civil rights issue in the supposedly utopian future. The story arc centers on Number One, who is revealed to be a member of the Illyrians, a species that practices genetic alteration to allow its members to thrive on different planets. Her heritage is exposed when she is the only crew member unaffected by the aforementioned light addiction, which was caused by Illyrian genetic engineering gone haywire. Captain Pike agrees to conceal her identity, which would result in her expulsion from Starfleet, but it is eventually discovered, and the first season ends with a cliffhanger when she is arrested ("A Quality of Mercy," SNW 1.10). One of the handful of tie-in comic miniseries directly follows up on this cliffhanger. They try to find ways to help their jailed colleague, resulting in the stunning revelation that the Illyrians actually took up genetic engineering at the behest of ancient Vulcans who had not yet embraced logic and apparently enjoyed messing with lesser species. While this information surely seems relevant, the writers—apparently chastened by their experience of being overwritten repeatedly by every other streaming show—contrive to keep it hidden by having an Illyrian leader beg Pike not to expose their treasured cultural practice as a sign of weakness and oppression.[22] Subsequent tie-in works have imitated the more purely episodic approach of their parent show.

Early in the second season ("Ad Astra per Aspera," SNW 2.2), Number One is put on trial and reveals that she reported herself to Starfleet because she did not want to hide her real self any longer. Fans know that the trial cannot end with the renunciation of the ban, which remains in place in all "future" shows. Instead, her lawyer (Yetide Badaki)—a fellow Illyrian and former friend who resents Number One's ability to pass in mainstream Federation society but nonetheless agrees to represent her—engineers a solution where Number One's revelation of her identity to Captain Pike amounts to a request for political asylum. As it turns out, the genetic engineering ban led to the often violent persecution of Illyrians by non-engineered Federation citizens, forcing them underground, and in her impassioned (and lengthy) arguments, Number One's lawyer draws implicit analogies to Black people, trans people, and even (by characterizing the genetic manipulations as cultural rituals) Jewish people. I agree with the NPR reviewer that the episode is "a little ham-handed and obvious."[23] The overabundance of symbolism gilds the lily, and although the exclusion of people who are genetically altered at birth does seem unfair, it is more than a little incongruous to propose that the *Star Trek* universe's worst form of discrimination is against people who practice eugenics. In a world where people argue that the removal of white nationalist hate speech from social media platforms is a major human rights violation, this allegory is perhaps ill-judged.

Much more successful is "Under the Cloak of War" (SNW 2.8), which focuses on the war trauma of Nurse Chapel and the chief medical officer, Joseph M'Benga (Babs Olusanmokun), who served together in a medical camp reminiscent of the setting of *M*A*S*H* (1972–83) during *Discovery*'s Klingon war. In this episode, we meet Ambassador Dak'Rah (Robert Wisdom), a Klingon defector whose visit to the *Enterprise* brings back unwelcome old memories, as he was a brutal commander who led attacks on the world where Chapel and M'Benga served. Over the course of a well-crafted and intricate plot, it is gradually revealed that Dak'Rah, who trades on his reputation for murdering his own Klingon officers for poor performance, had actually fled in cowardice and dishonor when M'Benga was sent on one last mission to decapitate Dak'Rah's command staff. Using the same knife that Dak'Rah claimed he used to murder his officers— killings that M'Benga himself had actually carried out—M'Benga ultimately kills Dak'Rah while making it look like self-defense. The moment is tense in a way that screen writing seldom is. For a moment, it could seem that M'Benga is merely going to symbolically kill the ambassador by revealing his lie and destroying his reputation. Adding to the tension is the fact that the two are alone in sick bay, meaning someone could easily walk in and interrupt. We know that M'Benga himself cannot die, since he later appears in two *Original Series* episodes ("A Private Little War," TOS 2.19, and "That Which Survives," TOS 3.17), but surely no one is thinking of that kind of trivia during such an engrossing scene.

When confronted by Pike, who suspects things are not quite what they seem, M'Benga is cagey but unrepentant, saying that he is glad Dak'Rah is dead. It is perhaps the most convincing portrayal in *Star Trek* history of the trauma and profound moral damage of war. Indeed, it arguably captures genuine moral ambiguity better than fan-favorite episode "In the Pale Moonlight" (DS9 6.19), in which Captain Sisko accepts complicity in the murder of an innocent Romulan ambassador in order to bring his people into the Dominion war on the Federation's side. The *Strange New Worlds* story is much simpler and more direct than Sisko's convoluted scheme, and the transformation of the normally affable M'Benga into a killer is much more chilling. Like *Discovery* season 1, the episode raises the question of whether some people really are irredeemable enemies while addressing the moral compromises required to respond to them, but it does it more elegantly, in part simply because it is compressed into a single episode. There could be no better proof that *Star Trek* can continue to break new ground and take bold risks precisely by staying within its familiar episodic format. The episode's gesture of pushing the series in such a dark and serious direction is all the more striking for being sandwiched in between two of the most lighthearted episodes of *Strange New Worlds:* the musical "Subspace Rhapsody" and the *Lower Decks* crossover "Those Old Scientists" (SNW 2.7)—a sequence that renders the range and ambition of the series unmistakable.

TIME-TRAVEL TRIBUTES

From a purely artistic perspective, then, I would count "Under the Cloak of War" as the best single episode of the late *Star Trek* era— even above the apparent fan favorite, *Discovery*'s time-loop outing in "Magic to Make the Sanest Man Go Mad" (DIS 1.7). Part of what makes it work so well is how self-contained it is. Though it draws on *Discovery*'s Klingon war arc, the viewer does not need that background—or really any background—to understand the basic dynamics at play. Naturally, the writers do not always strike such a perfect

FIGURE 7. (a) *The* Strange New Worlds *crew hosts a tense dinner with the Klingon ambassador, Dak'Rah ("Under the Cloak of War," SNW 2.8).* (b) *The* Strange New Worlds *crew involuntarily bursts into song ("Subspace Rhapsody," SNW 2.9).*

balance. In particular, problems seem to arise on the few occasions when they foreground the show's relationship to canon. "A Quality of Mercy" manages to extract a compelling tale of military strategy from its questionable premise of convincing Captain Pike that he cannot evade the fate set for his character in 1967. There are fewer redeeming qualities in "Tomorrow and Tomorrow and Tomorrow" (SNW 2.3), a time-travel episode featuring new character La'an

Noonien-Singh (Christina Chong), on whom the writers have in-explicably piled tragedy after tragedy. The sole survivor of a Gorn attack that resulted in her family and fellow colonists being left for dead as food for hungry alien hatchlings, she also carries the burden of having the genocidal dictator Khan Noonien-Singh as a distant ancestor. (Apparently the technology of changing one's name was lost in the post–World War III nuclear apocalypse.)

"Tomorrow and Tomorrow and Tomorrow" sees poor La'an first pulled into an alternate timeline where Earth never joined the Fed-eration but Kirk is nonetheless captain of the *Enterprise*. The two are then shifted back in time, where they enjoy a budding romance as they attempt to undo whatever has changed the timeline. Alter-nate Kirk is ultimately murdered by a Romulan temporal agent, whom La'an must stop by preventing her from killing her evil great-great-great-great- . . . grandfather Khan as a child. La'an's motivation here is unclear. She knows she is permitting genocide, and a survivor of the Klingon war and the depredations of the Gorn would hardly suspect that she is living in the best of all possible timelines. The episode is a clear homage to the classic time-travel episode "City on the Edge of Forever" (TOS 1.28), in which Kirk must refrain from saving the life of a charismatic peace activist with whom he has fallen in love so that she does not convince President Roosevelt to sit out World War II. However, refraining from murdering a pro-verbial baby Hitler does not hold the same emotional resonance or moral ambiguity. In the end, it feels like a nihilistic assertion that *Star Trek*'s history must happen, come what may. Yet even that mes-sage is undercut by the fact that Khan is a small child in 2023, when *Picard* season 2 had presented the Khan project as a thing of the past in 2024—an apparently intentional contradiction that the writ-ers explain as a by-product of the constant temporal meddling to which this decisive historical personage is subject. This rare attempt at larger-scale world-building on the part of the *Strange New Worlds* writing staff serves only to distract the audience from the intended emotional stakes of the episode.

Compared to most *Star Trek* shows, *Strange New Worlds* is remarkably sparing in its use of time travel. The only remaining instance is in the aforementioned crossover with *Lower Decks,* which opens with Mariner, Boimler, Tendi, and Rutherford (in their customary animated forms) assigned to investigate a mysterious portal that unexpectedly sucks Boimler into the time period of "Those Old Scientists" (SNW 2.7). Now in live-action format, Boimler spends the first half of the episode alternately geeking out and chiding himself for potentially corrupting the timeline as Pike's crew seeks a way to send him back to his proper time. When the moment comes, it turns out that the *Cerritos* crew has simultaneously been working on a similar project, leading to a misfire that brings Mariner (also in live-action form) back in time as well.

For me as a fan, the appearance of Mariner was a revealing moment. She is the true star of *Lower Decks,* lending the show much of its energy and setting the tone, and I was initially sad when the comparatively boring Boimler was the only one pulled into the future. When Mariner came out of the portal, I was more excited than I had been to see any legacy character in the streaming era—more excited than when Michael Burnham finally found Spock in *Discovery* season 2, more excited than when Riker and Troi unexpectedly showed up in *Picard* season 1, even more excited (if one could believe it) than when we finally saw the original bridge of the *Enterprise*-D in all its carpeted glory in the penultimate episode of *Picard* season 3. All the tributes in the world mean nothing if *Star Trek* cannot create new characters viewers are genuinely excited to see.

Though "Those Old Scientists" is a *Strange New Worlds* episode, it is told from the perspective of the *Lower Decks* characters, who are starstruck to meet such legendary figures but at the same time surprised that they have not yet grown into what they will become.

Most touching, perhaps, is Boimler's and Mariner's reaction to Number One—whenever they see her, they become uncharacteristically tongue-tied and seem almost scared. The viewer worries that it is because something tragic befalls her, as does Number One herself, but they ultimately reveal that she is quite literally the poster child for Starfleet, as her image adorns many recruitment materials. Over time, the *Enterprise* crew grows irritated at Boimler and Mariner's fawning attitude, until they realize that it would be like if they met Archer and the crew of the *Enterprise* NX-01. The *Strange New World* crew start tittering with excitement at the prospect of meeting their heroes, like Travis Mayweather and Hoshi Sato—a touching acknowledgment of two neglected characters. Indeed, the NX-01 turns out to directly save the day and allow Boimler and Mariner to go home, because we learn that a piece of the hull from the previous vessel to bear a given name is always integrated into the new ship, and the original *Enterprise*'s hull contained a rare alloy necessary to make the portal work.

In those few moments, the whole main stretch of *Star Trek* history from *Enterprise* to *Next Generation*—including *Discovery* too, because the current versions of Pike and Spock were introduced there—comes together in a moment of sincere tribute. In a sense, this moment marks the end of late *Star Trek*'s post-*Enterprise* era, simply because *Enterprise*'s place in the franchise is finally taken for granted, rather than deployed as part of a proxy battle over the shape of *Star Trek* canon. *Discovery* used *Enterprise* as leverage to pick a fight with the fans about *Original Series* literalism; *Star Trek Beyond* refers to *Enterprise* in an intentionally scrambled way to assert its independence; and *Picard* season 3 proclaimed that the commemoration of the events of *Enterprise* can only result in disaster. In contrast, this crossover between *Strange New Worlds* and *Lower Decks* makes a gesture of straightforward inclusion to normalize *Enterprise*'s status at last. This moment encapsulates *Lower*

Decks' approach to canon, implicitly raising a fan service question (Why doesn't anyone in the later *Star Trek* shows seem to know or care about the events of *Enterprise?*) and answering it with some self-aware world-building (they do—look at the way crews from the *Original Series* and *Next Generation* eras can bond over their adventures!). At the same time, it fits well with the easy and un-selfconscious way that *Strange New Worlds* generally inhabits *Star Trek* canon. In contrast to their recent predecessors, neither show is anxious to stake out a space for its creative freedom because each has hit on a distinctive blend of fan service and world-building that frees them to tell new and compelling stories with fresh (or freshly reimagined) characters—which is ultimately the only creative freedom that has any lasting value.

CONCLUSION

FROM MYTH TO FRANCHISE

I n the preceding pages, I have had many occasions to cite Ina Rae Hark's article "Franchise Fatigue?," which remains one of the most perceptive studies of the interplay of the *Star Trek* franchise's commercial and creative failures. Writing at the beginning of the long fallow period between the cancellation of *Enterprise* and the premiere of *Discovery,* Hark argues that "*Enterprise* failed not because of franchise fatigue—something that can be cured by taking a few years off before launching another series—but by franchise obsolescence."[1] This obsolescence was both creative and commercial. On the one hand, *Star Trek* remained stuck in the rut of one particular form of storytelling while other shows pushed the space opera concept in new and unexpected directions. On the other hand, after seizing the unique opportunity of a direct-to-syndication format, *Star Trek*'s owners had actually moved backward by attempting to use the franchise as an anchor for an ill-conceived attempt to launch their own broadcast network, thereby artificially limiting their reach even as the growth of cable TV was undercutting the broadcast market as a whole.

As I conclude my argument, *Star Trek* is not in such dire straits, because at least *Strange New Worlds* seems to have a bright future. Yet the franchise is at a turning point, as the tentpole series *Discovery* and *Picard* have come to an end and the studio has begun to make strange and erratic decisions (most notably the abrupt cancellation of *Prodigy* and the later decision to spin it off to another streaming service). What once seemed like an innovative and forward-thinking decision—to opt for a streaming model rather than traditional broadcast—now appears questionable amid industry-wide concerns about the profit model for streaming TV, as well as the fairness and sustainability of the changes it has wrought for the livelihoods of actors and writers alike. The second golden age of *Star Trek*—when a Paramount+ subscriber could expect to find not only a new episode most weeks but also an unprecedented variety of styles and storytelling approaches—was, in retrospect, part of the unsustainable pandemic-era boom in streaming TV, and we cannot expect such bounty going forward. Nevertheless, it is easy to imagine *Strange New Worlds* running more or less indefinitely, occasionally supplemented by an additional series (like *Starfleet Academy*) or a direct-to-streaming movie (like the Michelle Yeoh vehicle *Section 31*). However, especially in light of the 2023 joint writers and actors strike and the ongoing drama surrounding Paramount's decision to put itself on the market for a merger or acquisition, it is possible, if unlikely, that the fifth season of *Discovery* and the second season of *Prodigy*—which as of the time of this writing are the only unaired seasons to have completed filming—will be the final seasons of streaming *Trek* for the foreseeable future.

In this fraught moment, then, it is worth returning to Hark's prescient remarks about the future of the franchise amid its apparent post-*Enterprise* ruin:

The only way to tell for certain whether the Trek paradigm has become irrevocably obsolete is for someone with fresh ideas and enthusiasm for that universe to create the best possible new series that hews to the major principles of the franchise and is realistic about matching budget and audience projections to the expectations of the network on which it is broadcast. If such a series cannot succeed, it is time to end the franchise once and for all.[2]

We know that Hark does not believe that *Enterprise* met that standard. How do the other iterations of late *Star Trek* fare? The verdict is decidedly mixed. On the artistic side, in terms of the fully canonical film and TV productions, the franchise was able to draw on talented writers and producers—among whom Simon Pegg, Bryan Fuller, Mike McMahan, and Michael Chabon stand out for the combination of creativity and outside prestige they brought to bear—who took the franchise in new directions. There have been genuine creative triumphs. At the time of its debut, *Star Trek Beyond* was as good a *Star Trek* story as we had seen on-screen in fifteen years; the first season of *Discovery* was a quantum leap in sophistication and ambition for the franchise; and many individual episodes (above all "Magic to Make the Sanest Man Go Mad," DSC 1.7, and "Under the Cloak of War," SNW 2.8) stand among the best the franchise has seen.

At the same time, there have been inexplicable failures of both concept and execution. The creative teams have more than once seemingly burned through an entire season simply to arrive at a new status quo for the story they really want to tell. Even worse, there has been an almost inexcusable lack of planning. How could an inexperienced showrunner have been allowed to start shooting a heavily serialized narrative before he knew the story he was trying to tell in *Picard* season 1? How could the writing and production team for *Discovery*—even allowing for the turmoil surrounding the showrunner role—attempt to chart out the second season's arc without making some basic decisions about what the Red Angel was going to be? Why did seemingly no one recognize that the resolution to the Burn in *Discovery* season 3 was going to feel random and unsatisfying to most viewers? Why did they waste season 5 on a plot that concludes with the admission that it never should have happened in the first place? *Discovery* seasons 1 and 4—and, for all their faults, *Picard* seasons 2 and 3—show that it is possible to chart out a cohesive season-long *Star Trek* story, making it all the more baffling that four of the eight serialized seasons thus far fell short of those basic standards.

On the positive side, one area where the late *Star Trek* era has made an undeniable advance over even the *Next Generation* golden age is in the sheer variety of approaches to *Star Trek*. Over the course of a few short years, the franchise seemed to put out something for everyone—episodic and serialized stories, live action and animated, adult and youth oriented. This range shows *Star Trek* to be a more capacious concept than many would have expected, but there have also been signs that the creative team is becoming overextended as similar ideas are reused across different shows. A malevolent AI struck in *Discovery* season 2, then again in *Picard* season 1 (which aired immediately after), and then, as if for good measure, in *Lower Decks* season 3 as well. Starfleet was nearly destroyed by a computer virus that propagated itself through a networked fleet in *Prodigy* season 1 and then again in *Picard* season 3. *Picard* season 2 explores the lore surrounding the Eugenics wars; *Strange New Worlds'* premiere episode ("Strange New Worlds," SNW 1.1), which aired on the same night as the former's finale, has Captain Pike deliver a lengthy speech about the same topic. The repetition is sometimes even more fine-grained. In *Lower Decks* season 3, Rutherford learns that his cybernetic implant has actually erased his past memories and personality, and he has to fight his past self for control of his mind; in

Picard season 3 (which aired shortly afterward), Data goes through a similar struggle with his evil brother, Lore, for control of his mind (Figure 8). Number One faces expulsion from Starfleet for her genetically engineered DNA in *Strange New Worlds;* Dal faces exclusion from Starfleet for his genetically engineered DNA in *Prodigy*. In *Picard* season 2, Seven of Nine is freed from her Borg implants and transported to a time when no one has even heard of the Borg, allowing her to envision a life where strangers no longer automatically view her with suspicion; in *Strange New Worlds* season 2, La'an Noonien-Singh is transported back in time to an era where no one has heard of her evil ancestor, allowing her to envision a life where strangers no longer, etc.

These kinds of mistakes are emphatically not signs that the writers and producers are not up to the task. I continue to hold to my rule of trusting that the creative teams for the various *Star Trek* shows are made up of talented people who are doing their best. As with the dominance of disaster themes that I noted in the introduction, I believe these slips and repetitions are a symptom of working under tremendous pressure—and the 2023 writers' strike created greater awareness of streaming services' practice of attempting to squeeze as much writing as possible out of as few full-time writers as possible.[3] From that perspective, all the questions I ask above—why the first season of *Picard* was allowed to start shooting without a fully articulated plan, or why the writers pressed forward with *Discovery* season 2 despite not knowing what they were going to put in their mystery box or why they went forward with such a poor resolution to the Burn in season 3—have an obvious answer: they were not given enough time to develop their ideas properly. In principle, the streaming format, which is not beholden to the traditional release schedule of broadcast networks, could have allowed the studio to wait until they had the best possible product to present. In practice, the scheme to milk *Star Trek* completists (like myself) for

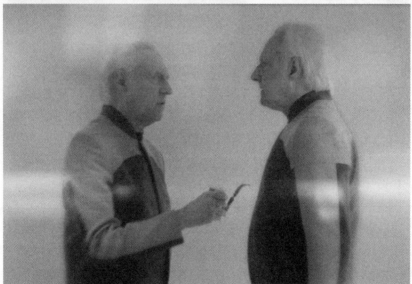

FIGURE 8. (a) *Ensign Rutherford confronts his former self in the virtual space of his brain implant ("Reflections," LDS 3.5). (b) Data confronts his evil brother, Lore, in the virtual space of their now-shared mind ("Surrender," PIC 3.8).*

year-round subscription fees drove them to do what Hark accused Rick Berman of doing in the waning years of the *Next Generation* era: "churn[ing] out mediocre product on which to slap the Trek brand for the sake of profit."[4]

The fact that so much of what has been churned out has nonetheless been so good is a testament to the inherent fruitfulness of the *Star Trek* concept and to the kind of dedicated and talented writers, producers, and performers the franchise attracts. Yet it is no accident, I think, that it is precisely in the highest-profile shows (*Discovery* and *Picard*) that the biggest problems have arisen, nor that arguably the most sustained long-term creative successes in the late *Star Trek* era were seen in the tie-in novels and comics rather than the canonical films and shows. A similar pattern has repeated itself throughout the franchise's history. During both major periods when the franchise was off the air—the 1970s and early '80s as well as the 2000s and 2010s—it reached new creative heights in the novels, which the studio treated with benign neglect. The most beloved *Star Trek* film, *The Wrath of Khan* (1982), was only given the initial go-ahead because it could be done cheaply. Even during the *Next Generation* period, *Deep Space Nine* was able to push *Trek* in new and unexpected directions because it was largely ignored by the corporate higher-ups.[5]

In contrast, when the corporate side becomes too entangled in the production process, things begin to fall apart. As we have seen, Berman and Braga were hamstrung above all by the demand to take a *second* stab at creating a *Star Trek* show that could support an entire new broadcast network. For all that he is demonized by fans, J. J. Abrams saw what would be necessary to make the Kelvin Timeline a substantial contribution to the franchise, namely a television show, but he was thwarted by corporate infighting between two competing intellectual property owners. Alex Kurtzman, in his role as streaming czar, seems genuinely open to a range of creative ideas in a way that previous generations of *Star Trek* producers have not, but the pressure he has been put under to produce wall-to-wall content has led to overextension of the franchise, and almost certainly to over-work on the part of the creative staff. And the poor novelverse was forced to write itself out of existence for the sake of a *Next Generation* sequel that turned out to be much less interesting than almost any of the stories the various authors had created.

Admittedly, this list of corporate restraints on storytelling mixes two different phenomena. What held back Berman, Braga, and Abrams in my account were highly idiosyncratic situations with clear culprits, while the pressure to produce ever more content and the tendency to periodically invalidate tie-in products are both more or less inherent to existing as a franchise. Both of the latter apply equally to Disney-era *Star Wars,* for instance, which de-canonized its vast catalog of tie-in novels to make room for the new trilogy that began with *The Force Awakens* (2015), and which has generated an equally relentless stream of new TV series on Disney+. In other words, the core problem is inherent to the very existence of an on-going shared universe in which an ever-growing body of fictional events is treated as binding canon for all future storytelling.

It is worth taking a step back and asking where this notion of a fictional canon with an internally consistent continuity came from. It is not intrinsic to the act of telling multiple stories with the same characters, even in a commercial context. There are any number of recurring characters whose individual adventures are more or less completely episodic and self-contained. This is often the case for fictional detectives. For instance, there is no *Columbo* (1968–2003) universe; the famously disheveled detective simply shows up in one murder investigation after another. Certain features recur—the dis-tinctive green cigars, the rumpled raincoat, the never-seen wife—but those are not binding canon in the same sense as the revelation that he met his wife on a certain date and therefore can never mention witnessing a historical event with his wife before that date. Even in ongoing shows that develop overarching soap opera–like narratives, like *Friends* (1994–2004), the continuity of Ross and Rachel's on-again–off-again relationship does not necessarily entail strict consistency when speaking about the various characters' backstories.

Practices become even looser when we look to precapitalist modes of storytelling. As a teacher in a Great Books program, I have experience teaching multiple versions of the same mythical story or character, and it is striking how readily students reach for franchise-style interpretations. For example, recently I taught *Gilgamesh* as well as a collection of myths about the goddess known variously as Inanna or Ishtar. Both characters appear in each other's stories, with at times contradictory traits. My students immediately began generating fan theories to explain away the discrepancies, as though the earliest known storytellers were already operating with the notion of a fictional canon. In reality, of course, they were simply different stories told by different authors for different purposes, with no necessary relationship beyond the reuse of familiar characters—a mode of storytelling that has been the norm for most of human history but that my students needed to be taught to recognize.

Along similar lines, I once started a social media thread jokingly asking whether Virgil's *Aeneid* is canon for the Homer Extended Universe. Amid many humorous responses, I received a serious answer: it does not matter. Outside of a capitalist context, the stories that are binding for a given author are those they choose to take up and use, and there are no limits to what they can do with them. Hence, Aeschylus's *Oresteia* trilogy can take up Homer's epic poems as pointing toward the foundation of the unique form of democratic governance found in Athens, a city that is hardly mentioned in the *Iliad* or *Odyssey*. For his part, Virgil can craft a sequel to Homer's epics that prophesizes the foundation of the Roman Empire while casting the Greek heroes of the earlier poems as aggressors and villains. Subsequently, Dante can incorporate both Homer and Virgil into a story centered on a religion (Christianity) that did not exist at the time that the latter were writing.

Storytelling practices more closely align with franchise norms in religious contexts, from which the idea of a binding canon is drawn.[6] However, even in the most canonical canon of them all, the Bible, there are multiple contradictory versions of the same stories, as well as passages that represent minority viewpoints (such as Ruth or Jonah, whose focus on the piety of non-Israelites dissents from the exclusivism of most other scriptures, or Job, who radically questions the justice of God). In that context especially, we find familiar franchise techniques like prequels or retcons. Perhaps most audaciously, the Gospel of John serves as a prequel to the Book of Genesis itself, revealing that the spiritual entity that would become incarnate as Jesus Christ (the Word) was eternally present with God and aided him in his act of creation. Many other passages in the New Testament (which recasts the Jewish Bible as the Old Testament, much as *Next Generation*'s success led to the retronym *The Original Series*) represent attempts to retrospectively change the meaning of earlier scriptural passages by interpreting them as symbolic anticipations of events in Christ's life. From this perspective, the Qur'an would represent a full reboot, which self-consciously attempts to eliminate all the accrued inconsistencies in the previous canon.

Using franchise-style terminology to discuss classic texts, much less sacred ones, may seem disrespectful. My goal, however, is not to diminish the earlier texts but rather to point out that storytelling techniques that are now regarded as proverbially inferior and even illegitimate are not only commonplace but actually foundational for many of the greatest works of world literature. Today it is taken for granted that reusing familiar characters and storyworlds is a recipe for redundancy and poor quality, but many of the most beloved works of all time are variations on existing stories. The explanation cannot be that the characters and storyworlds they were drawing on were somehow intrinsically better. As someone who has closely studied both, there is no greater inherent depth to Odysseus than to Captain Kirk, for instance, or to Achilles than to Batman. The quality of the stories we tell about those familiar characters depends on the ambition and talent of the authors taking them up, and for much of human history, quality largely determined which iterations of those stories would become durable points of reference for later authors.

What has changed in contemporary franchise culture is that the natural process of artistic evolution has been preempted by commercial concerns, foremost among them the existence of a binding fictional canon, usually defined as including every story told in a certain format (usually television or film, as for the *Star Trek* and *Star Wars* canons). This convention, which is so familiar to us today that my students instinctively use it as a framework for understanding ancient texts, is ultimately a marketing technique to compel fans to consume every new installment because it may become relevant for still later installments. The idea of large-scale continuity among different stories found its most natural home in genres—such as superhero comic books, science fiction, and fantasy—with the greatest emphasis on world-building. Stories were increasingly set up to reward fans' command of past stories, which effectively trained fans to read with an eye for consistency and modeled ways of resolving the inevitable inconsistencies that fans could then generate in their own speculative discourse among themselves.

There is an odd satisfaction that comes from generating these types of fan theories—an activity I have indulged in with sufficient vigor to be promoted to the rank of commander on r/DaystromInstitute, which prides itself on being the most intellectually rigorous fan community in existence—but it also prompts a kind of deformation of the intellect. Dedicated fan theorists run the risk of actively unlearning how to understand stories on their own terms, allowing the search for increasingly contrived connections between disparate episodes to override the inherent logic of the plots themselves. Perhaps the most striking example of this phenomenon is the tendency to claim that *every* time-travel story in *Star Trek* creates a forking timeline, even though the logic of essentially every time-travel story before the creation of the Kelvin Timeline depends on the idea that our heroes have endangered their own future through their interventions. The perceived benefit is that shattering the franchise's fictional timeline into dozens of forks provides a ready method of explaining away inconsistencies, especially when it comes to visuals. In other words, the drama and even meaning of some of the most beloved *Star Trek* installments of all time (such as "City on the Edge of Forever," TOS 1.28, "Past Tense," DS9 3.11–12, and *First Contact,* to name only a few) is sacrificed to the demand for a superficial consistency, thus ultimately destroying the unified fictional history that the concept of canon was originally meant to guarantee.

This mutually reinforcing dynamic between the promise of a consistent fictional canon and the development of a fan culture centered on quasi-scholarly knowledge of that canon would ultimately lead to any number of absurdities. Here I am thinking of the widespread fan shibboleths that changes in Klingon makeup must have an in-story explanation and that starship technology took an abrupt downward turn in the mid-2360s and that a vast global conflict centered on eugenics took place in the 1990s—but we could also point toward such excesses as the production of an entire blockbuster movie whose only purpose is to establish that past canon is no longer binding, or the development of multiple story arcs that aim alternately to explain or deny the in-universe relevance of the makeup budget of *The Original Series,* which reinforce the worst tendencies of fan culture. The specific approach to canon inculcated among the fans by the intellectual property owners also means that past installments can never be forgotten about or dismissed, no matter how unsuccessful they are. The death of Data in *Nemesis,* for instance, cannot be simply brushed off in a later installment (perhaps with a quick nod to the fact that he was resurrected after uploading his memories to B4). Instead, entire television seasons must be dedicated to exploring the full implications of a plot development that fans almost universally rejected as ill-conceived and unjustified. No bit of established lore can be left behind, no matter how reviled. Even *The Final Frontier* (1989)—which Gene Roddenberry himself regarded as so bad that it could not be treated as canon, and which was such a commercial and critical failure that it threatened to derail the franchise as a whole— has found an unexpected relevance for contemporary *Star Trek,* as *Strange New Worlds* centered one plot on Sybok, the previously unmentioned brother introduced in the widely panned film ("The Serene Squall," SNW 1.7).

Here fan culture and commercial imperatives rhyme. Just as the fans' investment of time in even the worst *Star Trek* outings must be rewarded, so too must the intellectual property owners' investment of money in acquiring them. The existence of the obsessive fan base as the most reliable revenue stream means that every attempt to win over new audiences, or simply to approach the material in a more creative and interesting way, must be followed by subsequent installments explicitly undoing the violation of fan expectations. We have seen this again and again. To highlight only the most egregious examples, *Enterprise*'s final season amounted to an ongoing apology for all the unexpected world-building the previous seasons had introduced, just as the second seasons of both *Discovery* and *Picard* served primarily to neutralize the implications of the first. The narrow-mindedness of fans is usually blamed for this tendency to privilege fan service over creative freedom, but their attitude is ultimately the product of the continuity-centered marketing strategy on which the franchise was founded. The same goes for the overreliance on high-stakes stories that claim to make decisive contributions to franchise world-building. As the volume of existing canon continues to increase, the perceived necessity to keep up with each new installment decreases—unless something big and unprecedented is happening.

It would be too simple, however, to say that the problem with the *Star Trek* franchise is simply the fact that it is a franchise. Many of its more specific misfortunes stem from its awkward status in the cultural landscape as at once an iconic cultural institution and a cult phenomenon. Hark speaks of "matching budget and audience projections to the expectations of the network on which it is broadcast,"[7] but the real challenge facing the franchise in recent decades has been that the intellectual property owners have consistently had unrealistic expectations that are effectively impossible for *Star Trek* to meet. They have been repeatedly tempted to overplay their hand, above all in the repeated attempts to press the franchise into service to carry an entire broadcast network and, more recently, a new streaming service. Those exaggerated financial stakes surely create a greater tendency for commercial interests to trump artistic ones. Even in the absence of direct corporate meddling in the writing or production process (likely unverifiable for recent *Trek*), the pressure to rush and overproduce is bound to hurt quality. In contrast, *Star Trek* has enjoyed its greatest artistic successes when its owners have simply left the creative staff to themselves, whether one thinks of shows that are (for whatever reason) a lower priority or of productions like novels and comics that exist outside the official canon.

Star Trek works best in the sweet spot where it is successful enough to have access to resources like high production values and full-time professional writers, which only corporate intellectual property owners can provide, without being so successful that it becomes a pawn in a misbegotten corporate scheme. From that perspective, the apparent obstacle of the sprawling fictional canon may actually be a benefit: it artificially limits the audience and keeps the franchise closer to cult status, where it will be left to its own devices. Such a steady state is difficult to attain under capitalism, especially in the more rapacious and short term–focused form it has taken in recent decades. Reliable profitability no longer suffices for an investor class privileging ever-accelerating revenue growth over long-term sustainability. I am optimistic that *Star Trek* will continue to endure in some form—after all, if its owners could not destroy it with the erratic and shortsighted decision-making they have displayed throughout the late *Star Trek* period, presumably no one can—but the franchise that has done the most to imagine a postcapitalist world ironically seems to be doomed to the familiar cycle of boom and bust. Faced with this grim reality, the franchise's creators may need to finally start thinking more seriously about the path from our neoliberal present to their postscarcity utopia, because ultimately the only way to guarantee the durability of *Star Trek*'s optimistic vision of the future will be to achieve it.

APPENDIX 1: *STAR TREK* SEASONS AND FILMS BY AIRDATE, 2001 TO PRESENT

2001
May 23: *Voyager* season 7 concludes.
September 26: *Enterprise* season 1 begins.

2002
May 22: *Enterprise* season 1 concludes.
September 18: *Enterprise* season 2 begins.
December 9: *Star Trek Nemesis* premieres.

2003
May 23: *Enterprise* season 2 concludes.
September 10: *Enterprise* season 3 begins.

2004
May 26: *Enterprise* season 3 concludes.
October 8: *Enterprise* season 4 begins.

2005
May 13: *Enterprise* season 4 concludes.

2009
May 8: *Star Trek* (2009) premieres.

2013
May 17: *Star Trek Into Darkness* premieres.

2016
July 22: *Star Trek Beyond* premieres.

2017
September 24: *Discovery* season 1 begins.

2018
February 11: *Discovery* season 1 concludes.

2019
January 17: *Discovery* season 2 begins.
April 18: *Discovery* season 2 concludes.

2020
January 23: *Picard* season 1 begins.
March 26: *Picard* season 1 concludes.
August 6: *Lower Decks* season 1 begins.
October 8: *Lower Decks* season 1 concludes.
October 15: *Discovery* season 3 begins.

2021

January 7: *Discovery* season 3 concludes.

August 12: *Lower Decks* season 2 begins.

October 14: *Lower Decks* season 2 concludes.

October 28: *Prodigy* season 1, part 1 begins.

November 18: *Discovery* season 4 begins.

2022

February 3: *Prodigy* season 1, part 1, concludes.

March 3: *Picard* season 2 begins.

March 17: *Discovery* season 4 concludes.

May 5: *Picard* season 2 concludes.

Strange New Worlds season 1 begins.

July 7: *Strange New Worlds* season 1 concludes.

August 25: *Lower Decks* season 3 begins.

October 27: *Lower Decks* season 3 concludes.

Prodigy season 1, part 2, begins.

December 29: *Prodigy* season 1, part 2, concludes.

2023

February 16: *Picard* season 3 begins.

April 20: *Picard* season 3 concludes.

June 15: *Strange New Worlds* season 2 begins.

August 10: *Strange New Worlds* season 2 concludes.

September 7: *Lower Decks* season 4 begins.

November 9: *Lower Decks* season 4 concludes.

2024

April 4: *Discovery* season 5 begins.

May 30: *Discovery* season 5 concludes.

July 1: *Prodigy* season 2 episodes are all released simultaneously on Netflix.

APPENDIX 2: KEY EVENTS
IN *STAR TREK*'S FICTIONAL HISTORY

A true timeline of *Star Trek*'s fictional history could extend for hundreds of pages, so I have focused on events that I actually discussed in this book. Dates of the series and films indicate the setting of the main action. Notable background and time-travel events are listed individually. Dates in the Kelvin Timeline are flagged as such; all others are within the Prime Timeline. All dates are taken from the Memory Alpha pages from the respective episodes, series, and films.

1957: A Vulcan survey crew is stranded on Earth and settles in the small town of Carbon Creek, Pennsylvania ("Carbon Creek," ENT 2.2).

1990s: Khan Noonien-Singh plays leading role in the Eugenics Wars ("Space Seed," TOS 1.22; *Wrath of Khan*).

2023: La'an Noonien-Singh (initially accompanied by an alternate version of James T. Kirk) travels back in time and meets Khan Noonien-Singh as a child ("Tomorrow and Tomorrow and Tomorrow," SNW 2.3).

2024: Benjamin Sisko ("Past Tense," DS9 3.11–12) and Jean-Luc Picard (PIC season 2) separately visit the dystopian past.

2063: Zefram Cochrane makes the first human warp flight, triggering First Contact with the Vulcans, aided by the time-traveling *Next Generation* crew (*First Contact*).

2151–55: Events of *Enterprise*.

2233 (Kelvin): Nero's incursion and destruction of the USS *Kelvin* (*Star Trek* 2009).

2254: Events of "The Cage" (unaired pilot featuring Captain Pike).

2256–58: Events of *Discovery* seasons 1 and 2.

2258 (Kelvin): Arrival of Prime Spock in Kelvin Timeline; destruction of Vulcan (*Star Trek* 2009).

2259 (Kelvin): Events of *Star Trek Into Darkness*.

2259–60: Events of *Strange New Worlds* seasons 1 and 2.

2263 (Kelvin): Events of *Star Trek Beyond*.

2264–70: Events of *Next Generation*.

2265–69: Events of *The Original Series*.

2266: Captain Pike's tragic accident ("The Menagerie," TOS 1.11–12; "Through the Valley of Shadows," DSC 2.12; "A Quality of Mercy," SNW 1.10).

2269–2375: Events of *Deep Space Nine*.

2270s–90s: Events of original-cast films.

2271–78: Events of *Voyager*.

2371–79: Events of *Next Generation* cast films.

2380s: Events of *Lower Decks*.

2383–85: Events of *Prodigy*.

2385: Synth attack on Mars shipyards ("The End is the Beginning," PIC 1.3); abandonment of Romulan evacuation effort, prompting Picard to resign in protest ("Remembrance," PIC 1.1).

2387: Spock and Nero pulled into Kelvin Timeline after failed attempt to halt Romulan supernova (*Star Trek* 2009); supernova destroys Romulan home world and beyond ("Remembrance," PIC 1.1).

2399–2402: Events of *Picard*.

2700s: Home time period of *Enterprise*'s Future Guy ("Broken Bow," ENT 1.1).

2800s: Home time period of *Enterprise*'s time-traveling space Nazis ("Storm Front, Pt. 1," ENT 1.26).

3000s (early to mid): Home time period of *Enterprise*'s Lieutenant Daniels ("Cold Front," ENT 1.11).

3000s (mid): Temporal Cold War breaks into outright temporal war; all time travel is banned in perpetuity after the war's conclusion ("The Hope That Is You, Pt. 1," DIS 3.1).

3069: Dilithium-powered vessels across the galaxy are simultaneously destroyed by the Burn, shattering interstellar civilization ("The Hope That Is You, Pt. 1," DIS 3.1).

3188–91: Events of *Discovery* seasons 3 through 5.

NOTES

INTRODUCTION

1. The classic statement here is of course that of Henry Jenkins, *Textual Poachers: Television Fans and Participatory Culture* (New York: Routledge, 1992).
2. Roughly speaking, we could trace this arc of criticism from Frederic Jameson, *Postmodernism, or The Cultural Logic of Late Capitalism* (Durham, N.C.: Duke University Press, 1992), to Anna Kornbluh, *Immediacy, or The Cultural Logic of Too-Late Capitalism* (New York: Verso, 2024).
3. Dan Hassler-Forest, *Science Fiction, Fantasy, and Politics: Transmedia World-building beyond Capitalism* (New York: Rowman & Littlefield, 2016), 5; emphasis in original.
4. Hassler-Forest, *Science Fiction,* 49.
5. I have explored the concept of canon in *Star Trek* and scriptural traditions elsewhere: Adam Kotsko, "The Inertia of Tradition in *Star Trek:* Case Studies in Neglected Corners of the 'Canon,'" *Science Fiction Film and Television* 9, no. 3 (2016): 347–70.
6. Peter Frase, *Four Futures: Life after Capitalism* (New York: Verso, 2016), 24.
7. Given the number of episodes that I will be citing in this work, I will adopt a streamlined citation style: the title, followed by the standard fan abbreviation of the series and the season and episode number (as established by the page for each series on the exhaustive fan wiki Memory Alpha, n.d., https://memory-alpha.fandom.com/wiki/Portal:Main). All quotations from pre-streaming series and films are taken from the widely used Chrissie's Transcripts Site, n.d., http://www.chakoteya.net/.
8. Here I draw on my own modest contributions to the genre of books with variations on the term "late capitalism" in their subtitles. See Adam Kotsko, *Why We Love Sociopaths: A Guide to Late Capitalist Television* (New York: Zero, 2012); and Adam Kotsko, *Neoliberalism's Demons: The Political Theology of Late Capital* (Stanford, Calif.: Stanford University Press, 2018).
9. Francis Fukuyama, *The End of History and the Last Man* (New York: Free Press, 1992).
10. In a strange turn of the screw, the indefinite dominance of neoliberal economic principles was eventually literalized, because, as Guynes and Canavan point out, a number of tie-in novels, written by a variety of authors, present the benighted

businessman from "The Neutral Zone" as the long-serving Federation secretary of commerce. See Sean Guynes and Gerry Canavan, "Novels," in *The Routledge Handbook of Star Trek,* edited by Leimar Garcia-Siino, Sabrina Mittermeier, and Stefan Rabitsch (New York: Routledge, 2022), 177.

11. Hassler-Forest, *Science Fiction,* 62.

12. Hassler-Forest, *Science Fiction,* 66.

13. Despite the importance of the *Star Trek Online* game to fan culture during the interregnum between *Enterprise* and *Discovery,* I feel I must unfortunately leave it aside for lack of expertise in game studies.

14. Dan Golding, *Star Wars after Lucas: A Critical Guide to the Future of the Galaxy* (Minneapolis: University of Minnesota Press), 121.

15. Hark provides arguably the most nuanced and interesting version of a narrative that can be found in many other commentators. See Ina Rae Hark, *Star Trek* (New York: Palgrave Macmillan, 2008).

16. Ina Rae Hark, "Franchise Fatigue? The Marginalization of the Television Series after *The Next Generation,*" in *The Influence of "Star Trek" on Television, Film, and Culture,* edited by Lincoln Geraghty (Jefferson, N.C.: MacFarland, 2007), 50.

17. Hark, "Franchise Fatigue," 41.

18. "Growing the Beard," TV Tropes, n.d., https://tvtropes.org/pmwiki/pmwiki .php/Main/GrowingTheBeard.

19. See Hark, "Franchise Fatigue," 43.

20. Hark, "Franchise Fatigue," 44.

21. Hark, "Franchise Fatigue," 44.

22. David K. Seitz, *A Different "Trek": Radical Geographies of "Deep Space Nine"* (Lincoln: University of Nebraska Press, 2023), 7.

23. Hark, "Franchise Fatigue," 47.

24. Hark, "Franchise Fatigue," 45.

25. Hark, "Franchise Fatigue," 45.

26. This comment—to which I will be returning later—originally appeared in response to my thread: Adam Kotsko, "What was it like watching the Xindi arc as it unfolded?," Daystrom Institute (Reddit), March 5, 2015, https://old.reddit .com/r/DaystromInstitute/comments/2y0ksy/what_was_it_like_watch- ing_the_xindi_arc_as_it/, but was subsequently removed. Thank you to user william_842 for helping me recover the full text from the Wayback Machine: https://web.archive.org/web/20210320231210/https://www.reddit.com/r/ DaystromInstitute/comments/2y0ksy/what_was_it_like_watching_the_xindi_ arc_as_it/cp5gnui/.

27. Although *Star Trek: The Animated Series* (1973–74) aired originally on Satur- day morning, it was largely a continuation of *The Original Series* in both tone and thematic content. Though few commentators have addressed this strange series in any detail, it had an important influence on the franchise, as I argue elsewhere; see Kotsko, "Inertia of Tradition."

28. Nellie Andreeva, "*Star Trek: Prodigy* Finds New Home at Netflix after

Paramount+ Cancellation," Deadline Hollywood, October 11, 2023, https://deadline.com/2023/10/star-trek-prodigy-netflix-pickup-paramount-plus-cancellation-1235569984/.

29. Alex Sherman, "Warner Bros. Discovery Halts Merger Talks with Paramount Global, Sources Say," CNBC, February 27, 2024, https://www.cnbc.com/2024/02/27/warner-bros-discovery-halts-paramount-global-merger-talks.html.

30. Indeed, as we will see in chapter 1, fan theories have devoted considerable effort to writing *Enterprise* out of the main *Star Trek* timeline—or, even worse, exclusively *into* the timeline created by the hated Abrams reboot films.

31. Seitz, *Different "Trek,"* 10.

32. Sharon Sharp, "Nostalgia for the Future: Retrofuturism in *Enterprise*," *Science Fiction Film and Television* 4, no. 1 (2011): 35.

33. The most thorough estimate I have been able to find is Michael McCarrick, "How Long It Would Take to Watch All of *Star Trek* (Yes, ALL of It)," CBR.com, January 21, 2021, https://www.cbr.com/star-trek-every-tv-episode-movie/. McCarrick puts the total at "651 hours and 48 minutes, meaning it will take over 27 days to watch them all uninterrupted." As of this writing, there have been four new seasons of the three recent live-action shows and one more of *Lower Decks* since that date, adding approximately forty-five more hours.

34. In the case of the most recent shows, the academic literature is obviously far from voluminous, though I try to cite whatever is available. As my account gets closer to the present, I rely more on reviews in the popular media in the absence of any significant scholarly resources.

CHAPTER 1

1. Alan Moore and Dave Gibbons, *Watchmen* (1987; reprint, New York: DC Comics, 2019), and Damon Lindelof et al., *Watchmen: An HBO Limited Series* (Burbank, Calif.: Warner Bros. Home Entertainment, 2020).

2. Lincoln Geraghty, *Living with Star Trek: American Culture and the Star Trek Universe* (New York: I. B. Tauris, 2007), 142–44.

3. Zaki Hasan, "Star Trek: Enterprise," in Garcia-Siino, Mittermeier, and Rabitsch, *Routledge Handbook,* 56–64.

4. Inattention to the different phases of the show's production (conflating the early introduction of the Temporal Cold War arc with the Xindi and time-traveling space Nazi plots) arguably undercuts Sharp's otherwise valuable critique of *Enterprise*'s conservative turn. Sharp, "Nostalgia for the Future."

5. Hark, *Star Trek,* 5.

6. Christopher L. Bennett, "ST: Enterprise, Rise of the Federation," Written Worlds (blog), n.d., https://christopherlbennett.wordpress.com/home-page/star-trek-fiction/rotf-a-choice-of-futures/. The popular fan podcast *Star Trek: The Next Conversation,* hosted by Matt Mira and Andrew Secunda, has been systematically reviewing *Enterprise* and coming to similar conclusions.

7. Hasan, "Star Trek: Enterprise," 62.

8. Sarah Böhlau, "'Lorca, I'm Really Gonna Miss Killing You': The Fictional Space

Created by Time Loop Narratives," in *Fighting for the Future: Essays on "Star Trek: Discovery,"* edited by Sabrina Mittermeier and Maeike Spychala (Liverpool: Liverpool University Press, 2020), 127–28.

9. Hark, *Star Trek,* 135.
10. Hark, *Star Trek,* 136.
11. Seitz, *Different "Trek,"* 41–51.
12. I had to scour the transcript to find the year of Q's trial, because the episode summary for "Encounter at Farpoint" on Memory Alpha—which is normally highly detailed—omits the date 2079 in favor of a vague reference to the late twentieth century. This is arguably an example of fans covering for the apparent continuity discrepancy introduced by *First Contact.*
13. Hark, *Star Trek,* 137.
14. Quoted in Hark, *Star Trek,* 140.
15. Sharp, "Nostalgia for the Future."
16. Donna Minkowitz, "Beam Us Back, Scotty!," *Nation,* March 7, 2002, https://www.thenation.com/article/archive/beam-us-back-scotty/.
17. David Greven, "The Twilight of Identity: *Enterprise,* Neoconservatism, and the Death of *Star Trek,*" Jump Cut 50 (2008), https://www.ejumpcut.org/archive/jc50.2008/StarTrekEnt/text.html.
18. Hasan, "Star Trek: Enterprise," 59.
19. Golding, *Star Wars after Lucas,* 90.
20. Hark, *Star Trek,* 142.
21. Hark, *Star Trek,* 142.
22. Qtd. in Memory Alpha, "Suliban."
23. Kotsko, "What was it like watching the Xindi arc as it unfolded?"
24. As I note in the introduction, this comment was subsequently removed from my thread. Thanks again to user william_842 for helping me retrieve the text.
25. Hark, *Star Trek,* 146–47.
26. Qtd. in Memory Alpha, "Zero Hour (episode)."
27. Hasan, "Star Trek: Enterprise," 58.
28. Hasan, "Star Trek: Enterprise," 61.
29. Hark, *Star Trek,* 149.
30. Qtd. in Hasan, "Star Trek: Enterprise," 61.
31. Qtd. in Hasan, "Star Trek: Enterprise," 62.
32. Hark, "Franchise Fatigue," 44.

CHAPTER 2

1. Diane Carey, *Broken Bow* (ENT) (New York: Pocket, 2001). The citation of *Star Trek* novels is necessarily awkward because their official titles include the title of the TV or book series of which they are a part. The more official title of Carey's novelization would thus be *Enterprise: Broken Bow*—or, if the producers had followed convention for the early seasons, *Star Trek: Enterprise: Broken Bow.* I have adopted the expedient of citing the book's unique title and adding the series code in parentheses after it.

2. Carey, *Broken Bow,* 9–10.
3. Carey, *Broken Bow,* 111.
4. Carey, *Broken Bow,* 113.
5. Carey, *Broken Bow,* 122.
6. Carey, *Broken Bow,* 195.
7. Carey, *Broken Bow,* 144; ellipses in original.
8. Carey, *Broken Bow,* 146.
9. Carey, *Broken Bow,* 149–50.
10. SpaceCadetJuan, "Brannon Braga: Not a Diane Carey Fan?," TrekBBS, March 31, 2013, https://www.trekbbs.com/threads/brannon-braga-not-a -diane-carey-fan.208597/.
11. Andy Mangels and Michael A. Martin, *Last Full Measure* (ENT) (New York: Pocket, 2006).
12. Andy Mangels and Michael A. Martin, *The Good That Men Do* (ENT) (New York: Pocket, 2007).
13. Sean Guynes and Gerry Canavan, "Novels," in Garcia-Siino, Mittermeier, and Rabitsch, *Routledge Handbook,* 176.
14. Guynes and Canavan, "Novels," 178.
15. Guynes and Canavan, "Novels," 182.
16. See andré carrington, *Speculative Blackness: The Future of Race in Science Fiction* (Minneapolis: University of Minnesota Press, 2016), chap. 5, and Seitz, *Different "Trek,"* 57–58.
17. Caroline-Isabelle Caron and Kristin Noone, eds., *Strange Novel Worlds: Essays on Star Trek Tie-in Fiction* (Jefferson, N.C.: McFarland, 2024). There is also a licensed reference work to the *Star Trek* literature from 1967 to 2006: Jeff Ayers, *Voyages of Imagination: The Star Trek Fiction Companion* (New York: Pocket, 2006). This work unfortunately fails to capture the most active period for the stand-alone novel continuity.
18. Guynes and Canavan, "Novels," 176.
19. Guynes and Canavan, "Novels," 176.
20. The most recent version of the full chart can be downloaded at 8of5, "Trek-Lit Reading Order Flow Chart," Trek Collective (blog), n.d.. https:// www.thetrekcollective.com/p/trek-lit-reading-order.html. Note that the most recent version is incomplete: the novelverse's concluding Coda trilogy has not been added.
21. Peter David, *Vendetta* (TNG) (New York: Pocket, 1991).
22. Peter David, *Imzadi* (TNG) (New York: Pocket, 1992).
23. Gene Roddenberry, *Star Trek: The Motion Picture* (New York: Pocket, 1979).
24. Guynes and Canavan, "Novels," 178.
25. Diane Duane, *Spock's World* (TOS) (New York: Pocket, 1988).
26. Diane Duane, *My Enemy, My Ally* (TOS) (New York: Pocket, 1984).
27. Diane Duane, *The Romulan Way* (TOS) (New York: Pocket, 1987).
28. John M. Ford, *The Final Reflection* (TOS) (New York: Pocket, 1984).
29. Angie Korporaal, "*Star Trek: Discovery* Designers Reveal Look and Colors Will

Evolve to Be More Like TOS," TrekMovie.com, September 3, 2017, https://trekmovie.com/2017/09/03/star-trek-discovery-designers-reveal-look-and-colors-will-evolve-to-be-more-like-tos/.

30. Guynes and Canavan, "Novels," 179.

31. S. D. Perry, *Avatar,* 2 vols. (DS9) (New York: Pocket, 2001).

32. Christie Gold, *Homecoming* (VOY) (New York: Pocket, 2003).

33. For an overview of the series with links to detailed summaries of each novel, see "A Time To . . . ," Memory Beta (wiki), n.d., https://memory-beta.fandom.com/wiki/A_Time_to.

34. Keith R. A. DeCandido, *Articles of the Federation* (New York: Pocket, 2005). This is one of a handful of novels that truly does not belong to any particular series.

35. Christopher L. Bennett, "ST: Enterprise—Rise of the Federation," Written Worlds (blog), n.d., https://christopherlbennett.wordpress.com/home-page/star-trek-fiction/rotf-a-choice-of-futures/.

36. Guynes and Canavan, "Novels," 180.

37. Christopher L. Bennett, *Watching the Clock* (DTI) (New York: Pocket, 2011). His voluminous annotations can be found by following the links at "DTI: Watching the Clock," n.d., https://christopherlbennett.wordpress.com/home-page/star-trek-fiction/dti-watching-the-clock/.

38. Bennett, *Watching the Clock,* 352.

39. Christopher L. Bennett, *Forgotten History* (DTI) (New York: Pocket, 2012), chap. 1.

40. Christopher L. Bennett, *Over a Torrent Sea* (Titan) (New York: Pocket, 2009).

41. Christopher L. Bennett, *The Captain's Oath* (TOS) (New York: Pocket, 2019).

42. Christopher L. Bennett, *Tower of Babel* (ENT) (New York: Pocket, 2014).

43. Christopher L. Bennett, *The Collectors* (DTI) (New York: Pocket, 2014). Naturally, he devotes considerable space in his annotations to the appearance of the *T. rex* (with feathers, in line with contemporary paleontology) and his decision to describe it as hissing rather than roaring (again, in line with fossil evidence). Christopher L. Bennett, "DTI: The Collectors Annotations," Written Worlds (blog), n.d., https://christopherlbennett.wordpress.com/home-page/star-trek-fiction/dti-the-collectors/dti-the-collectors-annotations/.

44. Christopher L. Bennett, *Uncertain Logic* (ENT) (New York: Pocket, 2015); and Christopher L. Bennett, *Live by the Code* (ENT) (New York: Pocket, 2016).

45. Peter David, *Before Dishonor* (TNG) (New York: Pocket, 2007).

46. Kirsten Beyer, *Full Circle* (VOY) (New York: Pocket, 2009).

47. Kirsten Beyer, *The Eternal Tide* (VOY) (New York: Pocket, 2012).

48. See Kirsten Beyer, *Unworthy* (VOY) (New York: Pocket, 2009).

49. Guynes and Canavan, "Novels," 182.

50. Kirsten Beyer, *To Lose the Earth* (VOY) (New York: Pocket, 2020).

51. "David Mack," Memory Alpha, n.d., https://memory-alpha.fandom.com/wiki/David_Mack; "Christopher L. Bennett," Memory Alpha, n.d., https://memory-alpha.fandom.com/wiki/Christopher_L._Bennett; "Kirsten Beyer,"

Memory Alpha, n.d., https://memory-alpha.fandom.com/wiki/Kirsten_Beyer. In what may count as evidence for his greater stature, Mack's books were automatically tabulated by the web page itself, while the other two authors' required me to count by hand.

52. David Mack, *Destiny #1: Gods of Night* (New York: Pocket, 2008), *Destiny #2: Mere Mortals* (New York: Pocket, 2008), and *Destiny #3: Lost Souls* (New York: Pocket, 2008).

53. Alex Perry, "Prelude to *Picard*—Retro Review: 'Destiny,'" Trek Core, January 19, 2020, https://blog.trekcore.com/2020/01/prelude-to-star-trek-picard-retro-review-destiny/.

54. David Mack, *A Time to Kill* (New York: Pocket, 2004); and David Mack, *A Time to Heal* (New York: Pocket, 2004).

55. David Mack, *Control* (Section 31) (New York: Pocket, 2017).

56. The first, and best, volume is David Mack, *Harbinger* (Vanguard) (New York: Pocket, 2005).

57. The first volume covers the majority of the Data resurrection story: David Mack, *Cold Equations: The Persistence of Memory* (TNG) (New York: Pocket, 2012).

58. David Mack, *Oblivion's Gate* (Coda) (New York: Pocket, 2021), 423.

59. Mack, *Oblivion's Gate,* 424.

60. David Mack, *Collateral Damage* (TNG) (New York: Pocket, 2019).

61. Mack, *Oblivion's Gate,* 424.

62. Dayton Ward, *Moments Asunder* (Coda) (New York: Pocket, 2021).

63. Exemplary here is a negative review by Thrawn (Malcolm Eckel), the creator of the novelverse flowchart, in which he pledges to never, ever again read a tie-in novel by Dayton Ward. See Thrawn, comment to "Coda: Book 1: Moments Asunder by Dayton Ward Review Thread," October 5, 2021, https://www.trekbbs.com/threads/coda-book-1-moments-asunder-by-dayton-ward-review-thread.309148/page-13#post-13911394.

64. James Swallow, *The Ashes of Tomorrow* (Coda) (New York: Pocket, 2021).

65. Mack, *Oblivion's Gate,* 223.

66. Mack, *Oblivion's Gate,* 223.

67. Mack, *Oblivion's Gate,* 422.

68. Una McCormack, *The Last Best Hope* (PIC) (New York: Pocket, 2020).

CHAPTER 3

1. Geraghty, *Living with Star Trek,* 1.

2. Following a common fan convention, I will continue to append the date to the title of this film going forward, to disambiguate it from the franchise.

3. Mike Johnson et al., *Star Trek: Countdown* (San Diego: IDW, 2009).

4. Anthony Pascale, "Exclusive: Orci Says Star Trek TV Talks Getting Real + Declares Movie Tie-in Comics and Game as Canon," TrekMovie.com, July 17, 2012, https://trekmovie.com/2012/07/17/exclusive-orci-says-star-trek-tv-talks-getting-real-declares-movie-tie-in-comics-game-as-canon/.

5.   Gerry Canavan, "Comics," in Garcia-Siino, Mittermeier, and Rabitsch, *Routledge Handbook,* 185.

6.   Canavan, "Comics," 185.

7.   Canavan, "Comics," 186.

8.   Megan Leigh, "Star Trek: How J. J. Abrams Ruined Everything," Pop-Verse, May 1, 2013, http://pop-verse.com/2013/05/01/star-trek-how-jj-abrams-ruined -everything/.

9.   William Proctor, "Star Trek (2009)," in Garcia-Siino, Mittermeier, and Rabitsch, *Routledge Handbook,* 144.

10. Dusty Stowe, "After 13 Years of Rights Issues, Star Trek Is Whole Again," Screen Rant, August 14, 2019, https://screenrant.com/star-trek-rights-viacom -paramount-cbs-merger-explained/.

11. Erin Horáková, "Freshly Remember'd: Kirk Drift," Strange Horizons, April 2017, http://strangehorizons.com/non-fiction/columns/freshly-rememberd-kirk -drift/.

12. Golding, *Star Wars after Lucas,* 90.

13. Nathan Jones, "Star Trek Into Darkness," in Garcia-Siino, Mittermeier, and Rabitsch, *Routledge Handbook,* 148.

14. Lynnette Porter, "Khanned: Whitewashing Khan in *Star Trek Into Darkness*"; Penelope Ingram, "Race, the Final Frontier: Star Trek, Trump, and Hollywood's Diversity Problem"; and Bart Bishop, "*Star Trek* Into Colonialism," all in *The Kelvin Timeline of "Star Trek": Essays on J. J. Abrams' Final Frontier,* edited by Matthew Wilhelm Kapell and Ace G. Pilkington (Jefferson, NC: McFarland, 2019).

15. Jones, "Star Trek Into Darkness," 151.

16. Porter, "Khanned," 29.

17. See Porter, "Khanned," 36; and Bishop, "*Star Trek* Into Colonialism," 59.

18. Jones, "Star Trek Into Darkness," 150.

19. Bishop, "*Star Trek* Into Colonialism," 58.

20. Hark, "Franchise Fatigue," 44.

21. Jones, "Star Trek Into Darkness," 151.

22. Jones, "Star Trek Into Darkness," 151.

23. Stowe, "After 13 Years."

24. Two of the novels—Alan Dean Foster, *The Unsettling Stars* (Kelvin) (New York: Pocket, 2020), and David Mack, *More Beautiful than Death* (Kelvin) (New York: Pocket, 2020)—were ultimately brought out during a period when the complex legal question of what the novelverse would do once its fictional timeline reached the date of the destruction of Romulus mentioned in *Star Trek* (2009) had brought the development of the novelverse to a standstill. A third, Christopher Bennett's permanently shelved *Seek a Newer World,* was reworked into the same author's *Original Series* novel *Face of the Unknown* (TOS) (New York: Pocket, 2016). See Christopher L. Bennett, "TOS: Face of the Unknown," Written Worlds (blog), n.d., https://christopherlbennett.wordpress.com/ home-page/star-trek-fiction/tos-the-face-of-the-unknown/.

25. The completist can turn to Robbert de Koeijer, "Star Trek: A Watching and Reading Guide to the Kelvin Timeline," Den of Geek, July 21, 2017, https:// www.denofgeek.com/games/star-trek-a-watching-reading-guide-to-the-kelvin -timeline/. Perhaps the most interesting tidbit from this truly exhaustive survey (which includes everything other than the final two *Boldly Go* volumes, as they had not yet been published) is that the writers even made an effort to include a tie-in video game in the Kelvin Timeline's quasi-canon by referring back to it in a later comic.

26. See Jackson Lanzing et al., *Star Trek: Year Five* (San Diego: IDW, 2019–21), and Scott Tipton et al., *Star Trek: The Next Generation—Mirror Broken* (San Diego: IDW, 2017).

27. Alex Kurtzman, Roberto Orci, Tim Jones, Mike Johnson, and David Messina, *Star Trek: Nero* (San Diego: IDW, 2010).

28. Mike Johnson et al., *Star Trek*, 13 vols. (San Diego: IDW, 2012–16). For convenience, I will refer to this series parenthetically by the volume numbers of the original trade paperback compilations, which remain the most readily available editions.

29. Mike Johnson et al., *Star Trek: Boldly Go*, 3 vols. (San Diego: IDW, 2017–18). Here I will follow the same convention as for the earlier series.

30. Mike Johnson, Roberto Orci, and David Messina, *Star Trek: Countdown to Darkness* (San Diego: IDW, 2013).

31. Mike Johnson, Claudia Balboni, and David Messina, *Star Trek: Khan* (San Diego: IDW, 2013).

32. Peter Goggin, "Star Trek Beyond," in Garcia-Siino, Mittermeier, and Rabitsch, *Routledge Handbook,* 155.

33. Simon Pegg, "A Word about Canon," Peggster (blog), July 11, 2016, https:// simonpegg.net/2016/07/11/a-word-about-canon/.

34. Craig Elvy, "Why Star Trek 4 is Happening Instead of Quentin Tarantino's Trek Movie," Screen Rant, February 17, 2022, https://screenrant.com/ star-trek-4-movie-not-quentin-tarantino-reason/.

35. Mark Donaldson, "Can Chris Hemsworth in Star Trek 4 Still Work?," Screen Rant, February 15, 2023, https://screenrant.com/star-trek-4-chris-hemsworth -still-possible/.

36. Proctor, "Star Trek (2009)," 146.

CHAPTER 4

1. James Hibberd, "Bryan Fuller on His *Star Trek: Discovery* Exit: 'I Got to Dream Big,'" *Entertainment Weekly,* July 28, 2017, https://ew.com/tv/2017/07/28/ bryan-fuller-star-trek-discovery/.

2. Sabrina Mittermeier, "Star Trek: Discovery," in Garcia-Siino, Mittermeier, and Rabitsch, *Routledge Handbook,* 71.

3. Andrea Whitacre, "Looking in the Mirror: The Negotiation of Franchise Identity in *Star Trek: Discovery*," in Mittermeier and Spychala, *Fighting for the Future,* 36.

4. Whitacre, "Looking in the Mirror," 32.

5. Sherryl Vint, "Preface: Unheimlich *Star Trek*," in Mittermeier and Spychala, *Fighting for the Future*, 2.

6. I owe this insight to Gerry Canavan (personal correspondence).

7. Mittermeier, "Star Trek: Discovery," 68.

8. "Star Trek: Discovery—First Trailer Analysis Thread," Daystrom Institute (Reddit), May 17, 2017, https://old.reddit.com/r/DaystromInstitute/comments/6brxvb/star_trek_discovery_first_trailer_analysis_thread/.

9. "'The Vulcan Hello' and 'Battle of the Binary Stars'—First Watch Analysis Thread," Daystrom Institute (Reddit), September 24, 2017, https://old.reddit.com/r/DaystromInstitute/comments/7284v8/the_vulcan_hello_battle_at_the_binary_stars_first/.

10. Hark, "Franchise Fatigue," 44.

11. Mittermeier, "Star Trek: Discovery," 68.

12. Tattersdill highlights this innovation and argues that fan-favorite episode "Magic to Make the Sanest Man Go Mad" (DSC 1.7) actively teaches viewers how to watch the show through the use of the time-loop trope. Will Tattersdill, "*Discovery* and the Form of Victorian Periodicals," in Mittermeier and Spychala, *Fighting for the Future*.

13. Mittermeier, "Star Trek: Discovery," 70.

14. Henrik Schillinger and Arne Sönnichsen, "The American Hello: Representations of U.S. Diplomacy in *Star Trek: Discovery*," in Mittermeier and Spychala, *Fighting for the Future*, 226.

15. Sabrina Mittermeier and Jennifer Volkmer, "'We Choose Our Own Pain. Mine Helps Me Remember': Gabriel Lorca, Ash Tyler, and the Question of Masculinity," in Mittermeier and Spychala, *Fighting for the Future*.

16. Williams_842, "The first nine episodes of Discovery are a model for what streaming era Star Trek should have looked like," Daystrom Institute (Reddit), June 20, 2023, https://startrek.website/post/66228.

17. These posts can be found at the following respective URLs: https://itself.blog/category/star-trek-discovery-event/ and https://itself.blog/category/star-trek-discovery-conversations/.

18. Mittermeier and Spychala, *Fighting for the Future*.

19. Kapell and Pilkington, *Kelvin Timeline*.

20. Mike Johnson, Kirsten Beyer, and Tony Shasteen, *Star Trek: Discovery—The Light of Khaless* (San Diego: IDW, 2017–18); Mike Johnson, Kirsten Beyer, and Angel Hernández, *Star Trek: Discovery—Succession* (San Diego: IDW, 2018); and Kirsten Beyer, Mike Johnson, and Angel Hernández, *Star Trek: Discovery*, annual #1 (San Diego: IDW, 2018).

21. David Mack, *Desperate Hours* (DSC) (New York: Pocket, 2017), and Dayton Ward, *Drastic Measures* (DSC) (New York: Pocket, 2018).

22. Mittermeier, "Star Trek: Discovery," 67.

23. Mittermeier, "Star Trek: Discovery," 67.

24. Justin Harp and Darren Scott, "Star Trek Boss Promises Discovery Will Sync

Up with Canon in Season 2—And Hints at Series Endgame," Digital Spy, January 3, 2019. https://www.digitalspy.com/tv/ustv/a25727485/star-trek-discovery-season-2-sync-ups-canon/.

25. Mittermeier and Volkmer, "We Choose Our Own Pain," 313.
26. Mittermeier and Volkmer, "We Choose Our Own Pain," 313.
27. Mittermeier, "Star Trek: Discovery," 66.
28. Una McCormack, *Wonderlands* (DSC) (New York: Pocket, 2021).
29. Si Sophie Pages Whybrew, "Queerness II: Transgender and Nonbinary People," in Mittermeier and Spychala, *Fighting for the Future,* 409. A later tie-in comic tries to smooth over this point from an in-universe perspective by revealing that Adira struggled to gain access to their memories after the implantation of the symbiont and only began to reconnect to their former self after meeting the *Discovery* crew; see Mike Johnson and Angel Hernández, *Star Trek: Discovery—Adventures in the 32nd Century* (San Diego: IDW, 2002), #2.
30. I specifically sought out the Georgiou-centered novel by John Jackson Miller, *Die Standing* (DSC) (New York: Pocket, 2020), to learn more about San, but there I found only another brief name-drop.
31. Mike Joest, "Jonathan Frakes Agrees *Star Trek: Discovery* Ending after Season 5 'Sucks,' Shares Thoughts on Plans for Finale and 32nd Century Timeline," Cinema Blend, March 7, 2023, https://www.cinemablend.com/interviews/jonathan-frakes-agrees-star-trek-discovery-ending-after-season-5-sucks-shares-thoughts-on-plans-for-finale-and-32nd-century-timeline.
32. Whitacre, "Looking in the Mirror," 36.
33. Hibberd, "Bryan Fuller," n.p.

CHAPTER 5

1. Hark, "Franchise Fatigue," 41.
2. Justice Hagan, "Star Trek: Picard," in Garcia-Siino, Mittermeier, and Rabitsch, *Routledge Handbook,* 75.
3. Hagan, "Star Trek: Picard," 76.
4. Mike Bloom, "*Star Trek: Short Treks* Flashes Way Forward to Reveal Discovery's Fate," *Hollywood Reporter,* November 2, 2018, https://www.hollywoodreporter.com/tv/tv-news/star-trek-short-treks-michael-chabon-aldis-hodge-interview-1158432/.
5. James Whitbrook, "*Star Trek: Discovery*'s Final Epilogue Was Almost Its Next Season Arc," Gizmodo, May 31, 2024, https://gizmodo.com/star-trek-discovery-ending-calypso-season-6-burnham-1851513349.
6. "Exclusive Interview—Michael Chabon, Alex Kurtzman, Akiva Goldsman, and Kirsten Beyer on *Star Trek: Picard,* What It Means to Treat *Star Trek* as a Franchise, and More," interview conducted by Alex Moreland, FlickeringMyth, January 23, 2020, https://www.flickeringmyth.com/2020/01/exclusive-interview-michael-chabon-alex-kurtzman-akiva-goldsman-and-kirsten-beyer-on-star-trek-picard-what-it-means-to-treat-star-trek-as-a-franchise-and-more/.

7. Chabon subsequently published a sketch of his view of Romulan culture: Michael Chabon, "Some Notes on Romulans," *Medium,* March 7, 2021, https://michaelchabon.medium.com/.

8. Hagan, "Star Trek: Picard," 77.

9. Christian Blauvelt, "*Star Trek: Picard* Review: Season 1 Finale Inspires Many Questions, Little Emotion," March 27, 2020, https://www.indiewire.com/features/general/star-trek-picard-season-1-finale-review-et-in-arcadia-ego-part-2-spoilers-1202220935/.

10. James Hibberd, "*Star Trek* Showrunner Discusses *Strange New Worlds* Plan, Evolving Q for *Picard*," *Hollywood Reporter,* April 12, 2021, https://www.hollywoodreporter.com/tv/tv-news/star-trek-producer-reveals-strange-new-worlds-plan-evolving-q-for-picard-4164064/.

11. Greg Cox, *The Eugenics Wars: The Rise and Fall of Khan Noonien Singh,* 2 vols. (New York: Pocket, 2001–2).

12. Kirsten Beyer, Mike Johnson, Michelle Hurd (narrator), and Jeri Ryan (narrator), *No Man's Land* (PIC), audio CD and digital download (Ashland, Ore.: Blackstone, 2021).

13. This trend was memorably critiqued by Parul Sehgal, "The Case against the Trauma Plot," *New Yorker,* December 27, 2021, https://www.newyorker.com/magazine/2022/01/03/the-case-against-the-trauma-plot.

14. Scott Collura, "*Star Trek: Picard*—Full Season 2 Review," IGN, May 5, 2022, https://www.ign.com/articles/star-trek-picard-season-2-full-review.

15. Christian Blauvelt, "*Star Trek: Picard* Season 2 Review: Finally, This Show Is What We Hoped It Would Be," IndieWire, March 3, 2022, https://www.indiewire.com/criticism/shows/star-trek-picard-season-2-review-1234703339/.

16. "With *Star Trek: Picard* (2020) (Sorted by IMDb Rating Descending)," IMDb, retrieved July 25, 2023, https://www.imdb.com/search/title/?series=tt8806524&view=simple&count=250&sort=user_rating,desc.

17. Lauren Coates, "*Star Trek: Picard* Season 3 Review: A Sendoff That's Much More than a Nostalgia Trip," A.V. Club, February 10, 2023.

18. Alex Cranz, "You Are Not Prepared for the Final Season of *Star Trek: Picard*," Verge, February 15, 2023, https://www.theverge.com/23594675/star-trek-picard-season-3-review.

19. Scott Collura, "*Star Trek: Picard* Season 3 Review," IGN, April 26, 2023, https://www.ign.com/articles/star-trek-picard-season-3-review.

20. Adam Roberts, "*Picard* Season 3 (2023)," Sibilant Fricative (blog), April 16, 2023, https://sibilantfricative.blogspot.com/2023/04/picard-season-3-2023.html.

21. Daniel Cooper, "Don't Watch *Star Trek: Picard* Season Three, It'll Only Encourage Them," Engadget, February 10, 2023, https://www.engadget.com/star-trek-picard-season-3-paramount-plus-preview-review-080010710.html.

22. "*Picard* Production Designer Says *Star Trek: Legacy* Spin-off Is 'Just a Nice Idea,'" TrekMovie, January 31, 2024, https://trekmovie.com/2024/01/31/picard-production-designer-says-star-trek-legacy-is-just-a-nice-idea/.

23. "Star Trek: Picard 3x10 'The Last Generation' Reaction Thread," Daystrom

Institute (Reddit), April 20, 2023, https://old.reddit.com/r/DaystromInstitute/comments/12smpvo/star_trek_picard_3x10_the_last_generation/.

24. See Kirsten Beyer, Mike Johnson, and Angel Hernandez, *Picard: Countdown* (New York: IDW, 2020), and Kirsten Beyer, Mike Johnson, and Angel Hernandez, *Picard: Stargazer* (New York: IDW, 2023), respectively.

CHAPTER 6

1. The franchise narrowly missed that landmark in 1994, the year *Next Generation* concluded, as *Voyager*'s debut was delayed until January of the following year rather than having the traditional fall premiere.

2. Roberts, "*Picard* Season 3 (2023)."

3. Aaron Bady (@zunguzungu), "I want friends solving space crimes in a supportive yet challenging workplace," Twitter (now X), January 23, 2023, https://twitter.com/zunguzungu/status/1220519545414094853.

4. See Samantha Coley, "*Star Trek: Lower Decks* Renewed for Season 5," Collider, March 28, 2023, https://collider.com/star-trek-lower-decks-season-5-renewed/; and Siobhan Ball, "Will *Star Trek: Strange New Worlds* Return for Season 3?," Mary Sue, June 20, 2023, https://www.themarysue.com/will-there-be-star-trek-strange-new-worlds-season-3-answered/.

5. Though it aired on Saturday mornings, the *Animated Series* featured plots that were largely indistinguishable from *Original Series* episodes.

6. Brian Lowry, "*Star Trek: Prodigy* Takes Off in Too-Familiar Animated Directions," CNN.com, October 28, 2021, https://www.cnn.com/2021/10/28/entertainment/star-trek-prodigy-review/index.html.

7. Zach Handlen, "*Star Trek: Prodigy* Offers a More Visceral Spin on *Trek*'s Utopian Ideals," A.V. Club, October 28, 2021, https://www.avclub.com/star-trek-prodigy-offers-a-more-visceral-spin-on-trek-1847954773.

8. Shamus Kelley, "Does *Star Trek: Prodigy* Work for More than Just Kids?," Den of Geek, February 15, 2022, https://www.denofgeek.com/tv/does-star-trek-prodigy-work-for-more-than-just-kids/.

9. See, for example, Hark, *Star Trek,* chap. 5.

10. Ramón Valle-Jiménez, "Star Trek: Lower Decks," in Garcia-Siino, Mittermeier, and Rabitsch, *Routledge Handbook,* 80.

11. Indeed, it is the mockery of the fan abbreviations on *Lower Decks* that inspired me to forego them in the present book.

12. Valle-Jiménez, "Star Trek: Lower Decks," 81.

13. Mike McMahan (@TNG_S8), "Wonder no more: All TNG season 8 writing is being channeled into Star Trek: Lower Decks—coming to CBS All Access this year," Twitter (now X), February 9, 2020, https://twitter.com/TNG_S8/status/1226739296226304001.

14. Mike McMahan (@TNG_S8), "A subspace rumple disables the Enterprise and blinds the crew. Data & Geordi's plan to build the perfect girlfriend backfires explosively," Twitter (now X), March 18, 2015, https://twitter.com/TNG_S8/status/574626763835211776.

15. Valle-Jiménez, "Star Trek: Lower Decks," 80.
16. Figures are drawn from the series' respective Wikipedia pages thanks to persistent difficulty loading Rotten Tomatoes directly.
17. Zack Handlen, "*Star Trek: Lower Decks* Sets Phasers to Charm in Season 2," A.V. Club, August 12, 2021, https://www.avclub.com/star-trek-lower-decks-sets -phasers-to-charm-in-season-1847451467.
18. Ryan Britt, "*Lower Decks* Season 3 is the Best Trek Show of the Year," Inverse, August 22, 2022, https://www.inverse.com/entertainment/star-trek-lower -decks-season-3-review-no-spoilers.
19. Eric Deggans, "*Star Trek: Strange New Worlds* Season 2 Is a Classic Sci-Fi Adventure," NPR, June 15, 2023, https://www.npr.org/2023/06/15/1182335025/ star-trek-strange-new-worlds-season-2-review.
20. Adrienne Westenfeld, "You Can't Bring *Star Trek: Strange New Worlds* Down," *Esquire,* June 30, 2022, https://www.esquire.com/entertainment/tv/ a40458654/star-trek-strange-new-worlds-review/.
21. Zack Handlen, "*Star Trek: Strange New Worlds* Succeeds by Going Back to Basics," *Variety,* May 2, 2022, https://variety.com/2022/tv/reviews/star-trek -strange-new-worlds-tv-review-paramount-plus-1235255901/.
22. Kirsten Beyer, Mike Johnson, and Megan Levens, *Strange New Worlds: The Illyrian Enigma* (New York: IDW, 2023).
23. Deggans, "*Star Trek.*"

CONCLUSION

1. Hark, "Franchise Fatigue," 56.
2. Hark, "Franchise Fatigue," 57.
3. See, for example, Michael Sainato and Lois Beckett, "Writers on Why They're Standing Up to Hollywood: 'This Is Fundamentally Broken,'" *Guardian,* May 4, 2023, https://www.theguardian.com/culture/2023/may/04/writers-on-why -theyre-standing-up-to-hollywood-this-is-fundamentally-broken.
4. Hark, "Franchise Fatigue," 57.
5. See Seitz, *Different "Trek,"* 7.
6. I pursue this analogy in detail elsewhere; see Kotsko, "Inertia of Tradition."
7. Hark, "Franchise Fatigue," 57.

INDEX

Italicized page numbers refer to illustrations.

"The Cage," unaired pilot, 149–50, 165, 218–19

Canavan, Gerry, 34, 69

Carey, Diane: *Broken Bow* (ENT), 66–68, 73

carrington, andré: *Speculative Blackness,* 70

CBS, 100, 109, 122; and corporate decisions for ST, generally, 233–36, 242; and DSC, 127

Chabon, Michael, 172

Chakotay: in franchise fiction, 84; in PRO, 203–4, 205

Changelings, 192–94

Chekhov, 34

Chen, T'Ryssa, 92

Coalition of Planets, 62

Cochran, Sean, 172

Cochrane, Zefram, 31–32, 39–40, 61

Cold War, fall of Soviet Union, 5

Columbo, 236

computer virus, 232

Control, 78, 151, 153, 179

Cornwall (Admiral), 130, 142

Coto, Manny, 28, 37, 53, 58–60

Covid-19, 161, 171, 181, 230

Cox, Greg, 182

Crusher, Beverly, 190–91, 192, *194*; and Picard, relationship with (franchise fiction), 78

Crusher, Jack, 191, 192–93, 196

Crusher, Wesley (aka the Traveler): in franchise fiction, 91; in PIC, 182

Culber, Hugh, 131, 143, 148–49, 156, 161

Dak'Rah, 222–23, *224*

Dal, 203, 205, 206, 233

Daniels (Lieutenant), 40–41, *42*, 54, 59, 153; in DSC, 164, 173; in franchise fiction, 80

Data: in *Countdown,* 96; in and Lal, franchise fiction, 93; in *Nemesis,* 21, 101–2,

171, 179, 240–41; in PIC, 169, 176–77, 179, 191, *194*, 232, *234*; resurrections, 89, 179, 191, 195, 240–41

David, Peter, 72; *Before Dishonor* (TNG), 83, 86; *Imzadi* (TNG), 72–73; *New Frontiers,* 75; *Vendetta* (TNG), 72

Dax, Ezri: in franchise fiction, 92

DeCandido, Keith R. A.: *Articles of the Federation,* 77

decline narrative, 12–13

Deep Space Nine: Avatar (Perry) franchise fiction, 76; as break from previous *Star Trek,* 1–2, 11, 24, 235; environs, exploration of, 52; and franchise fiction, 75–76; and LDS connections, 209–10; serialization, 52

——episodes: 3.11–12 "Past Tense," 38, 183; 5.6 "Trials and Tribble-ations," 61, 79, 133; 6.13 "Far Beyond the Stars," 93; 6.19 "In the Pale Moonlight," 223

Delphic Expanse, 37, 51–52

Delta Quadrant, 76, 78, 84–85, 200

Denobulans, 46

Department of Temporal Investigation: in franchise fiction, 78

Detmer (Lieutenant), 138

Devidians, 91–94

Discovery: artistic freedom, 28–29, 128–32, 139–45, 151–59, 163–64, 167; best episodes, 231; and "Calypso" *Short Treks* episode, 172; canon, apparent violation of, 125–28, 130–36; creative team, 127–28, 129, 147, 151; diversity of characters, 143; and ENT, 15, 125, 127–28, 131, 164; episodic versus serialization, 136–44, 160, 231–32; fan service, 28–29, 129, 139–45, 147–48, 164–66; and franchise fiction, 75, 146, 155; and Kelvin Timeline comparison, 163; and legacy characters, 149–52, 214–15; overshadowed by other

ST streaming shows, 129; pace of, 145, 155–58; political and social commentary, 144–46, 148–49, 158; and prequel status versus artistic freedom, 131–32, 151–59, 167; reinvention of franchise, weight of, 123–25, 130, 134, 199; series end, 230; and SNW, 165; social media, use of, 135–36; Starfleet uniforms and ship designs, 125; trauma, processing of, 148–49, 160–61; *Wonderlands* (McCormack) franchise fiction, 155; world-building, 28–29, 139–45, 157 59

——episodes: 1.1 "The Vulcan Hello," 123–25, *126*; 1.2 "Battle of the Binary Stars," 125; 1.3 "Context Is for Kings," *126*; 1.5 "Choose Your Pain," 141, 145; 1.7 "Magic to Make the Sanest Man Go Mad," 145, 231; 2.4 "An Obol for Charon," 151–52; 2.12 "Through the Valley of Shadows," 153; 3.1 "That Hope Is You, Pt. 1," 154; 3.2 "Far from Home," 155–56

Diviner, 203–4, 205–6

Dominion, 21–22, 144, 162, 213, 223

Duane, Diane, 74, 173

Eaglemoss, 97–98

Edison, Balthazar: in Kelvin Timeline, 118–19, 120. See also *Star Trek Beyond*

Elnor, 184–86

Emerald Chain, 19, 154

Enterprise: and artistic freedom, fan service, and world-building, 27–28, 32–43, 47–49, 51–57, 59, 60–62, 241; cancellation and series finale, 9, 62–65; character development as weak, 47–48; and continuity and canon, 15–16, 37–43, 64; and corporate decisions, 12, 55–56, 229–30; and fan relationship, 43, 56–57; fan response to, 41, 42–43, 64; and Federation, founding of, 50–52, 60, 63; and franchise fiction, 133; genetic engineering, 58–60; on human culture, 46; and Klingons, 33, 39; legacy of, 15–16, 51, 65, 128, 133, 136; loss and regret, theme of, 21; premiere of, 31; prequel dilemma, 35–44, 50–54, 57–58; production history of, 34, 35–37; as regressive, 43–47; on Romulan war, 50–52; serialization versus episodic, 37, 52–55, 62; in SNW and LDS, 227–28; social and political commentary, 49–50, 54–56; Starfleet uniforms and ship design, 46, 125; *and Star Trek* (2009), 100–101; and *Star Trek Beyond*, 118; and technology, treatment of, 46, 50; and terrorism theme, 17–20, 36–37, 54–56; title sequence and theme song, 33–34, 43–44; and TNG connection, 62–63; and TOS connections, 60–62; and Vulcans, 39, 44, 47–50, 60

——episodes: 1.1–2 "Broken Bow," 31, 40, 43–44, 62–63, 66–68; 1.5 "Unexpected," 49; 1.11 "Cold Front," 40; 1.17 "Detained," 49; 1.26 "Storm Front, Pt. 1," 41, *42*; 2.2 "Carbon Creek," 49–50; 2.4 "Dead Stop," 82; 2.9 "Singularity," 43; 2.22 "Cogenitor," 49; 2.23 "Regeneration," 39–40; 2.24 "First Flight," 50; 2.26 "The Expanse," 17, 53–54; 3.8 "Twilight," 53; 3.9 "North Star," 53; 3.10 "Similitude," 53; 3.11 "Carpenter Street," 54; 3.12 "Chosen Realm," 52; 3.18 "Azati Prime," 54; 3.24 "Zero Hour," 57–58; 4.1-2 "Storm Front," 58–60; 4.7–9 "The Forge," "The Awakening," "Kir'Shara," 60; 4.12–14 "Babel One," "United," "The Aenar," 60; 4.17 "Bound," 60, 62; 4.18-19 "In a Mirror, Darkly," 60–61; 4.20

Uhura, Nyota: first name of, 102; in Kelvin Timeline, 100, 112; in SNW, 217

uncanny doubles: in *Nemesis*, 139; in PIC, 176; in *Star Trek* (2009), 101. *See also* Mirror Universe

UPN, 12, 14, 55–56

V'ger: in Kelvin Timeline comics, 111–12

Voq (aka Ash Tyler), 134, 137–39, 143–45, 148–49

Voyager: and Braga, 36; conclusion of, 167; corporate failures of, 12; criticisms of, 206; dark themes of, 1–2; fan service, 204; and franchise fiction, 76; and PRO connections, 200, 202–7; and real-world timeline, 182. *See also* Janeway, Kathryn

——episodes: 7.25–26 "Endgame," 80, 174

——franchise fiction titles: *Full Circle* (Beyer), 83–84; *Homecoming* (Gold), 76

Vulcans: in ENT, 39, 44, 47–50, 60; in franchise fiction, 67, 74; in SNW, 221; as terrorists, 18; and trellium-D, 52

Ward, Dayton: Coda series (with Swallow and Mack), 91–94

warp drive, 31–32, 118. *See also* Cochrane, Zefram

Watchmen, 32, 137, 183

Worf: in *Countdown*, 96; in PIC, 191, *194*; in TNG, 132, 134

world-building strategy: explanation of, 24–25

World War III, 38

Wrath of Khan, 235; and *Star Trek Into Darkness*, 106–8

writers and actors strike (2023), 230, 233

Xindi, 37, 48, 51–57, 59, 63; in Kelvin Timeline, 118–19

Yelchin, Anton: death of, 116–17

Zaslav, David, 14–15

ADAM KOTSKO teaches in the Shimer Great Books School at North Central College. He is author of *Awkwardness* (2010), *Why We Love Sociopaths: A Guide to Late Capitalist Television* (2012), and *Neoliberalism's Demons: On the Political Theology of Late Capitalism* (2018), among many other books.